Contents

Preface

American industry shows much current interest in total quality management (TQM). The ASQC Quality Press publications catalog lists a number of books on statistical methods, benchmarking, reliability, and quality auditing. Yet there are relatively few books on the behavioral side of TQM, particularly human resources management (HRM)—even though proponents, such as Philip Crosby, J. M. Juran, and W. Edwards Deming, emphasize such human resources areas as leadership, teamwork, empowerment, training, and corporate cultural change.

This book is not a text in HRM for TQM. Rather it presents current ideas and research on areas of HRM that are particularly important for TQM to succeed. Each chapter examines an important human resources concern in TQM and is written by an industrial or academic expert in that area. Part I examines basic HRM issues affecting TQM: leadership and organizational culture; reward and recognition; performance evaluation; compensation; safety; and barriers and facilitators to HRM for TQM. Part II looks at how various sectors address HRM for TQM: manufacturing; medical; education; and government. Part III examines the emerging issues of internationalization and diversity management in HRM and TQM. Part IV ties it all together.

The book is directed toward two audiences: academicians and HRM practitioners. Academicians will find a number of theoretical frameworks with which to examine human resources concepts in TQM. Practitioners will find principles and new ideas for HRM practices in their TQM organization. It is hoped that this book will serve as a clearinghouse for both audiences. Indeed, it is hoped that this will be the first in a series that presents current practices and new ideas within the behavioral side of TQM.

Acknowledgments

First, I would like to thank the chapter authors for their enthusiastic response to my idea of putting together a book on current human resources issues in TQM. Almost every expert I contacted agreed to write a chapter. I would also like to thank my dean, Jan Duggar, and my department head, Bill Roe, who is also a chapter coauthor, for their support in compiling this book. And I would like to thank my graduate assistant, Bill Eden, for his editorial help.

Second, I would like to thank the staff of ASQC Quality Press, in particular Susan Westergard, Kelley Cardinal, Cathy Christine, and Mark Olson. They have an orientation to quality not only in the content of their publications but in the publication process itself.

Third, I would like to thank my family—my daughters Jessica and Andrea and my wife Teri—for their patience and encouragement during the process of making this book.

Introduction

The number of books and articles written on total quality management (TQM) is increasing at what seems to be an exponential rate. These works have taken TQM from its original emphasis on statistical tools into numerous diverse areas.

One significant area has been the human resources side, where writers have explored such topics as leadership, employee involvement, cultural change, and reward and recognition. Indeed, some argue that TQM often fails because it may only focus on TQM statistical tools (the "hard" side of TQM) while ignoring critical human resources variables (the "soft" side of TQM) (Wilkinson 1994). According to a number of writers these human resources variables may include the following (Blackburn and Rosen 1993; Bowen and Lawler 1992; Cardy and Dobbins 1996; Costigan 1995; Wilkinson, Marchington, and Dale 1993):

- Helping to devise the strategic plan around quality
- Serving as a change agent to help transform the organizational climate to a culture of quality
- Transforming individual job analysis to team analysis describing broad, flexible team activity statements
- Recruiting applicants with realistic previews of working in a quality-oriented organization
- Selecting employees with the quick ability to learn TQM tools and the interpersonal skills to participate in quality teams
- Training quality teams in TQM tools and teamwork
- Training team leaders and managers in coaching and facilitating skills
- Informally mentoring employees in TQM skills
- Creating communications, such as newsletters and videos, about quality

- Designing performance evaluation and reward systems that focus on quality improvement and customer satisfaction
- Devising career development programs that emphasize skill breadth and cross-functional career moves
- Creating surveys to measure employee involvement in and satisfaction with quality initiatives
- Working with unions to enhance labor-management partnering efforts in quality improvement
- Improving safety and enhancing the physical workplace to improve the quality of working life

As an indication of the importance of behavioral issues in TQM, the prestigious Malcolm Baldrige National Quality Award emphasizes human resources as one of its seven pillars for evaluating quality. Criterion 4.0 Human Resource Development and Management delineates four categories of excellence that a candidate for the award must demonstrate (National Institute of Standards and Technology 1996).

4.1 Human Resource Planning and Evaluation

4.2 High Performance Work Systems (including how compensation and recognition encourage employee contribution)

4.3 Employee Education, Training, and Development

4.4 Employee Well-Being and Satisfaction

Given the emphasis on human resources in the Baldrige Award criteria, it is surprising that more has not been written on human resources management (HRM) and TQM. Thus, there is a definite need for this type of book.

It should be stressed that this book is not a textbook on HRM melded with TQM. There are several texts already on the market, such as Noe et al. (1994), which integrates TQM topics into every chapter. Rather this book is an examination of the current state of the art of human resources issues that are vital to TQM.

I have specifically chosen experts in these various areas to present a diversity of views. They form a cross-functional, synergistic team of academics and practitioners. Some of these issues have been examined elsewhere, but the authors present a new approach or a new perspective. Other issues have not been developed before, and the authors present a new area for TQM. Thus, new concepts as well as new practices that show promise are presented.

The basic purpose of this book is to facilitate a benchmarking of concepts and practices about human resources and TQM. Indeed, a 1995

Quality Progress survey shows that HRM activities were the most bench-marked category of TQM practices during 1994 (Human resources is top benchmarking process 1995).

This book is divided into three parts: current concepts of human resources and TQM; applications in the public and private sector; and a special section on the international and diversity thrust that is receiving so much attention in HRM. Moreover, the global competition that underlies the thrust in the third part appears to be one of the basic drives for an organization to adopt TQM.

In Part I, "Basic Human Resources Management Issues in TQM," Bruce Avolio and Francis Yammarino lead off with a theoretical look at two concepts that form the groundwork of TQM—leadership and vision. I then elaborate on reward and recognition within a reinforcement theory framework. J. Bruce Prince examines the highly controversial area of performance evaluation, and Michael Cleary looks at compensation within TQM. Robert Reber then explores a new TQM area, safety management. Richard Blackburn and Benson Rosen close the first part with an analysis of barriers and facilitators to HRM under TQM.

In Part II, "Human Resources Management and TQM in Various Sectors," Laura Junod describes new practices at Granite Rock, a Baldrige Award winner. Paula Phillips Carson, Kerry Carson, and C. William Roe then examine HRM and TQM issues gaining prominence within the health care industry. Nancy Howard and Jacquelyn Rudolph look at HRM and TQM at Oregon State University, while Michael White and Delbert Nebeker describe a new performance management concept within the U.S. government.

Part III, "International and Diversity Issues," contains two international perspectives. Graham Godfrey, Adrian Wilkinson, Michael Marchington, and Barrie Dale examine HRM quality issues in the United Kingdom. Alan Brown and Amrik Sohal look at HRM and TQM in Australia. Then David Chretien and I describe the advantages and problems of workforce diversity within a TQM framework. I end the book with a chapter summarizing the various concepts and practices presented and offering new HRM ideas identified in the chapters that TQM organizations may wish to benchmark.

When one is putting together a book of this sort, there is always the hope that the material will fill a special need in the knowledge base of the discipline (here the cross-disciplinary areas of HRM and TQM). In the larger scheme of things, however, there is the hope that this book will set in motion a basic process that will improve both the fields of HRM and TQM. In essence, I would like to see this book as setting the stage for some type of annual volume that describes the state of the art of TQM. There are analogous volumes in the various behavioral sciences, such as the *Annual Review of Psychology* and the *Annual Review of Sociology,* where each chapter describes the current thought, research, and practices in the important areas of that discipline. Similarly, I would like to see a regularly published *Review of Behavioral Issues in Quality Management,* in which experts in major areas of TQM describe new directions of thought, cutting-edge research, and best practices upon which to benchmark. My hope is that the present book will spark interest in this idea.

REFERENCES

Blackburn, Richard, and Benson Rosen. 1993. Total quality and human resources management: Lessons learned from Baldrige Award-winning companies. *Academy of Management Executive* 7, no. 3:49–66.

Bowen, David E., and Edward E. Lawler. 1992. Total quality-oriented human resources management. *Organizational Dynamics* (spring): 29–41.

Cardy, Robert L., and Gregory H. Dobbins. 1996. Human resources management in a total quality organizational environment. *Journal of Quality Management* 1, no. 1:5–20.

Costigan, Robert D. 1995. Adaptation of traditional human resources process for total quality environments. *Quality Management Journal* (spring): 7–23.

Human resources is top benchmarking process. 1995. *Quality Progress* (April): 17.

National Institute of Standards and Technology. 1996. *Malcolm Baldrige National Quality Award criteria.* Gaithersburg, Md.: National Institute of Standards and Technology.

Noe, Raymond A., John R. Hollenbeck, Barry Gerhart, and Patrick Wright. 1994. *Human resources management.* Burr Ridge, Ill.: Irwin.

Wilkinson, Adrian. 1994. Managing human resources for quality. In *Managing quality,* edited by Barrie G. Dale. New York: Prentice Hall.

Wilkinson, Adrian, Mick Marchington, and Barrie Dale. 1993. Enhancing the contribution of the human resource function to quality improvement. *Quality Management Journal* (October): 35–46.

Part I

Basic Human Resources Issues in TQM

Chapter 1

Leadership, Vision, and Continuous Process Improvement Examined at Multiple Levels of Analysis

Bruce J. Avolio and Francis J. Yammarino

Over the last 20 years, many academics and practitioners moved from not seriously questioning total quality management (TQM) as a way of modeling organizations, to accepting it without question. In effect, TQM had become "received wisdom" in the field of management practices (Barrett 1972).

One unique feature of the TQM movement in the United States has been its near-universal application across sectors such as military, government, education, profit, and not-for-profit organizations (Bemowski 1995; Corrigan 1995; Dobbins 1995; Early and Godfrey 1995). TQM had overcome a common tendency among other management trends that were discounted because it was "not invented here." To the contrary, a substantial body of evidence has accumulated demonstrating the positive impact of TQM interventions across many sectors (Brown 1991). There are, however, some chinks in the armor that are now emerging. For example, Bleakley (1993) recently concluded that many companies have dropped their quality programs because no significant improvements were seen after a year or two of operation.

Several critical questions arise based on the emerging trend that Bleakley observed. First, what are the components of TQM that contribute to the lack of significant changes in quality performance? Second, how has leadership—at all levels—in these organizations contributed to the problems associated with TQM failures? Third, what criteria are used to assess TQM program effectiveness, and are those criteria being assessed at the appropriate time and level following implementation? Finally, what contextual factors, in which these TQM efforts are embedded, have impacted its performance? Taken together, each of these questions raises the importance of examining TQM efforts using a levels of analysis perspective.

To date, one of the missing links in discussions on TQM has been the link between macrolevel cultural change and the specific developmental process associated with continuous process improvement (CPI), observed at both high and low levels of analysis. A second problem concerns the impact that leadership (both at micro- and macrolevels) has on individual, group, organizational, and systemic changes with respect to quality improvement programs. A third problem addressed in this chapter concerns the range of operational definitions associated with TQM. Specifically, Reeves and Bedner (1994) concluded that "regardless of the time period or context in which quality is examined, the concept has had multiple and often muddled definitions and has been used to describe a wide variety of phenomena" (p. 419). Using a levels perspective, an attempt will be made to clarify a central component of TQM initiatives by operationally defining CPI at multiple levels of analysis. For the purpose of this chapter, CPI is discussed as one of the core components associated with TQM initiatives. Stated another way, TQM is the broader strategy and framework in which CPI is embedded.

OVERVIEW OF TQM AND CPI: TRENDS, FADS, AND NEW DIRECTIONS

After the film "If Japan Can, Why Can't We?" was introduced in the United States in the early 1980s, many organizations focused their energies on learning to apply statistical process control (SPC) to address a broad range of organizational ills (Deming 1986; Juran 1991; Walton 1986). SPC provided a concrete strategy and a specific set of tools that could be adapted in different organizational contexts to directly address problems with poor quality. SPC was quickly adopted by many prominent businesses and government agencies, including those that were at the high end of technology applications as well as those focused on general services (Dobbins, Cardy, and Carson 1991; Linkow 1989; Sashkin and Kiser 1991).

In contrast with most prior organizational change and development models, the concrete details of what needed to be accomplished with TQM to determine the root causes of problems and strategies for resolving them, were thought to be specific and trainable within short periods of time. Many managers held this view. Although many TQM writers advocated a focus on macrolevel processes, the framework that was developed to interpret these macroprocesses was often too simplistic, particularly in terms of how TQM was operationalized (Waldman 1994). For example, TQM has often been defined as representing cooperation between functional areas, emphasizing teamwork, involving everyone in the process, having strong leadership, and focusing on continuously improving systems and processes (Bemowski 1995; Corrigan 1995; Dobbins 1995; Early and Godfrey 1995). Although noteworthy objectives, the process to achieve these desired states was not clearly operationalized nor was it systemically discussed at the level at which the change was expected to be implemented. Some TQM efforts began at macrolevels—often ignoring the impact of change processes on the interpersonal processes within groups, groups within departments, and departments within organizations. Underestimating the embeddedness of TQM at each of these levels reduces the amount of information available, especially when one tries to explain why certain goals driven by TQM initiatives simply haven't achieved their full potential.

Typically, the process associated with groups was frequently mandated to change as part of a new approach to becoming a total quality organization. This was done without providing the necessary details on how such interpersonal processes should be changed. TQM advocates called for managers to create a team-oriented culture, to enable their workforce, to be risk-takers, to focus on systemic versus individual processes, to show leadership, and to ultimately change the process by which their organizations functioned. Although noteworthy goals, it was unclear how this should all be accomplished and at what level the process should begin. For instance, does strong leadership mean only at the most senior rank, or at all organizational levels? Can a TQM program be fully successful if the attention to leadership is only at the most senior level?

Such general operational definitions of TQM, and the CPI processes associated with these strategic efforts, raise two important questions. First, to what degree do these definitions provide a basis for accurately measuring the process of continuous improvement expected within a TQM organization? Second, is there a clear indication of the level of analysis at which these variables should be measured? Before specifically addressing these questions, the reasons why many TQM efforts have been successful will be examined. Then, some suggestions for integrating TQM with other organizational change processes will be offered.

Key Reasons for TQM Success

Some factors that have contributed to TQM's wide acceptance include that, unlike many organizational development interventions, improvements in performance quality occurred quickly and were quantifiable. Rapid turnarounds and significant advancements in quality reputations were often the norm, rather than the exception. Although top management commitment was deemed important to TQM implementation

(Brown 1991; Deming 1986; Waldman 1994), it has often not been necessary to achieve positive, significant changes in work system processes and performance.

Unlike many previous management trends, TQM came to the foreground with a history of successful application, particularly with many high-profile competitors of U.S. businesses. TQM practitioners advocated respect for employee knowledge and development, which are difficult points for most employees to argue against. Yet when it came to broad cultural or learning process changes, it was readily apparent that it would be difficult to quantify them. Nevertheless, TQM provided a way of thinking and the strategies necessary to fix problems. It also produced measurable results within very short time periods.

TQM also came along at a very fortuitous time in history. Many U.S. organizations were going through dramatic restructuring efforts, following the rapid growth of the 1980s. Often, organizations had to find ways to reduce layers of management to simply remain competitive. TQM was an ideal approach for flattening the organizational structures of the 1990s and to address the rapid globalization of markets. This is where the emphasis on clients and customers was critical to maintaining an organization's competitive position. TQM also gave hope and focus that things could be better once organizations had gone through this painful period of readjustment.

Indeed, TQM offered organizations what effective leaders often provide: a sense of purpose and direction during the most difficult crises (Bass 1985; Bennis and Nanus 1985; Burns 1978). TQM itself was endowed with leadership properties in that it provided structure, goals, a vision of a more desirable world, and the means to achieve it. TQM was quickly turning the threats of the 1980s into the opportunities for change in the 1990s. If a model or process can have charisma, then TQM certainly had the impact often associated with charismatic leaders; that is, those who lead organizations and nations out of deep crises with a new way of thinking and a vision of a better future, thus reducing fear and focusing people's energy to take on new challenges and opportunities.

The Emerging Criticism of This New Perspective

TQM's image, although still favorable in many sectors, has faded somewhat in the past several years. Most criticisms have stemmed from a lack of trust in top management's commitment to fundamentally change the way organizations make decisions, set agendas, and reward performance (Corrigan 1995; Dobbins 1995). The authors contend that there is nothing inherently wrong with TQM nor should it be counterproductive to individual, group, and organizational performance. What may be counterproductive, however, is to fail to systematically consider the impact such changes have over time on existing and emerging social processes within organizations. To some extent, TQM was damned if it did and damned if it didn't! Specifically, by simplifying organizational processes, quality can typically be improved; but by oversimplifying the social processes underlying improvement, the long-term outcomes expected from TQM may be elusive.

Thus, the debates surrounding the efficacy of TQM as a process and model for change greatly depend on the level of analysis used to both understand and evaluate its core concept—CPI. For example, in a comprehensive report on the outcomes of numerous TQM programs, Ernst & Young (1992) raised the issue of "received doctrine" with respect to TQM in the following statement: "The previously unchallenged assumption of the quality movement has been that any organization, regardless of its current performance, can benefit from widespread adoption of these management practices—the more widespread the better" (p. 7). Based on a study of more than 500 manufacturing and service organizations in the United States, Canada, Germany, and Japan, the Ernst & Young report concluded that practices that were beneficial at one level of organizational performance showed either no association or even a negative association at other levels. This report followed an earlier one on TQM efforts in a broad cross section of organizations. It showed that a majority of TQM programs had not lived up to initial expectations and, in the opinion of the author, had partially or, in some cases, completely failed (Holmes 1992).

It is certainly possible to build further evidence of failed TQM efforts, attributing those failures to fundamental problems with the TQM approach, lack of top management commitment, and/or the inability of the workforce to grasp the specific techniques and processes needed to be a total quality organization. Yet it seems equally crucial to evaluate TQM approaches and their application by first understanding that different levels of analysis may be involved when TQM's strengths, weaknesses, failures, or successes are discussed.

A Meso-Level Framework for TQM

A straightforward example of using a meso-level approach (House and Rousseau 1993) for examining TQM comes from an organization that attempted to drive TQM throughout all of its systems and processes. The organization's CEO was a Deming disciple, and would often interpret events as being linked to one of Deming's 14 principles. After putting the workforce through extensive training on SPC procedures, the CEO became increasingly frustrated with the lack of progress toward improving the overall quality of performance. The workers were completely intimidated by the CEO and only made changes when they were absolutely confident of their positive impact. This fear pervaded the entire culture and clearly affected the levels of continuous improvement observed by the CEO.

To explain this CEO's disappointment, consider the broader culture at one level of analysis and how it impacted individual behavior at another, more microlevel. Using a multilevel approach (Yammarino 1996) assumes that behavior observed at one level is embedded at a more macrolevel, and that can potentially help explain the target behavior observed. In this case, the employees' behavior was directly linked to the no-mistakes culture that the CEO created. Of course, the question that could have been asked is whether there was something inherently wrong with TQM.

Ironically, multiple levels of impact and interaction have been implied in many discussions of TQM, including those of Deming, where he discussed removing organizational-level barriers to individual development and performance (Anderson, Rungtusanetham, and Schroeder 1994). Other examples include the following:

- *Creating cooperation* across functional areas and between individuals, which would bring the focus down to a dyadic or one-to-one level
- *Continuous adaptation*, which may involve an individual picking up a new approach or an organization shifting to meet changes in the market
- *Using leadership* to create a constancy of purpose for organizations, groups, and, at a microlevel, in the minds of individuals

Waldman (1994) summarized the importance of using a levels perspective for examining CPI/TQM in his following comment (p. 517).

> It is important to note that system process and factors exist at multiple levels within an organization. Thus a system factor can be organization-wide, affecting the performance of all individuals within that organization. Alternatively, a system factor can emanate from a subsystem within that system and apply only to those individuals within that subsystem.

Using a levels of analysis framework to examine TQM/CPI, changes in behavior cannot be fully understood without including the context in which those behaviors were embedded. This fact was highlighted by Herb Simon (1969, 230): "An ant, viewed as a behaving system, is quite simple. The apparent complexity of its behavior over time is largely a reflection of the complexity of the environment in which it finds itself." Being aware of how the context or system impacts on organizational, group, dyadic, and individual behavior enhances an understanding of these phenomena (Simon 1969). Simply stated, behavior cannot be fully understood without reference to the next level and/or the context in which it is embedded.

A LEVELS OF ANALYSIS FRAMEWORK FOR EVALUATION OF CPI

Organizational theorists are currently revisiting the separation between macrolevel and microlevel views of organizational behavior (House and Rousseau 1993; Tosi 1992; Yammarino 1996). This has resulted in an intermediate link that is labeled *meso-level*. Using a meso-level approach, the changes intended by TQM with respect to CPI can be examined. This directs attention on the context—the specific changes undertaken in that context that can impact on behavior—and their interaction.

A logical starting point for discussing a levels of analysis framework is to refine the definition of *level* and how this concept can be applied to building successful models of organizational change. One way to interpret level is to consider qualitatively different entities such as individuals, groups, and/or organizations as representing different hierarchical levels of analysis (Miller 1978). Using this notion of levels, total quality may be viewed as an individual responsibility versus a group requirement versus an organizational goal. Different levels of analysis would require different operational definitions to accurately assess what is meant by total quality. Furthermore, the level at which total quality is defined and measured may vary over time, such as when an initiative to upgrade quality, begun at a senior management level, gradually cascades to other levels in the organization. How total quality is conceptualized at the top may vary significantly as it moves across and down organizational levels.

Deming and others have argued that the relevant level of analysis is the system. According to Deming (1986), the system accounts for 94 percent of the variance in performance, which he refers to as "common cause" factors. Using the system as the unit of analysis, it is likely that individual variation would be viewed as irrelevant (Deming 1986). Most, however, if not all, phenomena operate at multiple levels (House and Rousseau 1993; Yammarino 1996). Indeed, work performance itself can be affected by numerous systemic factors in which individuals, dyads (or pairs of individuals), work groups, divisions, and ultimately organizations are embedded.

For example, the type of culture that is conducive to CPI is one that supports creative problem solving and where mistakes are viewed as part of the learning process (Avolio 1994). Such interpretations can apply equally well at the organizational, group, and/or individual level. Yet culture must be measured in different ways, and perhaps with different methods, depending on the level of analysis chosen. Specifically, a group's culture may be supportive of learning from one's mistakes, but at an organizational level this linkage may break down. In a similar vein, the leadership that supports a culture where followers are encouraged to take time to learn from mistakes and develop their potential may be similar at all levels. It is measured differently, however, when examined at the most senior leadership versus peer-to-peer or dyadic leadership interactions at the lowest level of the organization.

In sum, it is easy to argue that the introduction of a CPI program, which starts at the top of two equally effective organizations, could be successful in one and a total failure in the other because of the configuration of the organization, its culture, its leadership orientation, and the relationships among groups and individuals within the organization. To accurately assess what determines the success or failure of these programs, it is necessary to focus the evaluation at the appropriate level of analysis, including the intersection of the person in his or her relevant context.

Integrating Leadership and CPI at Multiple Levels

Leadership is one of the most prominent factors specified in the criteria for the Malcolm Baldrige National Quality Award. The measurement of leadership and its impact on CPI can be examined at the individual, dyadic, group, and/or organizational level (Yammarino and Bass 1991; Yammarino and Dubinsky 1992). All of these analyses may be appropriate depending on the focus of operationalizing CPI.

For example, in an organization that has implemented TQM, supervisors may interpret one of their roles as continuously developing the potential of their direct reports. Different developmental strategies may be pursued for each follower, resulting in a greater impact on each follower's development of competencies. In this description of leadership, which Bass and Avolio (1994) refer to as individual consideration (a component of transformational leadership), the emphasis is on continuous individual development, which can be either at an individual or dyadic (one-on-one) level. At an individual level, each person views the leadership differently regardless of his or her unique relationship with the leader. At the dyadic level, the relationship of the leader with each follower may vary depending on the need of the follower. Thus, the relationship within each leader-follower dyad becomes the relevant unit of analysis.

For the purposes of this chapter, transformational leadership and its four components are used as the basis for operationalizing leadership. According to Bass and Avolio (1994), there are four core components of transformational leadership, with the first already identified as individual consideration. The second component is intellectual stimulation. Here the behavior of leaders is reflected in their ability to get followers (or peers) to question the way they are or have always done things, thus looking at problems from new angles and unique perspectives. A third component, inspirational motivation, is represented by the ability of leaders to generate excitement and to articulate a compelling vision of the future. The fourth component, idealized influence, represents the moral character exhibited by leaders, often shown by their willingness to transcend their self-interests for the interests of others.

The level of analysis can be readily escalated by examining individual consideration at a group versus an individual or dyadic level of analysis (Avolio and Bass 1995). At this level, the supervisor may work with one group to develop specific norms and expectations that may differ dramatically from another group that also reports to the same leader. Individual consideration can be applied to a group where the supervisor is attempting to raise the group's needs and expectations in order to improve its potential. Of course, to complicate matters, individual, dyadic, and/or group development may occur in parallel, making it more difficult to conceptualize and measure CPI. Yet in most instances the authors would argue for them to occur in parallel, regardless of the complexities associated with measurement.

Examining another central component of Bass and Avolio's (1994) model of transformational leadership, inspirational motivation, a CEO of a large organization may articulate a vision of total quality that becomes an organizationwide vision (Larwood et al. 1995). The vision may be understood by the entire workforce, may be seen as exciting, and may influence new employees to choose to work for the company. The vision results in a shared perspective held by the workforce regarding the importance of CPI, which becomes evidenced by new and innovative initiatives, higher performance, and a more creative, risk-free culture.

In contrast, a vision can also be viewed at an individual level with respect to its inspirational appeal. One worker may personally identify with the vision and become inspired by its potential, while another may be so threatened that he or she resists every attempt to implement the vision (Shamir, House, and Arthur 1994). In the first case, the individual employee may seek out educational opportunities to improve his or her core skills; he or she might devise ways to reduce work cycle time and to enhance the quality of relationships with customers and clients. Thus, the vision would be translated into measurable improvements at the individual level of analysis. Yet none of these improvements may have been observed in another employee, leading to an obvious question: At what level did the linkage or impact break down?

Sticking to an individual level of analysis, the two components of transformational leadership could be combined to help explain and advance the CPI efforts. Since inspirational leadership may be in the eye of the beholder, leaders may need to translate their message in different ways to capture employees' imagination and interest. By understanding the needs and concerns of each employee, leaders can adopt and modify their vision without changing its meaning to motivate each employee to strive for continuous improvement. At this point, a third component of transformational leadership, termed *intellectual stimulation,* is introduced (Bass and Avolio 1994). Here leaders may challenge the assumption of workers threatened by CPI to view it from a different perspective. Leaders may personalize the CPI effort to demonstrate the program's individual benefits. Indeed, leaders may demonstrate how personal development and CPI can work together, providing a desirable intervention for each worker.

Building on this example, depending on the level chosen to measure the impact of CPI efforts, the conclusions may differ. At an organizational level, strong and visionary leadership has been recommended by Deming and others to promote TQM/CPI initiatives (Corrigan 1995; Dobbins 1995). For some groups, the vision articulated by a strong leader may have the necessary appeal to achieve exemplary performance, while for others it may be ambiguous, threatening, and/or perceived as inconsequential. The conflict in perspective among employees may, over time, become so significant that any attempts at CPI will fail. No matter what the level of analysis is, by examining the effects of leadership at multiple levels, a much clearer view of how to intervene to keep the CPI process on track can be derived. Examining leadership at a global or systemic level would have overshadowed meaningful differences at individual levels that may have caused the CPI program to derail. Without understanding the developmental needs and perspective of each individual, and the groups to which they belong, the risk that a CPI program will be unsuccessful is increased. To develop this type of understanding, a multilevel analysis must be pursued.

Many models in organizational behavior and human resources management, including TQM, are inherently cross-level, yet few models include a levels of analysis framework in the operationalization measures and the model itself. Behling (1978) suggested that any model that takes into account the impact of the environmental context on individual behavior should be considered a "cross-level theory." Indeed, Schneider (1985) goes one step further, recommending that for each level of analysis at which behavior is examined, the next higher level of analysis is most likely to have a direct or indirect impact on that behavior. Schneider recommends that the unit of analysis be escalated to at least the next level to fully account for the system-level impact on behavior. While Deming essentially argues that individual variation is error and not worthy of consideration (only 6 percent of all variance according to him), Schneider makes the case for determining the unique variability that can be accounted for by the person (lower level), situation (higher level), and, of course, their interaction (cross levels). The fact that TQM efforts have tended to blur the boundaries between the customer/client and the organization is of itself a basis for developing a cross-level model (Spencer 1994). This approach would be consistent with arguments that there should be no boundaries between these two levels.

Developing a Cross-Level Framework

As noted, many propositions associated with CPI assume a cross-level or what Rousseau (1985) has called a "multilevel" effect. Specifically, certain relationships will hold at multiple levels, while other relationships only hold at one level and, therefore, are "level-specific" (Dansereau, Alutto, and Yammarino 1984). This does not make these relationships any less important; rather, it merely identifies where a particular relationship can be expected to occur.

There are four levels of analysis with respect to people in organizations that are relevant: (1) persons, (2) dyads, (3) groups, and (4) collectivities. Each of these can be described as four separate lenses for viewing behavior in organizations. As noted, however, a core aspect of using a levels of analysis framework is the embeddedness of these four levels within larger entities (or levels) and, more importantly, that organizations can be viewed as systems comprised of interdependent parts at each level.

Viewing behavior in organizations at higher levels of analysis, the number of entities is reduced, while the potential diversity or range (that is, number of elements) within a level increases. For example, individuals comprise dyads or groups, which comprise departments in organizations. The number of individuals is greater than the number of groups, which is also greater than the number of departments. The fact that Deming viewed organizations as systems that could produce "profound knowledge," in and of itself, indicated a levels of analysis perspective, but without a clear specification of embeddedness.

In many discussions of CPI and its measurement, the relevant level of analysis appears to be the organization (Bleakley 1993; Spencer 1994). A typical example is that the organization seeks out information from its external customers to improve on a continuous basis the delivery of its product. By examining CPI at a microlevel of analysis, such as the individual or group, the effective and efficient transference of information from external sources to various internal customers is indicative of CPI.

For example, how does information within the organization get transmitted from one unit to the next? How does information flow within groups? How do individuals use the information? How does that lead to continuous improvement with respect to the delivery of services? In each of these cases, several levels of analysis seem relevant as well as cross-level or multilevel influences. Moreover, should the process be operationally defined in different ways if internal customers are at different hierarchical levels within the organization? Depending on the level of analysis, the concepts of *CPI* and *customer* may take on different meanings and also may need to be measured in different ways.

The authors contend that all of the interpretations of CPI are central to the successful implementation of total quality improvement. The point is that *CPI implies different elements and translates to different criteria at various levels of analysis.* And, as Deming (1986) suggested, linking an individual's goals and perspective to the organization's goals and shared perspectives becomes a critical factor in the success of CPI efforts. To a large extent, CPI may provide a good vehicle for exploring the concepts of open systems and for helping researchers to learn more about cross-level relationships in organizations (Ashmos and Huber 1987).

This argument can be generalized to include a levels of analysis perspective by examining the specific dimensions comprising the Malcolm Baldrige National Quality Award and items contained in those dimensions. The indicators in the Baldrige Award criteria often represent processes as well as outcomes, which can operate at different levels of analysis, although they are not explicitly stated as such in the award criteria. For example, one specification of leadership in the Baldrige Award criteria is, "How the senior executives create and sustain a clear and visible quality value system along with the supporting management system to guide all activities of the company toward excellence." This statement includes several variables that can be operationalized at multiple levels, including the individual, group, and organization. Moreover, it also points to the importance of leadership in building internal and external (two levels) cooperation among different individuals and units (Anderson, Rungtusanetham, and Schroeder 1994).

Further Refinements to Developing a Levels Framework for CPI

A contingent relationship operates under some conditions and, therefore, defines the boundaries where an approach holds. For example, CPI performance relationships may hold in line or production areas, but not in staff or support areas. Given the conflicting findings regarding the impact of CPI programs, it is essential to specify under what conditions certain relationships linked to change processes associated with CPI would and would not be expected to occur.

Taking Deming's basic premise that the system accounts for most of the variability in organizational performance, there is substantial evidence to support his view. Yet whether his position applies equally well across levels within organizations, as well as across organizations that are people-driven (service) versus technology-driven (manufacturing), remains an open question. Certain boundaries to Deming's arguments might emerge if his position was systematically examined across different levels of analysis. Unfortunately, many total quality programs have been implemented as though they were independent of the context in which they were embedded, in contrast with almost every other contingency model of management (Dean and Bowen 1994).

Another important concept that can be used to examine CPI at different levels of analysis is referred to by Rousseau (1985) as an "ecological fallacy." Such fallacies occur when attempts are made to draw inferences about individual-level phenomena from relationships that exist at higher levels of analysis, such as dyads or groups. The reverse condition, "individualistic fallacies," exists when attempts are made to generalize from the individual level to a higher level (Glick and Roberts 1984; Pedhazur 1982). For example, it may be an ecological fallacy to argue that poor individual performance is invariably a function of the system. Some employees may work within the parameters of the system and/or avoid the parameters creatively in spite of the problems. In reality, the causes of variation in performance may exist at multiple levels and in varying degree over time. In some organizations, the culture, as opposed to standard operating procedures, may be more relevant to explaining variations in individual performance. Also, in other organizations, it may be the relationship of the immediate supervisor with his or her follower (dyadic relationship) versus the general philosophy of senior management. This leads to the idea that improving a system means something different at various levels of analysis, at different points in time, and depending on the unit of analysis (for example, person, group, and/or larger organizational unit).

Expanding CPI Visions to Multiple Levels of Analysis

The new paradigms of leadership discussed by Bass (1990) and Bryman (1992) all highlight the importance of vision to the future success of organizations. The concept of vision is also central to discussions of CPI and is one of the key variables/dimensions measured in the Baldrige Award criteria. Operational definitions of vision, however, often include multiple levels without clearly specifying how a vision differs when the focus is on a strategic vision versus an individual vision (Larwood et al. 1995). Complicating matters, many authors discuss the importance of a "shared vision" to ensure organizational, group, and individual success (Avolio and Bass 1988; Bennis 1991; Conger and Kanungo 1987; Kuhnert and Lewis 1987; Schein 1990).

For the sake of simplicity, a vision can be described as an articulation of a desired future state, regardless of level. The vision can be at a strategic or organizational level with respect to the image the organization wishes to create (for example, to be the industry leader in recyclable plastic products); markets to be explored (for example, to develop recyclable plastics for use in the health care industry); and in terms of the products to be produced (for example, to design recyclable products for prosthetic devices). In this example, if the organization's strategic vision evolves or is changed to "developing plastics products that can be configured to any form or strength," then the subsequent characteristics of the vision with respect to markets (for example, office construction) and products (for example, portable office cells) also may change substantially.

The concept of a vision can take on a distinctly different meaning if examined at the organizational versus group level. At the organizational level, the vision may serve the purpose of giving the firm a strategic focus, working toward offering potential investors information that would influence their decision to commit to the company. It also may signal potential customers what the organization is attempting to deliver to its markets, such as the type of product customers can expect to receive. The vision also may impact regulatory agencies and the types of judgments passed on the firm.

Looking inward, the vision helps groups and individuals within the organization decide how to allocate their resources. It aligns groups around a common mission and a set of shared expectations of what the future holds. As some authors have described, the vision may help develop a match between frames of reference held across levels, leading to alignment and a cohesive focus across individuals, groups, and larger entities (Ireland et al. 1987). A CPI vision can also challenge one's identity within a team or force individuals to question their own self-concept, perhaps changing it to be more in line with the global vision (Reger et al. 1994).

To this point, a vision at multiple levels of analysis that incorporates the organization, groups, and individuals within the organization has been examined. The environment in which the organization is embedded is part of the description of the vision's impact. A vision may also operate at multiple levels or cross-levels within the organization, such that the shared expectations conveyed at the organizational level are similarly conveyed at the group and individual level.

Each organization within a particular industry, however, could have a separate and distinct vision. Within a focal organization, all divisions may understand the vision and are able to articulate its uniqueness with respect to other organizations and visions. If there are differences within the organization with respect to the vision, then it is not yet fully shared or appreciated at all levels. This may mean that some divisions understand the vision and some don't, in terms of comparing it to other organizations within the same industry. Or, the vision may be articulated or modeled differently by various leaders in the organization's divisions. It also may mean that only some individuals, regardless of division, understand the vision and are able to articulate how it differs from other organization visions. In this case, there are vast individual differences in terms of each employee's ability to define the uniqueness of the organization's vision within its division or industry. Lastly, individuals within the organization may not know what the vision is or understand it as stated. Therefore, they would be unable to articulate its uniqueness with respect to other organizations. It is easily seen that a breakdown in the impact of a vision has many potential sources of explanation when viewing the articulation of a vision at multiple levels of analysis.

Complicating matters, the evolution of visions must be examined by including time in the levels of analysis (Early and Godfrey 1995). For simplicity sake, a snapshot of a vision, say at three points in time, will be taken. At time 1, a CEO articulates a vision for a CPI program. Because the exact meaning is not clear initially, there will be variation about the vision's meaning and intent within and between units at each level of the organization. Individuals in groups, and groups within the organization, will interpret the vision differently. Typically there is a lack of agreement about the vision in the workforce, among customers, and/or among the organization's competitors. At time 2, each group within the organization may achieve some consensus about the vision, but many groups may still differ in their interpretations. At a later point in time, when the vision has been repeatedly articulated and well-documented, it could be shared and agreed upon by all groups, individuals within all groups, and all groups within the organization. Thus at time 3, the vision is shared by all internal and external constituents, who can also articulate how it differs from other organizations' visions.

Using a levels of analysis framework can provide a strategy for senior managers for diffusing an organizational vision across all appropriate levels. For example, the CEO could roll out the vision assuming that there will be wide variations in its interpretation at all levels of analysis. As part of the CEO's strategy, he or she can meet with different entities within the organization to discuss the relevance of the vision to their particular work, while also attending to interactions with other areas/units and the accomplishment of the vision. Subsequent to these discussions, each leader of the respective areas could spend time with the CEO, as well as with members of their unit, further articulating how the vision has relevance to what each unit, and ultimately each individual employee, should do. Indeed, the purest test of a vision is whether it can be diffused in terms of its relevance to each individual's work, so that all share in its importance across levels of the organization.

Depending on the level of analysis and whether the focus is internal or external, the types of questions asked and measures taken to assess the vision's adoption may differ dramatically and change over time. The fact that individuals are unable to articulate the uniqueness of the organization's vision does not necessarily indicate that it is not unique or potentially useful. Perhaps it simply means that individuals within an organization are unable to explain it, because it requires an exact specification and examination of the appropriate level of analysis. For example, is the supervisor failing to translate the vision for his or her work group? Is it that the employees aren't motivated to pursue the vision? Is the CEO inconsistent with the main premise of the vision? Did the CEO fail to spend enough time with his or her direct reports when rolling out the vision?

Conversely, customers, which represent one segment of the external environment, may be able to clearly articulate the uniqueness of the vision because top management has expended a considerable amount of energy and time articulating the vision through its marketing efforts. This, however, may also change over time, as the organization's market matures and becomes more complex and diversified. Thus the evolution of a vision about CPI also becomes an important consideration in deciding the most appropriate level of analysis to assess the impact of a vision; how to improve its chances of success; and how to best educate the workforce about its implications for future organizational development.

A Multilevel Example of Continuous Process Improvement

The conceptual and operational definitions of CPI will vary if the focus is at the organizational, as opposed to the group, level of analysis. CPI at the organizational level may involve focusing on entire systems, such as the cost accounting system used by the organization. Over the last 40 years, the accounting field has focused organizational leaders' attention on measuring rates of output, as opposed to variables such as flexibility of inputs, as the best indicator of organizational performance (Johnson 1992). Within this accounting framework, volume of output determined unit cost. Thus, spreading overhead costs over more output meant lower cost per unit. This led to persuading the customer to purchase as much as the organization could produce. This strategy obviously created a great deal of waste and inefficiency in organizations. Marginally improving this accounting procedure would involve moving away from simply focusing on rates of output and including ways to assess the quality of inputs, resources, and outputs. Again, these could be specified and measured in different ways at the organization, group, and/or individual level.

Rather than simply look at CPI as an accounting process, it is possible to examine CPI as a learning process. For example, CPI has been broadly described as being represented by learning from one's mistakes, such as suggested in terms of "double loop" versus "single loop" learning (Argyris 1982). Entire organizations are described as having cultures that support a "learning from mistakes" environment, which promotes a more "holistic" approach to problem solving (Schein 1990; Waldman 1994). Groups in those organizations may, in turn, reinforce problem-solving strategies that encourage risk-taking behavior. Taking higher risks may result in more mistakes, yet the group would support the making of mistakes because it places a higher value on learning new and innovative methods. Of course, the concept of learning from mistakes can be easily applied to individuals within groups and the overall organization, taking on yet other foci or levels of analysis that affect conceptual and operational definitions.

Thus, learning from mistakes could be represented as an organizational value, a group or dyadic value, and an individual value, or some combination of these. Learning from mistakes may be seen as unique within an industry; understood by some divisions but not by others in an organization; practiced by different groups across divisions; practiced by some employee pairs, but not others within a unit; or simply as an individual-level phenomena. In the worst-case scenario, it may not be understood at all, because learning by mistakes may not have been clearly communicated by the leadership as being an acceptable practice. Again, the level that is chosen to define critical CPI components will determine the type of measures that need to be included and, most importantly, the conclusions that can be drawn from the data once collected on the success and/or failure of CPI programs.

IMPLICATIONS FOR CPI/TQM

In the last several sections, an attempt was made to apply a levels framework by precisely defining variables that are central to CPI. The authors' intent from the chapter's outset has been to refine the discussion of these variables so that they are precisely operationalized and measured. Operationally defining CPI at an organizational, group, and individual level are all equally valid and, in some instances, may represent important distinctions. Again, the concept of learning from mistakes may be seen quite similarly when discussing an organization, a group within an organization, dyads within a group, and an individual within a group or dyad. Yet whether learning from mistakes actually operates in similar ways at multiple levels in an organization is an empirical question to be tested rather than arbitrarily assumed.

To some degree, the inclusion of a levels of analysis framework into CPI models is consistent with the trend of examining organizations using a postmodern perspective. As Clegg (1992) suggests, "there are now different phenomena to be analyzed, phenomena that are not simply a linear progression of the past, but discontinuous with it" (p. 2). The postmodern view characterizes organizations as being more flexible and specifically targets principles of interaction and synthesis in its modeling of organizations. This postmodern view intersects with those ideas presented in this chapter because a focus on levels of analysis permits a differentiation of the whole and its parts, while examining both at various levels and across multiple levels.

Relatedly, Ackoff (1991) refers to a "holistic" perspective of organizations as representing "synthetic thinking." Specifically, consistent with the levels of analysis framework, things that are to be understood are examined as parts of a whole; identifying first the whole and then the parts. The whole is then disaggregated into its relevant parts (other levels) to explain the behavior of interest. Behavior and the properties of the parts are explained in terms of revealing the role of the behavior in the larger whole; for example, person within context or groups within organization.

According to Kuhnert (forthcoming), one of the best examples of the sort of thinking described by Ackoff (1991) is in models of CPI. Kuhnert refers to Lewin's (1947) comment to highlight the evolution of the field of organizational behavior and how it has paralleled other disciplines. Specifically, Lewin has argued,

> Throughout the history of mathematics and physics problems of constancy of relations rather than constancy of elements have gained importance and have gradually changed the picture of what is essential. The social sciences seem to show a very similar development. (p. 192)

There is every reason to believe that the shift in focus toward studying organizations and human behavior by incorporating a levels of analysis framework will continue to help refine conceptual and operational definitions of constructs and measures in organizational theory, behavior, and development, as well as human resources management. Rather than viewing this trend as being a de-evolutionary way of thinking, it has been argued that this trend is a distinct evolution where models of individual and organizational behavior have been integrated to help explain the successes and failures of TQM programs. It has also been argued that it would be inappropriate and counterproductive to cast aside the methods and model associated with CPI because of some instances of missed expectations and failure. On the contrary, the authors hope that specific boundaries can now be specified for CPI so that rigorous testing can be used to assess the model's overall construct validity. It is only through such refinements that one's understanding of individual behavior within complex systems can continuously improve.

Multiple levels of analysis provide a framework for accomplishing these advancements. Using this approach, there is now a historic opportunity to build on the work that has already taken place by integrating the system/context and groups/individuals in an inclusive model of organizational behavior, change, and development and human resources management, which heretofore has not been articulated. These efforts can have a profound impact on the models of organizational leadership and management that will take hold in U.S. organizations into the next millennium.

REFERENCES

Ackoff, Roger A. 1991. *Ackoff's fables: Irreverent reflections on business and bureaucracy.* New York: John Wiley & Sons.

Argyris, Chris. 1982. *The executive mind and double-loop learning.* New York: Basic Books.

Anderson, John C., Manus Rungtusanetham, and Roger G. Schroeder. 1994. A theory of quality management underlying the Deming management method. *Academy of Management Review* (July): 472–509.

Ashmos, Donde P., and George P. Huber. 1987. The systems paradigm in organizational theory: Correcting the record and suggesting the future. *Academy of Management Review* 12, no. 4:607–621.

Avolio, Bruce J. 1994. The alliance of total quality and the full range of leadership. In *Improving organizational effectiveness through transformational leadership,* edited by Bernard M. Bass, and Bruce. J. Avolio. Newbury Park, Calif.: Sage Publications.

Avolio, Bruce J., and Bernard M. Bass. 1995. Individual consideration viewed at multiple levels of analysis: A multi-level framework for examining the diffusion of transformational leadership. *Leadership Quarterly* 6, no. 2:199–218.

———. 1988. Transformational leadership, charisma and beyond. In *Emerging leadership vistas,* edited by James G. Hunt, Bajaram R. Baliga, H. Peter Dachler, and Chester A. Schriesheim. Lexington, Mass.: Lexington Books.

Barrett, Gerald V. 1972. Symposium: Research models of the future for industrial and organizational psychology. *Personnel Psychology* 25, no. 1:1–17.

Bass, Bernard M. 1985. *Leadership and performance beyond expectations.* New York: Free Press.

———. 1990. *Bass & Stogdill's handbook of leadership.* New York: Free Press.

Bass, Bernard M., and Bruce J. Avolio. 1994. *Improving organizational effectiveness through transformational leadership.* Newbury Park, Calif.: Sage Publications.

Behling, Orlando. 1978. Some problems in the philosophy of science of organizations. *Academy of Management Review* 3, no. 2:193–201.

Bemowski, Karen. 1995. TQM: Flimsy footing or firm foundation? *Quality Progress* (July): 27–28.

Bennis, Warren G. 1991. *Why leaders can't lead: The unconscious conspiracy continues.* San Francisco: Jossey-Bass Publishers.

Bennis, Warren G., and B. Nanus. 1985. *Leaders: The strategies for taking charge.* New York: Harper & Row.

Bleakley, Fred R. 1993. Many companies try management fads, only to see them flop. *Wall Street Journal,* 6 July, A1, A6.

Brown, Mark G. 1991. *Baldrige Award-winning quality.* White Plains, N.Y.: Quality Resources.

Bryman, Alan. 1992. *Charisma and leadership in organizations.* London: Sage Publications.

Burns, James M. 1978. *Leadership.* New York: Harper.

Clegg, Stewart R. 1992. Postmodern management? Paper presented at the National Meeting of the Academy of Management, August, Las Vegas, Nevada.

Conger, Jay A., and Rabi N. Kanungo. 1987. Toward a behavioral theory of charismatic leadership in organizational settings. *Academy of Management Review* 12, no. 4:637–647.

Corrigan, James P. 1995. The art of TQM. *Quality Progress* (July): 61–64.

Dansereau, Fred, Joseph A. Alutto, and Francis J. Yammarino. 1984. *Theory testing in organizational behavior: The varient approach.* Englewood Cliffs, N.J.: Prentice Hall.

Dean, James W., and David E. Bowen. 1994. Management theory and total quality: Improving research and practice through theory development. *Academy of Management Review* 19, no. 3:392–418.

Deming, W. Edwards. 1986. *Out of the crisis.* Cambridge, Mass.: MIT Institute for Advanced Engineering Study.

Dobbins, Greg H., Robert L. Cardy, and Ken Carson. 1991. Examining fundamental assumptions: A contrast of person and system approaches to human resource management. *Research in Personnel and Human Resources Management* 9:1–38.

Dobbins, Richard D. 1995. A failure of methods, not philosophy. *Quality Progress* (July): 31–33.

Early, John F., and A. Blanton Godfrey. 1995. But it takes too long. *Quality Progress* (July): 51–55.

Ernst & Young. 1992. *The international quality study: Best practices report: An analysis of management practices that impact performance.* Cleveland, Ohio: Ernst & Young.

Glick, William H., and Karlene H. Roberts. 1984. Hypothesized interdependence, assumed independence. *Academy of Management Review* 9, no. 4:722–735.

Holmes, Edward. 1992. Leadership in the quest for quality. *Issues and Observations* 12, no. 7:5–8.

House, Robert J., and Denise M. Rousseau. 1993. *On the bifurcation of OB or if it ain't MESO it ain't OB.* Working paper, Wharton School of Management, University of Pennsylvania, Philadelphia.

Ireland, R. Duane, Michael A. Hitt, Richard A. Bettis, and David A. dePorras. 1987. Strategy for relation processes: Differences in perceptions of strengths and weaknesses indicating an environmental uncertainty by management level. *Strategic Management Journal* 8, no. 5:469–486.

Johnson, Herbert T. 1992. *Relevance regained: From top-down control to bottom-up empowerment.* New York: Free Press.

Juran, J. M. 1991. *Juran on leadership for quality: An executive handbook.* Wilson, Conn.: Juran Institute.

Kuhnert, Karl W. Forthcoming. Leadership theory in post modernist organizations. In *Handbook of organizational behavior,* edited by R. T. Golembiewski. New York: Marcel Dekker.

Kuhnert, Karl W., and Phillip Lewis. 1987. Transactional and transformational leadership: A constructive/developmental analysis. *Academy of Management Review* 12, no. 4:648–657.

Larwood, Laurie., Cecilia M. Falbe, Mark P. Kriger, and Paul Miesing. 1995. Structure and meaning of organizational vision. *Academy of Management Journal* 38, no. 3:740–769.

Lewin, Kurt. 1947. Group decision and social change. In *Readings in social psychology*, edited by T. Newcomb, and E. Hartley. New York: Holt.

Linkow, Paul. 1989. Is your culture ready for total quality? *Quality Progress* (November): 69–71.

Miller, James G. 1978. *Living systems.* New York: McGraw-Hill.

Pedhazur, Elazur J. 1982. *Multiple regression in behavioral research.* New York: Holt, Rinehart & Winston.

Reeves, Carol A., and David A. Bedner. 1994. Defining quality: Alternatives and implications. *Academy of Management Review* (July): 419–445.

Reger, Rhonda K., Loren T. Gustafson, Samuel M. Demarie, and John V. Mullane. 1994. Reframing the organization: Why implementing total quality is easier said than done. *Academy of Management Review* 19, no. 3:565–584.

Rousseau, Denise M. 1985. Issues of level in organizational research: Multi-level and cross-level perspectives. *Research in Organizational Behavior* 7:1–37.

Sashkin, Marshall, and Kenneth J. Kiser. 1991. *Total quality management.* Seabrook, Md.: Ducochon Press.

Schein, Edgar H. 1985. Organizational culture. *American Psychologist* 48, no. 2:109–119.

Schneider, Ben. 1985. Organizational behavior. *Annual Review of Psychology* 36:573–611.

Shamir, Boas, Robert J. House, and Michael B. Arthur. 1994. The motivational effects of charismatic leadership: A self-concept based theory. *Organization Science* 4, no. 4:577–594.

Simon, Herbert A. 1969. *The sciences of the artificial.* Cambridge, Mass.: MIT Press.

Spencer, Barbara A. 1994. Models of organization and total quality management: A comparison and critical evaluation. *Academy of Management Review* 19, no. 3:446–471.

Tosi, Henry L. 1992. *The environment/organization/person (EOP) contingency model: A meso approach to the study of organization.* Greenwich, Conn.: JAI Press.

Waldman David A. 1994. The contributions of total quality management to a theory of work performance. *Academy of Management Review* 19, no. 3:510–536.

Walton, Mary. 1986. *The Deming management method.* New York: Dodd, Mead.

Yammarino, Francis J. 1996. A conceptual-empirical approach for testing meso and multi-level theories. In *Extensions of the environment/organization/person model,* edited by H. L. Tosi. Greenwich, Conn.: JAI Press.

Yammarino, Francis J., and Bernard M. Bass. 1991. Person and situation views of leadership: A multiple levels of analysis approach. *Leadership Quarterly* 2, no. 2:121–139.

Yammarino, Francis J., and Alan J. Dubinsky. 1992. Superior-subordinate relationships: A multiple levels of analysis approach. *Human Relations* 45, no. 6:575–600.

Chapter 2

The Reward and Recognition Process: A Reinforcement Theory Approach

Stephen B. Knouse

Reward and recognition is a vital process in total quality management (TQM). Motorola, a winner of the 1988 Malcolm Baldrige National Quality Award, states in its human resources policy, "A sound, integrated reward and recognition system is fundamental to an organization's ability to attract, retain, and motivate a best-in-class work force" (Donnelly 1992, 4).

Many TQM organizations have instituted a variety of financial rewards, awards, and innovative pay systems. Knouse (1995a) gives an extensive description. In this chapter, reward and recognition and their functions in TQM organizations will be defined. Then, using the framework of reinforcement theory, the reward and recognition process will be detailed. Finally, the organizational structure supporting the reward and recognition process will be examined.

CONCEPTS OF REWARD AND RECOGNITION

Reward

According to reinforcement theory, a reward is anything that increases the frequency of behavior (Skinner 1969). This is an operational definition; reward is defined in terms of how it operates on behavior. The key is that the reward dispenser (in the TQM organization, a manager or a team) must give out rewards that work—that is, those that actually improve employee behavior. There are a variety of possible rewards in any organizational environment. Table 2.1 summarizes examples of rewards, which are described in the following sections.

TABLE 2.1. Examples of types of reward and recognition.

Type	Focus	Organization
Cash bonus		
• Executive quality bonus	Quality performance	Federal Express
• Suggestion bonus	Improvement suggestions	Lou Ana Foods
	Cost savings	City of Phoenix
Noncash team rewards		
• Team names and T-shirts	Team orientation	Motorola's Quality Olympics
Recognition awards		
• Top executive's City Manager's Award	Quality excellence	City of Phoenix
Chairman's Quality Award	Quality performance	Motorola
• Performance area		
Quality Award	Problem solving	Oregon State
Beaver Award	Special projects	Oregon State
Great Performance Award	Exceptional performance	Oregon State
• Peer		
Peer-to-Peer Award	Quality performance	IBM
Crewmember Award	Team contribution	Lou Ana Foods
• Team		
Market Driven Quality Award	Use of quality tools	IBM
• Customer-oriented		
Customer Satisfaction Award	Customer satisfaction	Xerox
Gold Falcon Award	Customer service	Federal Express
• Publicizing		
Displays	Hall of fame	Millikan
• Customized		
Supervisor Award	Customized employee gift	Appleton Papers
Special Recognition	Time off, free travel	Shawnee Mission
Trifecta	Surprise gift, remembrance gift	IBM
Pay as reward		
• Profit sharing	Profits to teams	Johnsonville Foods
• Gain sharing	Specific improvements	General Motors Naval Supply Center
	Cost reductions	Evert Products
	Team skills	Polaroid
• Skill-based pay	Acquiring skills	Johnsonville Foods
	Developing competencies	StorageTek
• Equal raises	Contribution increase	Shawnee Mission

Types of Reward

1. *Cash* Most employees react favorably to cash. In fact, money is considered to be a generalized reinforcer that is effective with almost anyone. Cash rewards can be in the form of bonuses or raises or even cash on the spot in the form of brand-new bills (Milas 1995). For example, at Federal Express, a winner of the 1990 Baldrige Award, executives can earn up to 40 percent of their salary as quality bonuses (Blackburn and Rosen 1993). In addition, many organizations, such as Lou Ana Foods and the City of Phoenix, reward employee or team quality improvement suggestions with cash bonuses (Knouse 1995a).

2. *Nonmonetary rewards* There are several types of nonmonetary rewards: awards (plaques and certificates); social reinforcers (praise from supervisors or peers, attention of important persons in the company, publicity from in-house or outside in the form of customers or the public); and objects of personal value (decals, jewelry, pens that carry symbols or logos signifying accomplishments) (Drummond and Chell 1992; Harrington 1987).

3. *Team rewards* A reward variation that is becoming common in TQM organizations is team reward—one given to all members of a team that signifies a team accomplishment. A team reward can be a cash bonus or a token.

Team rewards are generally implemented when TQM has become firmly implanted in the organization. At this point teams are functioning well in problem solving and continuous process improvement. During TQM implementation, the organizational reward structure has progressed through a number of phases: first traditional pay for performance, like merit pay; then individual and key contributor incentives; then gain sharing and skill-based pay; and finally team rewards (Johnson 1993).

Functions of Reward

1. *Reinforce TQM behaviors* A managed reward system focuses on improving desired behaviors (Lawler 1987). In the case of the TQM organization, reward can improve TQM behaviors, such as using TQM tools (statistical process control (SPC), cause-and-effect diagrams, and Pareto charts), solving quality problems, and serving both internal and external customers.

2. *Reinforce teamwork* In TQM organizations reward is frequently focused on the quality team (Harrington 1987). Rewards may be directed toward the team, such as a dinner for team members or the opportunity for the team to present its quality improvements to an outside audience. In

addition, rewards to individual team members, such as T-shirts or coffee mugs, may carry the team symbol or logo. For example, many teams competing in the Motorola Quality Olympics have their own team names and distinctive T-shirts (Motorola 1992).

3. *Reinforce TQM culture* Corporate culture has several essential components—corporate values, leadership, and the reward structure of the organization (Trice and Beyer 1993; Lawler 1987). In a TQM organization the reward system reflects the corporate philosophy toward continuous improvement of quality and customer satisfaction. Moreover, reward strengthens employee commitment to the corporate values of quality and meeting customer needs. Indeed, reward serves to internalize organization values, such as quality, in employees (Drummond and Chell 1992). In Deming's (1986) terms, reward can help transform the organization toward a culture of quality.

Recognition

One type of nonmonetary reward, recognition, has been used extensively in TQM organizations. Juran (1992, 328) succinctly defines recognition as "public acknowledgment of success."

Types of Recognition

1. *Company awards* The most common form of recognition in TQM programs is some type of award conferred on individuals or teams for support of the quality effort. These have many names, such as President's Award, Excellence in Quality Award, Team Excellence Award, Idea Development Award, Contribution Award, Initiative Award, and Exceptional Effort Award. This type of award is usually in the form of a plaque or certificate. Many times it is presented at a formal recognition meeting, and TQM organizations publicize it in internal and external publications. In addition, firms like Milliken publicize winners in halls of fame (Schoenberger 1994).

The City of Phoenix has a City Manager's Award for Excellence (City of Phoenix 1992). Motorola has a Chairman's Quality Award, where the CEO flies to any unit in the world to present the award (Blackburn and Rosen 1993). Oregon State University has a series of awards: the Quality Award for problem solving; the Beaver Award (university mascot) for special projects; and the Great Performance Award for exceptional performance on a special task, such as handling a crisis (Coate 1991).

Several TQM companies have instituted creative team awards (Harrington 1987): family recognition picnics, team progress presentations to upper management or customers, company-financed team attendance at quality conferences, and team momentos (pens, calculators, or product models with team TQM logo).

2. *Peer awards* In a peer award, a coworker can nominate a peer for a quality award. IBM Marketing has a Peer-to-Peer Award where individuals receive $20 to buy a gift for a peer (Carder and Clark 1992). Lou Ana Foods has a Crewmember's Award given by peers to an individual for team contribution (Lou Ana Foods 1992).

3. *Team-managed awards* Several TQM companies offer quality awards where one quality team nominates another. In some companies the nominating team even creates a customized award for the winning team. Management provides the cash with which the nominating team then buys or makes something that uniquely characterizes the winning team—signs, tokens such as mugs or badges, or T-shirts with the team name or logo. IBM Marketing has a Market Driven Quality Award where a team nominates another for teamwork or use of quality tools (Carder and Clark 1992).

4. *Customer-oriented awards* Because TQM is based on meeting customer expectations, customer satisfaction awards should be prominent. In some companies customers are part of the award nomination and presentation process. Xerox Business Products Division, winner of the 1989 Baldrige Award, has a Customer Satisfaction Award. Federal Express gives the Golden Falcon Award for customer service (Blackburn and Rosen 1993).

Functions of Recognition

1. *Public indicator of achievement* Awards publicly show that the individual or team has achieved some degree of success with TQM (Milas 1995). They are indicators of quality efforts visible to both peers (internal customers) and clients (external customers).

2. *Feedback* Recognition is also a form of feedback about the results of individual or team efforts (Carder and Clark 1992). They show the individual or team that they are progressing toward quality goals. Recognition as feedback can come from one's own team, other teams, managers, or external customers in the marketplace.

3. *Reinforce a culture of appreciation* IBM has come to understand that TQM cultures are "recognition rich," while traditional corporate cultures tend to focus on productivity rather than their people and are thus recognition poor (Carder and Clark 1992).

In a TQM organization, recognition serves to publicize employees and teams who make a definite contribution to the TQM effort. As a reinforcer, recognition stimulates further effort in employees (Harrington 1987).

PAY AS REWARD

Traditionally, organizations reward their employees through the pay system, particularly with wages. Interestingly, even Frederick Taylor, the father of traditional American management practices, advocated worker bonuses for increased productivity. Deming, of course, was against any pay structure, such as management by objectives (MBO) or merit pay, that set up individual competition and decreased cooperation toward organization quality efforts (Knouse, Carson, and Carson 1993). Thus, TQM organizations have experimented with several variations to the traditional salary.

Profit Sharing

Profit sharing takes a portion of the company's profits for a year and divides them equally among employees. Deming's (1986) emphasis on equivalent pay is thus stressed. Furthermore, profit sharing logically follows from Deming's view that quality improvement should result in profitability. Since expensive rework is reduced, quality improvements lead to cost efficiencies, and a reputation for quality will increase market share for the company. Johnsonville Foods has a profit-sharing program where company teams divide the profits (Sashkin and Kiser 1991). Wainwright Industries, a 1994 winner of the Baldrige Award, also issues profit-sharing payments to its associates (Robbins 1994).

Gain Sharing

Gain sharing is usually more narrowly focused than profit sharing. Employee teams make improvement suggestions, which result in a cost savings when implemented (Welbourne and Gomez Meija 1995). The team then shares part of the cost savings. Generally, the entire organization does not participate in gain sharing (Sashkin and Kiser 1991). The advantage of gain sharing over profit sharing is that it focuses on producing cost efficiencies and cost savings from quality improvements, rather than emphasizing any means that produces a profit. Surveys show that gain sharing appears to be team- rather than individual-oriented. For example, General Motors requires that 95 percent of gains go to teams rather than to individuals (Schoenberger 1994).

The Naval Supply Center in San Diego has a gain-sharing program where teams get 50 percent of the cost savings arising from quality improvement suggestions (Naval Supply Center 1991). At Evart Products, an automobile parts firm, gain sharing reduced the defective products rate, increased supplier quality assurance survey scores, and helped Evart win several quality awards from customers such as Chrysler and Volkswagen (Ross and Hatcher 1992).

Pay Based on Skill Acquisition

Skill-based pay fits well into TQM's emphasis on employees with multiple skills (TQM tools, teamwork, and problem solving) working on quality teams. Indeed, a number of TQM organizations use some variation of skill-based pay (Lawler, Ledford, and Chang 1993). Further, multiskilled employees are flexible and innovative and thus better able to meet changing customer demands.

Johnsonville Foods gives salary increases for acquiring needed skills (Sashkin and Kiser 1991). StorageTek has competency-based pay for skill development (Stratton 1992; StorageTek 1991).

A major disadvantage of skill-based pay is that it increases labor costs, to pay for the salary increases, without immediately offsetting increases in worker productivity (Lawler 1990). At the same time, skill-based pay builds a flexible, multiskilled workforce for the long term. As TQM further develops, several variations on skill-based pay will likely evolve to balance its costs and advantages (Knouse 1995b).

One variation is skill-based bonuses. One-time bonuses reward skill training without permanently increasing the pay base. A paper company gave one-time bonuses as a reward for skills training because promotions were temporarily blocked (Meng 1992). Another variation is team-oriented, skill-based training where team members are rewarded for acquiring team skills. According to the *Economist* (1991), Polaroid implemented an applied knowledge pay program where team members were rewarded for skills they acquired for meeting team goals.

Contribution Increases

Shawnee Mission Medical Center gives everyone the same raises as "contribution increases" to the overall TQM effort (Burda 1992). Other companies are giving pay raises for meeting or exceeding goals on collaborative performance. In some companies this is looked upon as a one-time bonus and thus not included in base pay. The implication is that the bonus may increase or decrease depending on performance toward quality goals (Lawler, Mohrman, and Ledford 1992).

REINFORCEMENT THEORY APPROACH TO REWARD AND RECOGNITION

Reinforcement theory states that behavior is controlled by the environment surrounding behavior (Skinner 1969). Graphically, this would be as follows:

$$\text{Antecedents} \rightarrow \text{Behavior} \rightarrow \text{Consequences}$$

Specifically, events immediately preceding behavior (antecedents) and events immediately following behavior (consequences) control behavior.

Antecedents are organizational indicators that lead to quality behaviors. Antecedents include policy statements, statements from supervisors, and team-initiated efforts. Quality behaviors include correct use of TQM tools, such as SPC, team behaviors (information seeking, encouraging others, problem-solving behaviors), and customer-oriented behaviors (asking customers questions on quality, prompt response to customer problems, and solving problems for customers). In addition, innovative behaviors, such as suggestions for improvement, are encouraged by TQM organizations.

Consequences are the important factor here. Reinforcement or reward is the most significant consequence since it increases desirable behavior (Skinner 1969). From the operational definition given, reinforcement is anything that increases the desirable behavior: bonuses, praise, publicity, increased responsibility, or symbolic tokens. In reinforcement theory there is a concept termed *prior reinforcement history*. In essence, individuals or teams have a set of reward preferences based on their prior experience with various types of rewards.

ORGANIZATIONAL BEHAVIOR MODIFICATION

There are many studies that show that reinforcement theory is effective in improving organizational behaviors, such as absenteeism, safety behaviors, customer interactions, and reducing production errors (a quality measure) (Luthans and Kreitner 1985; O'Hara, Johnson, and Beehr 1985).

Organizational behavior modification (OBM) is essentially a problem-solving approach to improving behavior. It consists of a series of steps.

1. *Define the target behavior.* Define the problem in terms of specific behaviors that are observable and measurable. For example, poor selling technique translates into a low frequency of salesperson eye contact with the customer and a low frequency of asking the correct questions to discern customer needs.

2. *Baseline the behavior in its natural state.* Graph the frequency of behavior over a period of time to understand its variability.

3. *Do a functional analysis.* Analyze antecedents and consequences in the environment that can control the behavior.

4. *Intervene with a reinforcement program.* Use some combination of reinforcers to attempt to increase the target behavior.

5. *Evaluate the program.* Graph the results and compare them to the baseline data to determine if the behavior actually improved.

OBM Parallels to TQM

In a special issue of the *Journal of Organizational Behavior Management* (Mawhinney 1987), parallels between OBM and TQM were identified. Both programs focus on measurable variables and emphasize data collection. Both analyze causes—the functional analysis step in OBM; common and special causal analysis in TQM. Both are essentially problem-solving approaches to improving the situation.

PRINCIPLES OF REINFORCEMENT THEORY APPLIED TO REWARD AND RECOGNITION

Several basic principles of reinforcement theory for improving behaviors have direct application to the reward and recognition process. Examples are given in Table 2.2.

Contingent Reinforcement

One of the most important principles of managing reinforcers is contingency. In essence, reinforcers must be given immediately after the desired behavior, and they must be associated with the desired behavior by the individual (Skinner 1969). For example, supervisory praise of an employee is effective because it is generally given right after an employee does something well, and the employee can associate praise with good work.

Many reinforcers in the workplace are ineffective because they are noncontingent on the behavior they are supposed to be improving. Annual raises and holiday bonuses usually occur at the same time each year—frequently months after the behavior occurred that they are supposed to reward. Consequently, in many companies, bonuses and pay raises are looked upon as an employee right rather than a reward for good work.

TQM organizations should strive to give the reward as soon after the behavior as possible. For example, at Federal Express, supervisors can give immediate cash awards for performance (Blackburn and Rosen 1993). At Appleton Papers supervisors are empowered to give immediate cash awards

TABLE 2.2. Examples of reinforcement theory principles in the reward and recognition process.

Reinforcement principle	Example	Organization
Contingency	Immediate rewards	Appleton Papers
Valued reward	Customized rewards	Appleton Papers
	Time off	Shawnee Mission Medical Center
	Trifecta	IBM
	Choice of bonus or time off	Duke Power
Social reinforcement	Recognition dinner	Motorola
	Recognition day	Granite Rock
	Expo fair	Florida Power & Light
	Quality fair	Oregon State
Shaping	Effort awards	Stuller Settings
Team competition	Total quality awards competition	Westinghouse
	Quality Olympics	Motorola

to employees. The supervisors have their own reward accounts (Caudron 1993).

Valued Rewards

Based on prior reinforcement history, individual employees and teams have their own unique reinforcement history that indicates preferences for certain rewards. The important point is that rewards can be customized to satisfy differing preferences. At Appleton Papers supervisors not only can give immediate rewards but they can also customize the reward for individual employees (Caudron 1993).

Shawnee Mission Medical Center is experimenting with valued rewards, such as time off and paid travel (Burda 1992). According to *Personnel Review* (1994), Duke Power gives employees a quality award where they choose either $100 or a half day off with pay.

In addition, team input into the award process should be encouraged. After all, team members know one another's preferences better than supervisors or human resource managers. For example, IBM Marketing has a team award budget that allows teams to customize awards for other teams.

Its Trifecta Award consists of a cash bonus, a surprise gift to the employee's home, and a remembrance (tickets to dinner or a show) (Carder and Clark 1992).

Social Reinforcers

As noted, social reinforcers, such as praise, are particularly contingent by their nature. TQM organizations draw from a number of possible social reinforcers: formal presentations of awards including ceremonial dinners; items in company newsletters; items in local newspapers; and award announcements to external customers. Motorola has a formal recognition dinner for its award winners and displays them in publications (Motorola 1992). Granite Rock Construction Company, winner of the 1992 Baldrige Award, has a recognition day for awards (Bemowski 1993).

Frequently the chance to present TQM successes to others is highly reinforcing. At Florida Power and Light quality teams saw bonuses as too small and not impacting enough, so they proposed a quality fair where teams could showcase their quality efforts to other teams and the community (Walton 1990). Oregon State University has a similar quality fair (Coate 1991).

Shaping

A unique reinforcement principle is shaping, where increasingly better approximations to the final behavior are reinforced. The idea is that behavior should be learned in short, rather than long, steps. Some TQM organizations mirror this concept with the idea of reinforcing small gains as well as large successes (Bowen and Lawler 1992). This is particularly important if the organization desires that individuals and teams take risks and show innovation in solving quality problems. Individuals and teams must realize that good efforts are appreciated as well as accomplishments. To illustrate, Stuller Settings, which won the U.S. Senate Productivity Award, evaluates quality suggestions on ingenuity and effort as well as cost savings (Stuller Settings 1993).

Competition

Competition between groups is highly motivating and has been used in a number of OBM studies, such as at Weyerhauser. A number of TQM organizations have a formal competition among quality teams for best TQM efforts. Westinghouse, winner of the 1988 Baldrige Award, has a Total Quality Awards competition mirroring the Baldrige Award, where units are evaluated on customer orientation, human resources issues, and leadership

(Westinghouse 1992). Motorola has a quality Olympics that it terms Total Customer Satisfaction Team Competition, where teams vie for gold and silver awards (Blackburn and Rosen 1993; Motorola 1992).

ORGANIZATIONAL STRUCTURE FOR REWARD AND RECOGNITION

The reward and recognition process, similar to any other TQM process, requires monitoring and continuous improvement. Just as clients are external customers, employees are internal customers who have continually changing demands that must be satisfied. Two important TQM teams provide this monitoring and improvement function (Knouse 1995a).

TQM Steering Committee

The TQM steering committee directs the organization's TQM effort. Its members are typically top managers who lay out the basic TQM focus through the strategic plan. The committee also charters the major process teams, including the reward and recognition team. The steering committee also allocates resources for major operations, including the reward and recognition effort.

Reward and Recognition Team

The reward and recognition team monitors and improves the reward and recognition process. It is composed of members from the major departments of the organization, worker representatives (including labor unions, if applicable), and external customers. There should be a cross function of all the important parties to reward and recognition. Human resource management can provide technical expertise for compensation programs and facilitators for team skills, but the team itself should elect its own leader. A member of the steering committee should be on the team to ensure continuity with overall TQM efforts.

The purpose of the reward and recognition team should be continuous improvement of the reward and recognition process. For example, StorageTek (1991) has the following team charter and mission philosophy.

> The charter and mission of the Rewards and Recognition Task Force is to determine the most effective methods for rewarding and recognizing employees for their involvement and contributions to StorageTek success and to revise the performance appraisal process to reinforce the values of quality, teamwork, and participative management.

The Naval Supply Center (1991) in San Diego has the following recognition team mission.

> Align awards/recognition and performance evaluation with the TQM implementation plan to promote cultural change.

Team Duties

1. *Analyze and monitor the reward and recognition process.* Using existing organizational procedures, employee survey data, and customer data, the team should diagram the reward and recognition process in depth.

2. *Identify problem areas.* Based on the diagram, the team should identify problems and charter temporary teams to resolve specific problems with reward and recognition. To illustrate, new awards or improvements to existing awards could be handled by temporary teams.

3. *Benchmark other organizations.* The reward and recognition team should continually collect data from other organizations on innovative reward and recognition programs. In addition, the team should keep abreast of national quality awards, such as the Baldrige Award, and state quality awards that could provide criteria for evaluating reward and recognition programs.

To illustrate, StorageTek (1991) lists the following duties for its reward and recognition team.

- Definition of the rewards and recognition philosophy to support StorageTek strategic goals and excellence through quality

- Identification of system process improvements to support StorageTek cultural changes

- Development of the rewards and recognition proposals and product lines

- Development of a road map and communication plan

- Sponsorship of pilots to evaluate progress against the rewards and recognition plan

- Ongoing evaluation

CONCLUSIONS

TQM organizations have developed a rich variety of financial rewards and recognition awards for reinforcing both individual and team quality behaviors. From a reinforcement theory framework, effective rewards and awards must be contingent (immediate and associated with quality performance); valued by individuals and teams; reinforced by social events (formal presentation dinners, ceremonies, and team quality competitions); and must reinforce efforts as well as successes.

Similar to any other TQM process, however, the reward and recognition process must be continually improved. The reward and recognition team must monitor award programs and improve them, as well as introduce new programs in order to meet the changing needs of the organization's internal customers—its employees.

REFERENCES

Bemowski, Karen. 1993. Ceremony honors the 1992 Baldrige Award recipients. *Quality Progress* (February): 27–32.

Blackburn, Richard, and Benson Rosen. 1993. Total quality and human resources management: Lessons learned from Baldrige Award-winning companies. *Academy of Management Executive* (August): 49–68.

Bowen, David E., and Edward E. Lawler. 1992. Total quality-oriented human resources management. *Organizational Dynamics* (spring): 29–41.

Burda, David. 1992. Hospital employs TQM principles to rework its evaluation system. *Modern Healthcare* 22 (August): 60.

Carder, Brooks, and James D. Clark. 1992. The theory and practice of employee recognition. *Quality Progress* (December): 25–30.

Caudron, Shari. 1993. How HR drives TQM. *Personnel Journal* (August): 48B–48O.

City of Phoenix. 1992. *City Manager's Award for Excellence.* Phoenix, Ariz.: Office of the City Manager.

Coate, Larry E. 1991. *Implementation of TQM in higher education.* Corvallis, Oreg.: Oregon State University.

Deming, W. Edwards. 1986. *Out of the crisis.* Cambridge, Mass.: MIT Center for Advanced Engineering Study.

Donnelly, James. 1992. *Total quality at Motorola.* Schaumburg, Ill.: Motorola.

Drummond, Helga, and Elizabeth Chell. 1992. Should organizations pay for quality? *Personnel Review* 21, no. 1:3–11.

Harrington, H. James. 1987. *The improvement process.* New York: McGraw-Hill.

Johnson, Sam T. 1993. Work teams: What's ahead in work design and rewards management. *Compensation and Benefits Review* (March/April): 35–41.

Juran, Joseph. 1992. *Juran on quality by design.* New York: Free Press.

Knouse, Stephen B. 1995a. *The reward and recognition process in total quality management.* Milwaukee: ASQC Quality Press.

———. 1995b. Variations in skill-based pay for total quality management. *SAM Advanced Management Journal* (winter): 34–38.

Knouse, Stephen B., Paula Phillips Carson, and Kerry D. Carson. 1993. W. Edwards Deming and Frederick Winslow Taylor: A comparison of two leaders who shaped the world's view of management. *International Journal of Public Administration* 16, no. 10:1621–1658.

Lawler, Edward E. 1987. The design of effective reward systems. In *Handbook of Organizational Behavior,* edited by Jay W. Lorsch. Englewood Cliffs, N.J.: Prentice Hall.

———. 1990. *Strategic pay.* San Francisco: Jossey-Bass.

Lawler, Edward E., Gerald E. Ledford, and Lei Chang. 1993. Who uses skill-based pay, and why. *Compensation and Benefits Review* (March/April): 22–26.

Lawler, Edward E., Susan Mohrman, and Gerald E. Ledford. 1992. *Employee involvement and total quality management.* San Francisco: Jossey-Bass.

Lou Ana Foods. *Quality management.* Opelousas, La.: Schaum.

Luthans, Fred, and Robert Kreitner. 1985. *Organizational behavior modification and beyond.* Glenview, Ill.: Scott, Foresman.

Mawhinney, Thomas. 1987. Special issue on OBM and statistical process control. *Journal of Organizational Behavior Management* 9, no. 1:1–159.

Meng, G. J. 1992. Using job descriptions, performance and pay innovations to support quality. *National Productivity Review* (spring): 247–255.

Milas, Gene H. 1995. How to develop a meaningful employee recognition program. *Quality Progress* (May): 139–142.

Motorola. 1992. *Total customer satisfaction team competition.* Schaumburg, Ill.: Motorola.

Naval Supply Center. 1991. *Recognition process action team action plan.* San Diego: Naval Supply Center.

New Ways to Pay. 1991. *Economist,* 31 July.

O'Hara, Kirk, C. Merle Johnson, and Terry A. Beehr. 1985. Organizational behavior modification in the private sector. *Academy of Management Review* 10, no. 4:848–864.

Robbins, David. 1994. *Wainright Industries: 1994 award winner.* Malcolm Baldrige National Quality Award pamphlet. Gaithersburg, Md.: National Institute of Standards and Technology.

The role of rewards on a journey to excellence. 1994. *Personnel Review* (December): 53–55.

Ross, Timothy L., and Larry Hatcher. 1992. Gainsharing drives quality improvement. *Personnel Journal* (November): 81–89.

Sashkin, Marshall, and Kenneth J. Kiser. 1991. *Total quality management.* Seabrook, Md.: Ducochon Press.

Schoenberger, Richard J. 1994. Human resource management lessons from a decade of total quality management and reengineering. *California Management Review* (summer): 109–123.

Skinner, B. F. 1969. *Contingencies of reinforcement.* New York: Appleton Century Crofts.

StorageTek. 1991. *Reward and recognition task force.* Louisville, Colo.: Storage Technology Corporation.

Stratton, A. Donald. 1992. It's more than statistics. *Quality Progress* (July): 71–72.

Stuller Settings. 1993. *Stuller Settings' quality program.* Lafayette, La.: Stuller Settings.

Trice, Harrison M., and Janice M. Beyer. 1993. *The cultures of work organizations.* Englewood Cliffs, N.J.: Prentice Hall.

Walton, Mary. 1990. *Deming management at work.* New York: Putnam.

Welbourne, Theresa M., and Luis R. Gomez Meija. 1995. Gainsharing: A critical review and a future research agenda. *Journal of Management* 21, no. 3:559–609.

Westinghouse. 1992. *George Westinghouse total quality award guidelines.* Pittsburgh, Pa.: Westinghouse Productivity and Quality Center.

Chapter 3

Building Performance Appraisal Systems Consistent with TQM Practices

J. Bruce Prince

Quality management authors have frequently argued that the process of evaluating individual performance and related processes, such as merit pay, create more problems than they solve. Deming (1986) and others, such as Scholtes (1987), Starcher (1992) and Gerst (1995), pointedly argue that such practices represent a deadly disease and should be purged from the earth. This advice deviates considerably from traditional human resource management (HRM) thought. Human resources specialists (Bernardin et al. 1995; Bretz, Milkovich, and Read 1992; Latham and Wexley 1993; Latham et al. 1993) generally see the appraisal of employees' performance as a centerpiece in the organization's HRM activities and a key mechanism in achieving organizational effectiveness. A review of case studies of total quality management (TQM) introductions suggests that those implementing TQM changes are torn by this conflicting advice, but generally resolve the conflict by including some form of performance appraisal (PA), in which employees' contributions are assessed. These contributions can include effort, job knowledge, skill or proficiency levels, and work strategies and techniques that contribute to successful individual performance outcomes as well as direct measures of the quantity and quality of those outcomes (for example, units produced, scrap rate, and utilization rates). The often-referenced case of TQM implementation at Ford (Scherkenbach 1985; Walton 1986) is illustrative of the attempt to resolve the dilemma created by this conflicting advice. In that case, the appraisal system was changed considerably, but not eliminated as Deming and others have demanded.

The conflict between TQM- and HRM-based advice suggests the question: Is PA consistent with TQM? The most direct answer is yes—and

43

no. Supervisor-driven systems that narrowly focus on individual performance and require fine discriminations among similarly performing employees, with an inflexible rating scale that is out of touch with the continuously improving work system requirements, are inconsistent with TQM. Such systems, however, also face severe criticisms on contemporary HRM criteria. Presenting a caricature of poor appraisal practice hardly bolsters the argument that all appraisal practices should be eliminated (Deming 1986; Scholtes 1987). Effective HRM requires that the various system design features be congruent with the organizational setting. Therefore, the more pertinent questions are: What kind of context does TQM create? and How can organizational performance management systems be designed to reinforce and fit unique features of organizations well down the TQM implementation road?

THE UNIQUE APPRAISAL CONTEXT OF TQM ORGANIZATIONS

TQM comes in many shapes and forms. Thus, while the performance management systems of TQM organizations should generally be different from non-TQM organizations, they should not be exactly the same. In spite of the potential evolvement of a number of variants or types of TQM organizations, these are likely to have many general distinguishing characteristics that should be considered in designing a context-appropriate appraisal system.

From Hierarchical to Horizonal Organizations

One striking characteristic of TQM organizations is that they are less hierarchical than traditional organizations. The increased use of structures that parallel traditional managerial levels, such as quality councils, implementation teams, and cross-functional planning mechanisms, will naturally augment and supplant traditional hierarchical control (Graham and LeBaron 1994). Additionally, work itself in TQM organizations is likely to be organized around teams (Lawler, Mohrman, and Ledford 1992; 1995). This is sometimes the direct result of TQM-directed work simplification efforts. With work teams come additional lateral or peer influence processes that lessen the need for close supervision. Sometimes these teams are formally designed as autonomous or self-directed teams (Mohrman, Cohen, and Mohrman 1995), and the decrease in supervision is even more dramatic.

The increased dominance of lateral or horizontal information and influence processes extends beyond organizational peers. Customer monitoring and increased interactions with external clients are frequently characteristic of TQM organizations. Customers directly interact with an increased range of contact points where information is exchanged and problems are solved (Bounds et al. 1994).

In summary, the increased dominance of horizontal patterns of information and influence exchanges has many sources. It results in a reduced need for traditional hierarchical control, and thus displaces traditional supervisory oversight. This has direct implications for appraisal system design. For example, a clear tenant of effective HRM practice is that those with unique performance-relevant information should be involved in the rating process. Requiring supervisors to be the sole driver of the appraisal process in organizations dominated by horizontal processes conflicts with both TQM logic and traditional HRM thought.

From Individual to Team-Based Organizations

The team orientation of TQM organizations also has an additional implication. In companies where responsibilities are narrowly organized into individual jobs, and where individuals are uniquely responsible for a whole piece of work, the historical focus on individual performance makes sense. But as TQM organizations set up teams and other horizontal processes and make teams of individuals jointly responsible for a cluster of responsibilities and outcomes, then the historical sole focus on individual performance is, at best, incomplete. At worst, it can introduce dysfunctional dynamics that will lower team performance. If individuals on a team feel that higher ratings for other individuals will necessarily result in lower ratings for themselves, then they will be motivated to withhold help from their team peers (and overtly make them look bad) and focus on highly visible contributions that are easily attributed to their own initiative. Such games will be obvious to others, and they will be motivated to respond in kind. Teams need cooperation and teamwork. Team performance will only be hurt if members jockey to maximize personal outcomes at the expense of others. All individual rating approaches are vulnerable, in varying degrees, to this prospect. Such methods as individual ranking and forced-choice, however, come close to guaranteeing negative dynamics in team-oriented organizations. Given the widespread tendency to focus on individual performance, it is understandable why some TQM theorists see performance appraisal as inherently flawed. There are, however, alternatives to the traditional sole focus on individual performance, and there are additional ways to make appraisal systems sensitive to the need for cooperation and teamwork.

Recognizing and Interpreting Variation

TQM organizations are likely to make employees more sensitive to variations in work performance and the multiple causes of performance-related problems. TQM-trained employees understand that it is normal for performance to vary around a mean. They appreciate that a few extreme events, such as making an unexpectedly large sell or missing a deadline, should not be heavily weighted in evaluating overall performance. As employees learn sampling and statistical control methods to analyze the variation in work processes, it is natural for them to be critical of evaluators who focus on these extreme examples of their performance and fail to notice the much more frequent or typical examples of how well they accomplish their job responsibilities. Similarly, using TQM analytical tools to understand the full range of causes of performance deficiencies naturally makes employees skeptical of appraisal systems that ignore work system determinants that constrain the extent that employees' contributions—including effort, skill, knowledge, and work methods/strategies—will result in high work unit performance. Such constraints can include poorly designed production methods, poorly maintained tools, adequate or untimely information, or uncooperative coworkers or supervisors. The result is that PA systems that do not adequately sample the full range of relevant employee contributions, or address the work system sources of performance variance, are easily seen as simply lotteries where winning depends on luck. Over the long run everyone, except the extremely lucky, loses.

PA researchers have been trying to remedy these problems for years. It is easy for human observers to overcount atypical events. Arguably, the individualistic culture of North America predisposes people to overweigh human skill and effort in evaluating performance. HRM efforts to get evaluators to limit these biases have included the following:

1. Improving the rating scale format (for example, using behaviorally anchored rating scales (BARs))

2. Increasing rating frequency (for example, having supervisors keep diaries)

3. Using multiple raters

4. Training raters using a variety of approaches (for example, frame-of-reference training)

Thus far, no single appraisal improvement is so powerful that it eliminates bias and other sources of rating invalidity. Arguably, each technique, if implemented, simply adds a marginal improvement in overall appraisal accuracy or validity. Thus, invalidity and accuracy remain problems. The implication is that system designers should not assume that fine distinctions in performance are practically detectable. This is most true of performance in a performance distribution's middle range. A few selectively noticed, extreme performance events, such as a recent unexpectedly large sell or detection of a previously missed design flaw, can easily result in different PA evaluations for employees who are really very similar performers. Differentiating very similar performers understandably creates skepticism and pessimism about the whole appraisal process. Having to differentiate every performer in a group (that is, ranking them) or using rating scales with many shades of average performance (such as 10-point rating scales) forces even the most dedicated and talented appraiser into making inaccurate assessments.

Continuous Improvement Means Continuous Change

An additional distinguishing feature of TQM organizations is the philosophy of continuous improvement. This translates into efforts to continuously adapt and improve the way work is done. The implication for PA design is that employee requirements and performance standards are inherently dynamic. A basic principle of effective HRM is that PA criteria directly reflect job requirements. Being evaluated as a poor performer on criteria irrelevant to accomplishing one's job understandably violates employees' sense of fairness and can only lead to alienation and poor motivation. The continuously changing work system offers a moving target that demands a flexible system that can adapt to changing work requirements. Often appraisal systems try to sidestep these complexities by including generic performance criteria that are generally applicable to nearly every job (for example, quality and quantity of performance). The vagueness of such scales does not satisfy the job relevancy criterion and only evokes a sense of unfairness. In short, TQM organizations create a context that emphasizes unique and dynamic performance criteria. To respond to these realities, appraisal systems need to incorporate relevant criteria and include mechanisms for adapting and communicating relevant quality and quantity standards.

CREATING EFFECTIVE APPRAISAL SYSTEMS

Creating a PA system consistent with TQM requires attention to both the designing process and the features of the eventual design. While research and theory provide useful insights into the choice of design features, these decisions are complicated. First, the design must fit the culture and strategy of the organization and also the nature of the TQM management strategy. This is not completely knowable by external experts; people inside the organization must participate. Second, commitment to the eventual design is critical to its success. Simply hiring external consultants with a good PA package will not guarantee that people critical to the implementation of the new system will embrace it or that those being appraised will automatically respect the new PA system's legitimacy. Content, or correct design choices, and the process used to make those choices, go hand in hand.

Managing the Design Process

The design process is infrequently mentioned in PA literature. Other literatures, ranging from organization change to leadership, however, acknowledge the key role of process in fashioning any appraisal system design. There are several principles that should guide the design of the decision process used to create the appraisal system (Mohrman, Resnick-West, and Lawler 1989).

Get the right people involved. This principle argues that people with various types of expertise should be on the design team. Clearly, experts in PA and how appraisal system design choices are constrained by a commitment to TQM need to be involved. Human resources department professionals, independent of their PA expertise, need to be involved, since the appraisal system will interface with other HRM systems and activities, such as compensation, selection, and training (Von Glinow et al. 1983). HRM personnel will also be involved in setting up the eventual system, and participation in the design process will help them in their implementation role. PA system users must be represented. This includes both managers who will be appraisers and employees likely to be appraised by the new system. Good choices can only be reached if the design team is aware of the political realities of the organization and can respond to the many constituencies that the appraisal system will affect. Forming such a team is also consistent with TQM practices.

Look at design as an educational process. In the early stages of the design process, two educational or research thrusts are important. First, team members need to be informed about general PA issues, ranging from legal requirements to traditional validity concerns to design features consistent with TQM. (This is presented later in this chapter.) Human resource specialists or external consultants are likely to lead this process. Second, the design team must reach out to the rest of the organization. Interviews, focus groups, and surveys are mechanisms for discovering current practices, gathering perceptions about what works or does not work, and testing out some design ideas with different constituencies. There is a two-way communication process inherent in this research strategy. Besides getting information about the larger organization (and being better able to ground the new design in the current organizational reality), asking questions starts to communicate to the larger community the issues and choices they are considering. Involving the organization in this fashion will help legitimize the eventual design. This strategy also expresses trust, openness, and respect for all employees. These are all qualities that are consistent with TQM. More than one round of interviews may be needed as the design team moves from preliminary considerations to final design choices.

Connect system choices to strategic goals and key organizational values. The decision to pursue a TQM management process is only one important strategic direction that must be considered in designing a PA system. An appraisal system is a tool for achieving the organization's strategic goals. Thus, other strategic goals and related values also need to be considered. For example, a high-growth strategy focused on moving into new business areas may mean that the appraisal system needs to be an important tool for recognizing and rewarding entrepreneurial behavior and developing organizational talent to move into new growing businesses. A slow-growth strategy focused on improving organizational cost efficiencies provides a completely different frame and places a different set of demands with which the appraisal system must be consistent.

Clearly define the appraisal system's purpose and objectives. Clearly understanding the larger organization's strategic direction provides the basis for defining the appraisal system's objectives. PA system objectives must facilitate the achievement of the organization's strategy. There are many generic purposes appraisal systems can address. Designers must decide what mix of these general purposes makes sense, and design a system with those priorities in mind. Possible objectives for an appraisal system include the following:

- Plan performance improvements, including work system redesign.
- Give employees feedback and let them know where they stand.
- Gather information for employee development and training.
- Direct career planning activities by the employee or organization.
- Gather information used to make personnel decisions (for example, transfers, promotions, or retention).
- Facilitate human resource planning activities.

It is quite typical that different people will see the current appraisal system as focusing on different objectives (Mohrman, Resnick-West, and Lawler 1989; Prince and Lawler 1986). An important outcome of the high-involvement strategy implicit in the guidelines is that conflict about the purposes of appraisal be surfaced and resolved. If these conflicts stay underground and a clear consensus on the purpose of appraisal does not develop, then the problems are inevitable. It is quite conceivable that, given the points of tension between many traditional appraisal practices and TQM, it could make sense to narrow the range of purposes the PA system is designed to address. That is, smaller may be better. Other administrative practices may need to be developed to fill the void that this will create. The process of getting clear on system objectives and acting consistent with that plan is quite consistent with TQM philosophy.

Be experimental, rigorous in evaluation, and flexible. PA system design activity is best thought of as a redesign process. Designers need to put an evaluation strategy in place that gives them information on how their design choices are working. Opportunities to learn and make mid-course changes must be explicitly designed into the implementation process. The research-oriented decision process of the early design phase should carry over into testing, evaluation, and redesign phases. Small-scale pilot tests of different PA systems in different locations often make sense. An evaluation plan will help guide the assessment of information on how different parts of the design are working and what units are having difficulties. This will maximize opportunities to learn and evolve PA systems that fill both local contingencies and larger organizational purposes.

Design Options for a TQM-Consistent Appraisal System

Expertise in the PA system design choices must inform and guide the participative design process. It should focus on the broad array of choices within the general constraints defined by research and theorize on the unique demands of appraisal systems in TQM organizations. A small but growing literature offers explicit guidelines on these choices (Bushe 1988; Dobbins, Cardy, and Carson 1993; Henry and Redman 1990; Kane and Kane 1992; Prince 1994; Waldman and Kenett 1990). The following section identifies general PA system features consistent with TQM.

Rating scale length. How fine should be the discriminations required of raters? In general, fewer performance categories are better than many. Extreme performance that is either high or low is most easily detectible and least likely to be a function of work system constraints that are out of the employees' control. Performances in the middle range are most likely to be primarily system driven, and differentiating between such performers is likely to be inaccurate and invalid. Designers should address the question: Why is it important or necessary to differentiate average, slightly below average, or slightly above average performers? Often no great purpose is served. Habit and history have driven organizations to select, without much thought, 7- to 10-point scales. Where there are important purposes served by such fine distinctions, then organizations need to appreciate that additional time and resources need to be invested in the process if evaluators are going to accomplish this difficult task with adequate accuracy and validity. The cost of developing a system for differentiating middle-range performers is expensive. If such investments are not made, then it will probably be done poorly. Often organizations are unwilling to make the required investment. Creating a system that does a poor job of accurately rating performers is usually worse than not doing it at all. In short, a three-category system with the extreme 10 percent to 20 percent in each tail and the majority in the middle category should be closely considered. Departures from this to four- or five-category (or more) rating scales should be driven by explicit organizational considerations. Also, a clear commitment to invest in a more expensive system to design and support it, with the necessary ongoing training, should be made.

Who evaluates performers? Given the increased lateral communications and team orientation of TQM organizations, simply relying on the direct supervisor to be the only appraiser should not be considered. Others who have direct information and are in a position to accurately evaluate performance should be included in the process. The ideal of 360-degree appraisals (Cardy and Dobbins 1993; Nowack 1993) should be a starting point in the decision of who is included on an evaluation. This view argues that knowledgeable peers, subordinates, hierarchical superiors, and employees' clients (either inside or outside of the company) should be involved in the evaluation process. Self-ratings also help provide the basis for accurate ratings and useful discussions (Campbell and Lee 1988). While there is a wide range of ways the 360-degree idea could be carried out, simply polling people around the performer and having the direct supervisor as the sole authority to analyze, summarize, and present the evaluative conclusion is not adequately responsive to the unique nature of TQM organizations.

What gets evaluated? Employees should be evaluated on criteria relevant to job requirements. Many behavioral and outcome rating dimensions often used in PA systems are not inappropriate as much as they are incomplete. In a total quality organization, the way work gets done changes. Dimensions such as team skills and cooperation become increasingly relevant. Similarly, quality- and customer satisfaction-related criteria should also be considered. Baldrige Award winner Xerox Business Products and Systems' revision of its evaluation system incorporated many of these dimensions (Blackburn and Rosen 1993). Continuous improvement means changing and increasing standards. Changing requirements can be partially anticipated with management by objectives (MBO) or a similar goal-setting process; however, frequent review sessions become increasingly important in a TQM organization. It is critical that the focus of performance discussions be on the work planning process rather than fixated on past work outcomes. Easton's (1993) critique of Baldrige Award winners notes the importance of joint problem solving and planning in the evaluation process. Flexibility and the revision of performance objectives should be a distinguishing feature of the PA system.

Work team or group versus individual evaluations. As TQM organizations become increasingly team-based, the relative emphasis on team versus individual performance should grow. In a mature team-based organization (Mohrman et al. 1995), evaluation and discussion of team performance should be more dominant than individual-focused discussions. Teams need formal mechanisms to guide their actions. The team appraisal should include not only a discussion of past performance strengths and weaknesses, but should also focus on future performance requirements. This latter discussion should identify deliverables, milestones, time required for various subtasks, and errors or problems historically typical of these types of tasks. Price and Chen (1993) have noted the importance of these types of discussions for teams in high-technology organizations. Discussing individual and team performance is not inherently incompatible with each other, but more research is needed to explore the culture and other organizational characteristics that best support jointly evaluating individual and team performance.

Frequent performance review discussions. As suggested, the focus on future work planning discussions should be more dominant than the evaluation of past performance. Understanding past performance is an opportunity to learn and develop. The historic PA advice to separate evaluation and developmental discussions overstates the incompatibility of these objectives and has not been supported by research (Prince and Lawler 1986). Individual and team performance discussions should reflect the 360-degree appraisal concept by including a range of people in the discussion. For individual evaluations, the review discussion should include the supervisor, peers or work team representatives, and possibly customer representatives. Team evaluations should include supervisors and others affected by the team's performance such as customer representatives.

A broad range of perspectives in the meeting has several benefits. Such a group is more likely to discover problems in the work system that are constraining work performance and contributing variance. All performance problems, however, should not be assumed to be work system-based. Individual abilities and motivation, and team norms and characteristics, make a difference and must be discussed. Also, using a group discussion format makes it less likely that people will play the blame game so typical in boss-subordinate interviews, where subordinates become defensive and blame all performance difficulties on external events. Discussion groups allow an informal discussion of both external and individual or group-caused performance problems. With these groups, the supervisor has a unique responsibility to follow through on identified work system problems and initiate corrective action.

Separation of promotion/transfer and PA administrative systems. Future job potential is the key factor in making a promotion/transfer decision. Performance-in-current-job information from the PA system process is useful input for such decisions. Often, however, relevance of current and past performance is overstated. Performance potential is a function of the skills, knowledge, and aptitudes demanded by job requirements. Placing too much emphasis on past performance in these decisions encourages well-intentioned raters to misuse the appraisal system. If high past performance guarantees that candidates otherwise poorly qualified will get the new position, it is likely that those making performance ratings will try to protect the organization—and themselves—by underrating performance in the current position. To those uninvolved in the process, this seems quite unfair and leads to distrust and many more problems. PA systems are always subject to skepticism. Most employees need very little negative information to throughly distrust the system. The administrative process used to make promotion/transfer decisions must clearly identify characteristics of qualified applicants and be specific about how those characteristics relate to past PA ratings.

CONCLUSION

Implementing a TQM strategy without rethinking and changing the organization's PA system is likely to result in a disaster. Traditional PA practices conflict with various elements of typical TQM practice. Doing both will make both ineffective. Redesigning the appraisal system presents many challenges. First, like any major organizational change, it must be carefully managed. This requires careful attention to the process used to make design decisions. Second, designing an appraisal system involves trying out new practices that are only partially developed in the literature. Setting up a TQM-consistent design requires a commitment to innovation and experimentation that extends well beyond the development of a new PA system design.

REFERENCES

Bernardin, H. John, Jeffrey S. Kane, Susan Ross, James D. Spina, and Dennis L. Johnson. 1995. Performance appraisal design, development, and implementation. In *Handbook of human resource management*, edited by Gerald R. Ferris, Sherman D. Rosen, and Darold T. Barnum. Oxford, England: Blackwell Publishers.

Blackburn, Richard, and Benson Rosen. 1993. Total quality and human resources management lessons learned from Baldrige Award-winning companies. *Academy of Management Executive* (August): 49–66.

Bounds, Greg, Lyle Yorks, Mel Adams, and Gipsie Ranney. 1994. *Total quality management: Toward the emerging paradigm*. New York: McGraw-Hill.

Bretz, Robert, George Milkovich, and Walter Read. 1992. The current state of performance appraisal research and practice: Concerns, directions, and implications. *Journal of Management* 18, no. 2:321–352.

Bushe, Gervase R. 1988. Cultural contradictions of statistical process control in American manufacturing organizations. *Journal of Management* 14, no. 1:19–31.

Campbell, Donald J., and Cynthia Lee. 1988. Self-appraisal in performance evaluation: Development versus evaluation. *Academy of Management Review* 13, no. 2:302–314.

Cardy, Robert L., and Greg H. Dobbins. 1993. The changing face of performance appraisal: Customer evaluation and 360 appraisals. *Human Resources Division News* 16, no. 2:17–18.

Deming, W. Edwards. 1986. *Out of the crisis*. Cambridge, Mass: MIT Center for Advanced Engineering Study.

Dobbins, Greg H., Robert L. Cardy, and Kenneth P. Carson. 1993. Examining fundamental assumptions: A contrast of person and system approaches to human resource management. *Research in Personnel and Human Resources Management* 9:1–38.

Easton, George S. 1993. The 1993 state of U.S. total quality management: A Baldrige examiner's perspective. *California Management Review* 35, no. 3:1–9.

Gerst, Robert M. 1995. Assessing organizational performance. *Quality Progress* (February): 85–88.

Graham, Morris A., and Melvin J. LeBaron. 1994. *The horizonal revolution: Reengineering your organization through teams*. San Francisco: Jossey-Bass.

Henry, Gordon O., and William K. Redman. 1990. The effects of performance feedback on the implementation of a statistical process control (SPC) program. *Journal of Organizational Behavior Management* 11, no. 2:23–46.

Kane, J. S., and K. F. Kane. 1992. TQM-compatible performance appraisal: An American cultural imperative. *Journal of Management Systems* 4, no. 1:11–28.

Latham, Gary P., Daniel Skarlicki, Diane Irvine, and Jacob P. Siegel. 1993. The increasing importance of performance appraisals to employee effectiveness in organizational settings in North America. In *International Review of Industrial and Organizational Psychology* Vol. 8, edited by Cary L. Cooper and Ivan T. Robertson. Chichester, England: John Wiley & Sons.

Latham, Gary P., and Kenneth N. Wexley. 1993. *Increasing productivity through performance appraisal.* Reading, Mass.: Addison-Wesley.

Lawler, Edward E., III, Susan A. Mohrman, and Gerald E. Ledford. 1995. *Creating high performance organizations: Practices and results of employee involvement and total quality management in Fortune 1000 companies.* San Francisco: Jossey-Bass.

———. 1992. *Employee involvement and total quality management: Practices and results in Fortune 1000 companies.* San Francisco: Jossey-Bass.

Mohrman, Susan A., S. G. Cohen, and Allan M. Mohrman, Jr. 1995. *Designing team-based organizations: New forms for knowledge work.* San Francisco: Jossey-Bass.

Mohrman, Allan M., Jr., Susan M. Resnick-West, and Edward E. Lawler, III. 1989. *Designing performance appraisal systems.* San Francisco: Jossey-Bass.

Nowack, Kenneth M. 1993. 360-Degree feedback: The whole story. *Training and Development* (January): 69–72.

Price, Michael J., and E. Eva Chen. 1993. Total quality management in a small high-technology company. *California Management Review* 35, no. 3:96–117.

Prince, J. Bruce. 1994. Performance appraisal and reward practices for total quality organizations. *Quality Management Journal* (January): 36–46.

Prince, J. Bruce, and Edward E. Lawler III. 1986. Does salary discussion hurt the developmental performance appraisal? *Organizational Behavior and Human Decision Processes* 37, no. 3:357–375.

Scherkenbach, William. 1985. Performance appraisal and quality: Ford's new philosophy. *Quality Progress* (April): 40–46.

Scholtes, Peter. 1987. *An elaboration on Deming's teachings on performance appraisal.* Madison, Wis.: Joiner Associates.

Starcher, Ronald. 1992. Mismatched management techniques. *Quality Progress* (December): 49–52.

Von Glinow, Mary Ann, Michael Driver, K. Brousseau, and J. Bruce Prince. 1983. The design of a career-oriented human resource system. *Academy of Management Review* 8, no. 1:23–32.

Waldman, David, and R. Kenett. 1990. Improve performance appraisal. *HRMagazine* (July): 66–69.

Walton, Mary. 1986. *The Deming management method.* New York: Dodd, Mead & Company.

Chapter 4

Compensation Systems: Putting Deming's System to the Test

Michael J. Cleary

> *Remove barriers that rob the hourly worker of his right to pride of workmanship. The responsibility of supervisors must be changed from sheer numbers to quality. Remove barriers that rob people in management and in engineering of their right to pride of workmanship. This means* inter alia *abolishment of the annual or merit rating and of management by objective.*
>
> —W. Edwards Deming

BACKGROUND: DEMING'S POINT 12

When it comes to raising and educating children, even the most enlightened parents are apt to wrestle with the issue of rewards or allowances. On the one hand, parents want young people to become adults who are motivated by sheer joy in their work; on the other hand, parents know that rewards provide at least short-term external motivation and communicate a sense of participation in the family's financial picture.

Organizations, too, struggle with these issues. Offering incentives, commissions, and bonuses is often seen as the standard way to motivate people in companies. Indeed, some employees respond to reward systems that emphasize individual performance. But leaders often have a growing sense of contradiction between their company's encouragement of teamwork and pride of workmanship and the organization's compensation system with its emphasis on individual merit and performance (Cleary and Cleary 1993).

In fact, for those who are struggling with the day-to-day implications of the management ideas posited by W. Edwards Deming (1986), the application of point 12 of his 14 points for management presents one of the greatest challenges to traditional ways of doing business. Additionally, it has perhaps the greatest financial implication for employees. While its emphasis is on pride of workmanship, its impact is on pay and benefits and on the ways in which managers provide feedback to employees about their jobs and performance levels. In point 12, Deming would reconnect these three aspects of work life—feedback, pride in work, and pay and benefits—and dismantle the artificial separations that have grown around them.

The quality philosophy that Deming developed and left as his legacy evolved over years of experience and learning. It did not spring full-flown from his mind, nor can it be reduced, as some would wish, to a simple list of things to do. This observation applies to the 14 points that he articulated as well. These 14 points, important as they are, do not represent the complete Deming philosophy, which is too rich and too far-reaching to be reduced to such a list.

So although this chapter addresses, in very specific terms, the application of one of Deming's 14 points—the 12th one—it is to be remembered that none of the points can be applied to an organization out of context or without an understanding of the entire quality philosophy. This discussion will present a general analysis of compensation systems and pay schemes, and then offer three case studies that represent different approaches and interim steps toward equitable compensation systems that instill pride of workmanship and eliminate merit rating practices.

Systems problems often inhibit joy in work. Poor machinery, materials, or training, for example, and managers' demands for numerical quotas inhibit workmanship by making it impossible to produce quality products. The shortcomings of traditional management approaches in creating pride in workmanship take many forms. As William Scherkenbach (1986) points out, "[management] must first take the lead in examining every management system and operating procedure to determine if it supports or inhibits continuing improvement." The need to design systems that reflect a commitment to statistical thinking and the long-term goals of an organization is nowhere more pressing than in creating compensation systems. The focus in this 12th point, then, lies in the connection between pride of workmanship and incentive systems.

Pay and Pride in Work

No other single factor is as significant to employees as the pay schematic: The failure of an incentive system can have broad-reaching effects on a company and on its most important resource—its employees. While

Deming provides some guidelines for defining compensation systems, creating a workable and equitable system that reflects an organization's commitment to its employees and to the Deming philosophy is not easy; however, the potential rewards of a positive benefit system are many. Besides pride in workmanship and better quality, a compensation system can enhance teamwork, innovation, commitment, and good faith in management. With these rewards in mind, I examine the problems inherent in defining such a system.

Determining the relationship between employee compensation and achievement represents one of the most serious challenges that an organization can face. No good incentive system exists, although most people assume, if only unconsciously, that it does, and that with enough adjustment, such a system will not only serve to adequately compensate workers but will also simultaneously inspire a sense of justice and equity. On the contrary, it is clear that a reward system will introduce distortion in every case. Peter Scholtes (1987), Alfie Kohn (1993), and others have demonstrated the destructive effects of reward and incentive systems in organizations, and these are well documented. A few observations will illustrate these destructive effects. Imagining for a minute a kind of one-dimensional array of all possible payment systems, one sees that these can be grouped according to their rigidity, with the most formal systems ascribing exact relationships between standards of performance and pay. The spectrum of pay systems that exist is best described by examining the two extremes.

Commissions and Quotas

On the one extreme, assume that pay is exactly proportional to specific, quantifiable achievements. The best examples of this are commission or quota systems. If a salesperson sells a car, then he or she is entitled to a percentage of the profits on that sale. After all, the salesperson has put the product into the hands of the customer. Thus, the more products that the sales representative sells, the greater the rewards he or she ought to expect.

Upon examination, the negative effects of this system are immediately apparent. The first effect is discerned in customer relations. While the employer hopes that the commission will inspire a positive interface with customers, actual employee behavior moves away from intended behavior. Getting the product out the door becomes the orientation of the salesperson who sells products without fully understanding the system of identifying and serving customer needs. Long-term customer-supplier partnerships are undermined by such a system. Further, this system undermines any spirit of teamwork within the organization and denigrates the contribution of other employees to customer satisfaction. Thus, it will undermine opportunities for joy in work and pride in one's job. The work of the marketing staff, for example, that has developed brochures and placed advertisements may have contributed more to the sale than the efforts of the sales representative, who may have only answered the customer's phone call. How will the designer of an attractive ad feel when the rewards of the sale are distributed in proportionally greater amounts to the sales representative?

In other settings, a rigid pay system is designed to meet defined criteria that are articulated in such a way as to be benchmarks of performance. In such a reward system, however, these criteria have lost their relationship to real performance. One example is a production reward scheme where employees are rewarded 100 percent of their salary for full production (meeting their production quotas) and 1 percent extra for each percent in production up to 150 percent, at which point the quota will be reset at a higher level to avoid excessive payments. Clearly, the firm's goals are not being met when nearly all of the employees are mysteriously producing at 149 percent of their quota, maximizing their revenue. The ideal of maximum production within a reasonable quota is lost as employees curtail output rather than create higher quotas and concomitantly lower pay. And yet, from the point of view of an employee in such a system, the behavior is certainly rational.

Similar stories of incentive distortion in pay systems are legion, and the failures of a quantitative evaluative system have been a reality at one time or another for most employees. Even if selected statistical benchmarks are reliable indicators of individual contributions (a doubtful proposition at best), the relationship between real performance and such values becomes distorted when the reward system is formally associated with these values.

It is important to emphasize that such employee behavior is neither devious nor evil. Rather, the employee understands that he or she is being paid to do a job. It is entirely rational for an individual to maximize personal financial benefits. To place the blame at this level indicates a failure to understand the lack of workmanship as a system problem. To criticize employees for acting in their own self-interest in a system created by management is outrageous in light of the national emphasis on workplace control, choice, and the rationales of capitalistic behavior. In fact, in a rigid reward system, it is one's own pay that becomes the standard by which an employee comes to evaluate his or her contribution to the company, and not vice versa. In the absence of other indicators, such as job evaluations and descriptions, employees are often forced to accept the workings of the pay system as the only account that they have of their worth to the company and of how their work should be completed. Employees reason that maximizing individual pay will automatically maximize their value to the firm; after all, that is why an incentive system exists.

A further impact of such assumptions in a compensation system lies in its effect on actual workmanship. Reducing workplace appraisals to a single statistical evaluation may appear to be simple, but if employees internalize the importance of such figures, they will ignore other aspects of their jobs. It may appear to them that these other tasks are not considered important to the system since they are not commensurately rewarded. A sales representative may choose to respond to mail-in requests for information rather than reviewing his or her database and contacting old customers to develop long-term goodwill for the company. Sometimes what ensues is a trade of quality for quantity. Despite the problems that playing the system can cause, after all, it is the only possible response with limited information. Unfortunately, such a rigid scheme may distort the necessities of performance to the extent that it actually destroys the company, in spite of excellent performance within the schematic of the reward system. Additionally, diminished communication from what have been called street-level employees means a loss in valuable input. The hands-on experience of salespersons with respect to their interaction with customers on a day-to-day basis, for example, is lost in the absence of a continued information flow. This valuable communication will never reach the design and decision-making level, since the individual employee's appraisal marks represent greater value (translated into rewards) than the good of the organization as a whole.

Fixed Salaries

On the other extreme is the system where salaries are simply fixed, regardless of performance. Whether the individual does nothing or works 80 hours a week, he or she receives the same pay. One can imagine the impact of such a system on morale. The issue of justice will inspire those who perceive that they are doing a better job than someone who is receiving the same pay to adjust performance accordingly. The only ultimate safety valve in this system is that of firing nonproductive employees. As in the case of the rigid quota system, the distortion in this system is dramatic. The employee realizes that as long as he or she meets some minimum level of achievement, no one will care what kind of work is done or at least not enough to change salaries. Pride in workmanship becomes impossible; seat time or just being there counts equally with exceptional performance. Because the employee's welfare is linked neither to his or her own performance nor to the achievement of the company, the employee is no longer concerned with either his or her own progress or that of the organization.

The workplace becomes a place to spend a minimum number of hours a day and to collect a paycheck. The abandonment of quota systems for a strict salary system becomes just as problematic for the survival outlook of the firm.

The solution, however, does not lie in simply creating a system where performance evaluations and standards are not revealed to employees. In this kind of system, the rationale becomes that employees will work hard because they are no longer able to play games and instead must simply try to meet job requirements, with the hope that the benchmarks that management has chosen are incidentally met. The problems with such an approach are clear. Not only does this system reflect lack of faith by management and foster suspicion among employees, but it also introduces additional complexity: the game now becomes guessing what the payment system will reward. One employee might maximize sales at the expense of business practice in the hope that the system has been based on straight sales; another would emphasize quality over potentially big deals because he or she thinks that customer satisfaction has been the basis. In any case, two conclusions can be reached: (1) that employees must be made aware of the basis for payment systems; and (2) that structuring pay systems does not mean simply finding a solution to the payroll every week. Instead, it involves defining how each employee will understand his or her own goals, the company's goals, and the relationship between the two.

The reward system in an organization can undermine any commitment to the company's purpose or vision; a poorly defined system cannot convince employees to put their best efforts toward achieving that purpose. Employees are entitled to a clear articulation of the reward system within which they operate and to a compensation system that is consistent with personal as well as organizational vision. Ultimately, the limitation of information in a system under any pretext is costly. Every employee must understand the company's mission, philosophy, and methods. This understanding will help employees make decisions that have a positive impact on company goals and contribute to pride in their contributions to those goals.

Annual Ratings

Even when job objectives and requirements are well defined and clearly articulated, the merit or annual rating system that Deming describes can inhibit the factors necessary for success. The annual performance appraisal has deleterious effects on the organization and on the individual who is part of that organization. Evaluation by coworkers and supervisors introduces fear and inhibits healthy risk taking, with employees focusing on psychological gains within the organization instead of substantive gains in company success. The problems with performance evaluation systems are well documented, notably by Peter Scholtes (1987) and Alfie Kohn (1993). What needs to be examined is how pay schemes can be organized to be consistent with a Deming philosophy of management. The solution lies in creating a system that will tie long-term goals of the company to personal incentives and rewards.

Because employees in most cases do not own the company in which they work, there is an inevitable tension between their own rational interests and those of the owners. Employees must be convinced that it is in their own best interests to understand the goals of the company as these goals relate to each individual. Although employee stock ownership plans (ESOPs) and profit-sharing schemes do much to reinforce this connection, they cannot be seen as the end-all solution to designing benefit systems. The speculative nature of such investments and the fact that stock values have little to do with individual performance can discourage individuals from associating company progress with their own commitment. Similarly, although profit-sharing plans have worked well in some instances, there is a danger in relating short-term progress to what is perceived as a dividend.

Although organizational goals need to be emphasized, so do individual goals. The problems with solutions that place too much emphasis on company and not individual achievement are illustrated by Hardin's "tragedy of the commons" paradox (1977). In this example, readers are asked to imagine a village commons where all of the villagers' sheep can graze freely. The problem arises in the absence of government or other restraints, when each villager acts rationally by adding sheep to his stock. An increased number of sheep will mean destruction of the green. Still, it lies in each farmer's best interest to continue to add sheep, at least until the marginal revenue of one more sheep is outweighed by the marginal costs that degradation of the commons will have for the farmer's entire flock. Since each farmer is simultaneously making decisions, the number of sheep skyrockets, the commons is depleted of grass, and everybody loses.

Similarly one can imagine a company with 10 employees; each owns one-tenth of the company (through an ESOP) or will have benefits that hinge directly on company profits (profit sharing). For instance, each will receive a bonus that is 5 percent of the company's profit. The problem arises when one individual realizes that the marginal cost of not doing any work—a small impact on the company's overall profit position and thus on his or her wages—is outweighed by the marginal personal benefit of never coming to work, and instead going to the golf course. If, however, this exchange is rational for one individual, it is rational for all, and the company will fail. If ESOPs and profit-sharing plans are not linked to individual standards of performance, the results could be disastrous. While this may be an extreme example, it illustrates the flaw in such systems. They fail to convince employees that they will be rewarded in proportion to their exertions. In fact, payment plans need to be the nexus for reconciling company goals and individual goals, for making the individual aware of the relationship between the two, and of rewarding the progress of the individual in such efforts.

The key to improvement in performance, both for the individual and for the organization, lies in ongoing, regular feedback and interaction. When a supervisor saves observations about employee performance for an artificially determined deadline and then dumps all of these observations on the employee, both positive and negative feedback is diluted by its disconnection from actual events. "You were late for work several times last spring," is a criticism leveled so long after the fact that it can have only negative impact, and assumes inappropriate significance by being taken out of the original context. If, on the other hand, the supervisor had noted the tardiness on the day that it had occurred, the employee would have had an opportunity to correct the behavior, explain the special cause for a single incident, or correct the supervisor's perceptions about tardiness. Such interaction would have provided an opportunity for growth if it had taken place in a timely way. Instead, it assumes a sense that the employee has been watched, rather than supported in his or her efforts to improve performance.

Standards and Evaluations

A variety of ways are available to enhance the system of evaluation within an organization. One is to make the evaluative system interactive, not only at the end stages but up front in the development of the job description. An employee who has helped to define the job description will not only be more committed to performing that job, but will also have a clear understanding of what characterizes positive performance in that job. Emphases on numerical or formulative approaches should be tempered by integration of individual and company goals. What is too often forgotten is that there is a dialectic between employee and company (or even market/industry) performance. The impact of an industry downturn, poor product management, or inadequate marketing programs should not be expressed as a reduction in sales and be reflected in the personal revenue of the individual salesperson.

Once this understanding is in place, organizations may be tempted to move toward evaluative standards; that is, standards based on some measure of an individual's contribution to an organization. These standards often introduce another hazard, that of subjectivity in the system. The danger of softening strictly defined systems of pay is that the subjective standards become more important as less flexible, objective benchmarks are abandoned. Problems of fairness and perceived fairness will undermine the effectiveness of evaluative forms. Particularly in large companies, the problems of subjective variation become significant, given the all-too-frequently documented recurrence of personal and institutional bias.

Additional questions are raised by the system of evaluative standards. For example, different thinking styles exist among various disciplines in an organization. This variation is, of course, vital to the success of the organization, since it represents different kinds of contributions and a variety of perspectives. In specific situations, however, certain styles will be preferred over others. How can this diversity be encouraged when styles that are similar to management attitudes may receive higher ratings than styles that represent divergent approaches? The rational employee is likely to conform his or her own style to the type of thinking perceived to warrant the best evaluation. For instance, a dynamic risk-taker may make a better product salesperson, but the personal style that creates this dynamism may be incomprehensible to the management teams assigned to evaluate performance. This points to the necessity of consistent relationships in team format among interacting management-employee units. A blurring of this distinction is necessary not only to improve innovation by enhancing employee contributions, but also for positive, active relationships to develop.

Good Faith: Creating a System of Commitment

It becomes clear when addressing even very complex pay systems that some sort of distinction is inevitable when trying to instill employees with incentives that exactly parallel company goals. The challenge is not one of designing the perfect system, but instead of attempting, in an ongoing process, to minimize these distortions, and convincing employees to do their best in spite of disincentives often created by poor system design. This process relies on management's commitment to explaining—and perhaps more importantly to interactively formulating—pay schemes with all employees. Creating good faith becomes very important. The ability to convince employees that management is honestly concerned with developing and implementing evaluative progress requires dedication and hard work. Management needs to be aware of what each employee is doing and must communicate the objective of the job and the company. Employees need to know that management is acting in good faith. Such a systems approach is necessary in considering employee efforts, experience, and educational background as part of the compensation scheme. But the systems approach also suggests that examining objectives, observing progress toward achievement of objectives, and understanding the impact of the systems in which progress occurs must be considered. These factors are often left out of pay matrices in favor of level-specific or education-specific guidelines for pay.

In return for the commitment to such a system, the employer can expect that employees will accept the company's goals as their own, that in good faith the individual employee will not maximize products at the expense of process, that ultimately the employee's welfare is tied to the company in a win-win relationship. An additional benefit of good faith pay systems is increasing efficiency in evaluation and personnel systems. With the understanding of employee commitment to company goals, the issues of constant supervision and evaluation, and of careful calculation of benefits, is no longer necessary. When employees learn to take pride in their own work, take leadership in their own areas, and expect commensurate good faith treatment by the company to whose goals they are committed, the outcome can be described only as a win-win scenario.

The shortcomings of real-life systems arise out of flawed assumptions in human relations and variability, particularly with regard to the accuracy of evaluative systems, the objectivity of such systems, the reinforcement of mediocrity, and the destruction of teamwork within and between departments. Clearly, any benefits system will induce distortions in behavior because it is impossible to create an all-encompassing system that will be internalized by each employee in working for the ultimate good of the company.

Returning to Deming's 12th point, however, there is now a more accurate understanding of the importance of reviewing incentives systems and making them consistent with the Deming approach. The majority of American benefits systems are not, in fact, consistent with this philosophy. Because employees' concerns often center on payment schemes, the adoption of the 12th point is not an optional but a vital process. The difficulties in inspiriting the reciprocally altruistic benefits of good faith relations can be achieved only by patient and ongoing commitment to employee involvement and enforcement of the relationships between personal growth and performance and that of the company. The team aspect is enhanced when employees realize that their rewards are linked to personal commitment in a team effort. This is the benefit that is promised by ESOP and profit-sharing systems. A combination of linkages to company goals (ESOPs and profit sharing) and personal goals (established through interaction with management and evaluated in a variety of dimensions) provides a pay system that will minimize distortion of employee incentives and foster the concentration of company purpose. This must be created in an open environment where information is freely shared. Reduction of competition among departments should result when tensions created by pay systems are removed. Most importantly, good faith and well-designed incentive systems should return pride in workmanship and enhance teamwork and company position in a framework of total commitment to the Deming philosophy.

THREE FACTORS IN COMPENSATION SYSTEMS

Deming has been clear about the relationship between an organization's treatment of people and the quality of its products. Among his concerns have been the use of annual evaluations by American managers and the devastating effect these evaluations have had on quality improvement efforts. Peter Scholtes (1987) has communicated that message to a variety of audiences. Further discussion has been offered by Scherkenbach (1986), Jenkins (1990), and others. The problem is far from being solved, but it is certainly being addressed.

A second, equally important area for consideration is the link between the reward system of any organization and the quality of its products and services. If employees perceive that they are not being treated with reasonable levels of equity, either internally or externally, their pride in work will decline. Because evaluation appraisals occur just once a year, and payday is at least once each month, employees are regularly reminded of perceived injustices. Thus, the reward system itself can be even more important to quality than annual evaluations.

A company's compensation system is made up of three distinct factors: salary, benefits, and other rewards such as profit sharing, stock options, and so on. Salary is a forward-looking concept, since it represents an agreement between an employee and an employer about the amount of salary to be paid in the future based on the employee's skills, chosen career, the skills required by the company, the employee's experience, and the supply and demand levels for these skills and experiences in the marketplace. Since salary is a forward-looking concept, the more precisely employees can predict present and future salary, the greater will be their confidence in the compensation system.

The curve that represents salary (Figure 4.1) takes on a shape reflecting continuous increases, but at a decreasing rate. The actual shape of the curve will vary depending on the specific job skill an individual possesses. For example, Figure 4.2*a* illustrates that the entry-level file clerk may reach a plateau rather quickly, since the skills necessary for this job can be developed in a comparatively short period of time. The mechanic (Figure 4.2*b*) has a higher ultimate market value, since the time necessary to develop mechanics' skills is longer than that of a file clerk. A physician (Figure 4.2*c*) has an even higher potential maximum market value, but since substantial

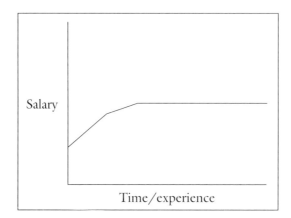

FIGURE 4.1. Salary curve.

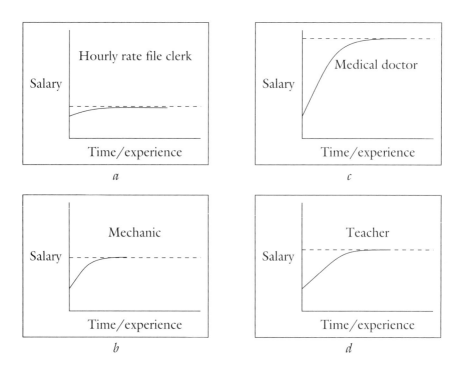

FIGURE 4.2. Different job skill salary curves.

preparation and education are demanded for this position, the time to reach this maximum is longer. A teacher (Figure 4.2*d*) may have a considerably lower maximum market value, in spite of the fact that the preparation required is substantial. These examples illustrate the concept of movement to maximum market value. The assumption in these curves is that the job remains the same; of course, if an employee's set of skills or knowledge has changed, or if the position is altered, the entire curve is reexamined and recalibrated according to the description of the new job or skill set.

A second aspect of compensation is that of benefits. Employees view benefits in the context of external equity rather than internal equity. That is, employees may compare their organization's benefits to those of other companies, not with others in the same organization. Individuals may not be satisfied with an organization's benefits package, but they understand that they have not been singled out. This is an important difference since research suggests that employees tend to be more concerned about internal than external equity issues. Managing the benefits package does not generally become an issue of internal equity.

A third leg of compensation is the reward system. This can be represented by profit sharing, commissions, stock options, and other plans to compensate employees. If salary is a forward-looking concept, a reward system is, in a way, a backward-looking system, since it evaluates some outcome of the actions of individuals, groups, and the entire company. Based on this outcome, rewards may be given, withheld, or given at a partial level determined by agreements reached about these rewards. It is important to distinguish between individual and group rewards. Commissions, for example, represent a kind of individual reward that can have a destructive impact on individuals' motivation. Those who receive commissions may feel that the organization is manipulating them by means of the commission system. At the same time, those who do not receive commissions may feel that their contributions to the product or service are not worth as much as the effort of the commissioned sales staff. Companywide profit-sharing plans, on the other hand, represent a kind of reward system that builds group morale and teamwork.

THREE CASE STUDIES

A Company

One firm is in the process of attempting to develop a compensation system that would best reflect the Deming philosophy. In order to determine the effectiveness of such a system, the firm developed criteria by which the compensation plan would be evaluated. All three aspects of compensation—salary, benefits, and rewards—must accomplish the following:

1. Be fair with respect to both internal and external equity.
2. Be easy to understand.
3. Align individual success with organizational success.
4. Foster teamwork.
5. Separate salary from evaluation of performance.
6. Tie skills to starting salaries.
7. Offer profit sharing to all employees.
8. Make salary a nonissue in the company.

In developing a policy to deal with all three aspects of compensation, one goal is reflected in the final criterion (8). Efforts were made to reduce anxiety about compensation. Employee time and creative energy are often diverted to discussions of salary and benefits. If equity could be achieved in the compensation system, these discussions would be minimized, and energy could be directed to more fruitful tasks.

This company is a full-service firm dedicated to providing software, training, and consulting to help organizations in their quality improvement efforts. It is a young company founded less than 10 years ago, and its founders continue to be the managing force in the company. Employees are professionals in consulting and computer development as well as administration and marketing. They tend to be young; the average age is 34. The company has experienced rapid growth, brought about through reinvesting most of its profits into expansion.

Formerly, salaries were determined by reviewing, every quarter, what all employees were paid and making adjustments as appropriate. Details of this procedure were not communicated to employees. A benefits package was similar to those offered by companies of the same size in the surrounding geographic area.

Once the company became profitable after its early survival stage, a profit-sharing plan was developed. The plan was loosely defined in terms of how much went into the plan and how it was to be divided among employees. They were informed in general terms about this process, understanding that salary and longevity with the firm were key factors in the distribution system. In addition to these factors, however, management also gave additional profit-sharing dividends to some employees based on the managers' judgments about individual performances. No public recognition of such awards was made. In its beginning, the company had used a commission system in the sales department, but this process had been eliminated after the negative factors associated with commission systems became apparent. The transition from commission to noncommission required a great deal of education and patience.

Objectives. The objectives of the policy were clearly outlined and shared with employees. Among these objectives were the following:

1. To establish a compensation system that will be fair with respect to both internal and external equity

2. To educate employees about the system and keep channels of communication open

3. To foster an atmosphere of teamwork

4. To minimize, as much as possible, dissatisfaction about individual levels of compensation

5. To tie salaries to those skills required to perform a certain job and to what the market will pay for these skills

6. To separate the connection between employees' pay and the evaluation of their performance

7. To create a profit-sharing system that represents an addition to, not a substitute for, an employee's compensation

8. To make a clear connection between the profits of the company and the profit sharing of its employees

The two objectives that most clearly set this system apart from traditional methods of compensation, and the most difficult to achieve, are (5) and (6). To separate pay from evaluation of performance is clearly the most radical departure from other systems. To achieve this objective, it was clear that evaluation must be made on an ongoing, immediate basis, so that it would not be tied to annual salary setting. This demands a great deal from managers. They must be aware of what their teams are doing and of how well they are performing, so the managers can give immediate feedback. In a sense, the evaluation system shifts from an emphasis on *detection* to one of *prevention*—a concept long familiar to quality management professionals.

The objective of establishing salaries through assessment of skills (5) demands constant monitoring not only of the market—so that market changes will be reflected in salaries—but also of employees' individual skills. If employees improve their skills and thus their usefulness to the company, their salary profiles must change to reflect this improvement.

Salaries. After studying comparable salary data in appropriate markets, it was determined that salaries would be set at 5 percent above the average (or at the 55th percentile) of people performing like work in the local region. A benefits package would be commensurate to those of companies similar in size and scope. And 35 percent of after-tax profits would be designated for profit sharing, to be distributed to all employees. The amount received would be based entirely on current salary and longevity with the company, a formula that each individual employee can calculate.

A great deal of energy has been invested in developing the new compensation system for the company and in assuring that information about actual market values for employees is kept up-to-date. The system has been operating for more than two years now, with fine-tuning of processes and job descriptions receiving ongoing attention. It must be remembered that regardless of the ultimate outcome of change, it is nonetheless change, and generates some level of anxiety that must be addressed along with the mechanical aspects of the compensation system itself.

Change is hard work, and there will always be some level of resistance to any change. Furthermore, these changes have been made in the most sensitive area of the organization's operation—that of dealing with and rewarding employees. Often, an individual's own sense of worth is tied to his or her paycheck. Therefore, there has been some level of sensitivity to the change, and some discomfort with the idea of experimenting with people's paychecks. In general, however, employees have seen the change as an improvement. Many of the problems generated by the old system have been eliminated. Managers are learning that they cannot depend on the compensation system to evaluate their employees, but instead must take an active role in the growth and development of their teams. This process has been difficult, but in itself represents a change for the better.

This firm does not claim to have the answer to the dilemma of compensating employees. It sees itself as investigating the relationship between the compensation system and the quality of products and services of an organization, and the implications of the Deming philosophy on the salary-benefits-reward system of a company. One adjustment, which has been made, relates to the language used in referring to the compensation. Somehow, although the system established salaries that were 5 percent above the average for firms of the same size, the expression *55th percentile* that employees used came to sound like less than 100 percent of what pay should be.

The company compensation plan is still in the early implementation stages, and thus it is too soon to determine its long-term implications. The firm is attuned to immediate responses to the changes, recognizing that the compensation system itself is a pioneering effort and will generate opportunities for new growth and learning about the application of the Deming management principles. The company emphasizes that the system is not meant to be only an experiment to determine the effects of change itself. Rather, the system represents a genuine attempt to improve the ways in which an organization's employees—its most important resources—are recognized and compensated for their investments in the company's future.

Application to a School

A second application of this compensation system is being pursued at an independent school in Ohio. It has about 400 students from early childhood through high school and 60 faculty and administrative staff members. The school offers a nonresidential, college-preparatory program in a suburban environment. Compensation, especially in the form of salary, has always been an unsettling issue in the school. While the school has not placed its compensation system within the framework of a commitment to the Deming philosophy, its approach demonstrates ways in which a firmly entrenched, emotionally charged compensation system can be improved by using Deming principles, regardless of what they are called.

In the school's traditional compensation system, teachers were observed in the classroom by their respective principals and given written feedback about their teaching and other responsibilities. This happened once each year. Unfortunately the actual process was not well documented, and there was a great deal of inconsistency between principals from different levels (elementary, middle school, high school). Faculty evaluations and the concomitant pay reflected a great deal of inequity and inconsistency. Though pay was not directly or formally tied to evaluation, salary decisions were made by the headmaster based on his own judgment about individuals' overall performance. At one time, this was called *value to the school*. Inequities developed for a variety of historical reasons. For example, some teachers had greater skill in negotiating their entry salaries or annual raises than others (the squeaky wheel syndrome); variation had developed among their perceived needs. Thus, entry-level salaries reflected great disparity over time.

For many years, the weeks following evaluations and contract release were miserable. Salaries were low to begin with, which was a function of the profession itself as well as the school's fledgling status as an institution and its lack of endowment support to sustain ongoing needs. Increases were minimal. But even more detrimental to morale was the sense of mystery of the process. No one really knew how salary decisions were made, but there was a great deal of speculation and suspicion about the process.

Real and perceived inequities exacerbated these difficulties, and rendered faculty concentration for part of every spring term abysmal.

To address the situation, a task force was created to examine the possibilities of creating change in the compensation system. A team headed by a member of the school's board of trustees included representatives from the elementary, middle, and high school teaching staff. A second board member, who joined the team later, was conversant with the Deming approach and practiced it in his own organization, but was sensitive to the school's limited acceptance of the philosophy. An administrator and the school's business manager were also on the team. Meeting regularly for a year, the group grappled with a number of issues.

- What should comprise the basic compensation system in the school?

- What is a reasonable target for salary levels for the school?

- How should advanced degrees be considered in the salary scheme?

- How should extracurricular activities be compensated?

The group arrived at a system that addressed some of the changes that would need to be made, but not all of them.

Because teachers in independent schools receive salaries that are traditionally lower than teachers in public schools, the first commitment of the team was to reduce the gap with public education. Its recommendation, accepted by the board of trustees, was to commit to assuring that teachers in this school would be paid at the rate of 85 percent of what teachers in commensurate positions in local suburban school districts received. Data were accumulated, and salary figures for several districts were averaged to reach a target salary level for the school. It took two years from the time the board accepted the 85 percent recommendation to the time when that target figure was reached by all teachers. Even before the plan was funded to that extent, however, there was a noticeable improvement in teacher morale. The committee's work improved faculty morale by

- Assuring teachers of the school's commitment to improved salaries.

- Establishing the possibility of internal equity—the most important faculty concern.

- Providing an opportunity to eliminate merit pay and salary curves developed by public school counterparts. This also eradicated the "squeaky wheel" effect generated by the former system.

- Diminishing the impact of the annual performance evaluation.

Some of these effects had not been anticipated. By utilizing research done in public school districts, the school leaped, as it were, to internal equity in ways that would have taken years if it had depended on the school's developing its own data and establishing salary curves internally. Just as in the case of the consulting company, pay became a nonissue for discussion in the spring. Unlike public schools, individual salaries in independent schools are not published, and teachers are encouraged not to discuss them with their colleagues. This system often engendered suspicion and mistrust, as one might expect. In the new system, however, everyone understands salaries in terms of defined ranges. A teacher who has been in the system for seven years, for example, knows that he or she is being paid an amount that is very similar, if not identical, to others with the same educational and experience-based background. There is nothing to discuss, once this understanding is reached.

It should be noted that a second outcome of the compensation system was one of renewed attention to the evaluation system, moving toward a separation that is implicit in the salary curves themselves. While the classroom observation and written evaluation are still part of the teacher's records, additional feedback (not recorded in the file) is given by means of peer observation and review and department chair evaluation. Student evaluations are solicited but not shared beyond the classroom. The onus of coaching and providing feedback is clear, particularly for weak performers, where the supervisor (principal) must become involved in evaluation on an ongoing basis rather than leaving it to an end-of-the-year session where the possibility of contract nonrenewal suddenly looms. As with the consulting company, this is the key link in the system, since the issue of poor performers who continue to receive compensation at the same rate as their counterparts creates resentment among other teachers and ultimately destroys the system itself. Unacceptable practices must be observed and counseled in immediate ways by the employee's supervisor.

A University Study

A third application of parts of this compensation system is represented in the efforts of a college of business at a university. A group of faculty and administrators had spent nearly a year meeting to discuss quality management in general and the Deming philosophy in particular. Initial meetings included a general education about the quality movement and the history of Deming's influence on that movement. The group had formed voluntarily and did not represent an official appointment of the college. The group members' interest led them to meet for an hour each week, with a core group of regular participants and a number of others who attended less often.

In structuring these meetings, the preferred format that developed was to share tapes from the Deming Library series and then discuss the ideas that they represented. Often these discussions were lively, and many of them challenged participants' long-held ideas about a variety of management approaches. The annual performance evaluation, a traditional component of the compensation and reward system in many organizations, was a topic of one of the discussion sessions, and the dialogue ultimately led to the compensation system of the university.

As in the case of most evaluation systems, the stated goal of the university's policy was to provide feedback to faculty. In its application, however, it formed the basis for salary decisions. Each department in the college had developed its own system of weighting each of the three areas in which faculty are traditionally assessed: teaching, research, and service. Each year, the department chairperson in one of the five departments would send a written evaluation to each faculty member. This included the chairperson's evaluation of that faculty member in each of the three areas and a numerical assessment for each of the areas. An overall evaluation number was then assigned, representing a mathematical combination of the numerical evaluation of the three areas.

An overall department average appraisal, as well as averages for each area, was published annually, assuring that half the faculty would feel like failures (since no one wants his or her performance to be considered "below average"). The evaluation itself was returned to the department chairperson after the individual faculty member had signed it. No oral interaction was required by the system. It was, however, available when a faculty member requested it and scheduled an appointment with the chairperson to discuss the evaluation.

Each department had its own approach to the process, but the key ingredients were essentially the same. The predictable outcome of communicating that half the faculty was below average was serious morale problems among those individuals. Another concomitant outcome, however, occurred among those who were determined to be above average: Each was aware of how far he or she was from the number that would render an individual the year's "superstar." In addition to the department allotment for pay, the dean had his own fund that he would distribute to those who were the highest achievers in the college.

Although most faculty members knew that this system was indeed flawed, they had no theory by which to develop a new system or to challenge the traditional approach. After the Deming group meetings and dialogue with the administration of the college, some changes were made in the system. The college still demands a written evaluation, and the university requires that faculty be designated by four categories.

1. Meritorious

2. Effective

3. Needs improvement

4. Unacceptable

To minimize the effects of ranking, one department agreed to encourage the chairperson to designate all 18 members of the department as "effective" in performance. The chairperson agreed to do this, still completing the written evaluations, but designating all members as "effective." This meant that they would all receive the same percentage in salary adjustment. Some departments were not as adamant about such identical ranking, but by and large, most faculty members in the college were ranked in that way. An entirely new paradigm—representing pride in work through improvement and response to feedback rather than through the relatively minor percentage differences in salary increase—developed among faculty members.

Much of what has happened to change the system is informal, and does not address many of the problems fostered by the old system, such as that of internal equity among faculty members. Nonetheless, there seems to be awareness of the possibility for change and a genuine movement away from the old, flawed system.

CONCLUSION

Just as traditional compensation systems demonstrate a great deal of variety, moving toward systems that contribute to pride in workmanship is represented in several ways in organizations. The challenges of change are very real, but two are especially critical.

The first challenge is a philosophical one. An organization must have a commitment to pride in workmanship and improvement of processes, or the steps that are taken to change its compensation system will have no purpose. Clearly, a commitment to the Deming management philosophy provides the most solid basis upon which to create a new approach to compensation. And the organization that embraces Deming's ideas must include its approach to compensation in its transformation.

A second challenge is represented in the daunting task of developing market curves, such as those utilized by the consulting company in the first case study. Keeping these data current is a part of the challenge as well; both assembling the information and revisiting it with current data occupy a great deal of energy within the organization. As the data are gathered, an organization will need to address a number of decisions, including the following:

- Determining the number of job classification that will be necessary
- Developing acceptable curves and using traditional market salary data

- Placing individual employees on the appropriate curves
- Adjusting curves when employees change positions within the organization
- Determining accurate descriptions of all jobs through written survey and follow-up interviews

Regardless of the point at which an organization finds itself in the quality transformation, its leaders must focus attention on the internal processes that fundamentally affect its members and the joy they find in their work. If not, the transformation can never be considered complete. On the road to creating a quality organization, attention given to the compensation system provides a critical ingredient to further success.

REFERENCES

Cleary, Michael J., and Timothy J. Cleary. 1993. Designing an effective compensation system. *Quality Progress* (April): 69–72 and (May): 97–99.

Deming, W. Edwards. 1986. *Out of the crisis*. Cambridge, Mass.: MIT Center for Advanced Engineering Study.

Hardin, Garritt James. 1977. *Managing the commons*. San Francisco: W. H. Freeman.

Jenkins, Mary G. 1990. The application of statistical principles in the design of people systems. Paper presented at the Fourth Annual International Deming Users Group, August, Cincinnati, Ohio.

Kohn, Alfie. 1993. *Punished by rewards*. New York: Houghton-Mifflin.

Scherkenbach, William W. 1986. *The Deming route to quality and productivity: Road maps and roadblocks*. Washington, D.C.: CEEPress.

Scholtes, Peter R. 1987. *An elaboration on Deming's teachings on performance*. Madison, Wis.: Joiner and Associates.

Chapter 5

TQM and Safety Performance Management

Robert A. Reber

Preventing occupational injuries and illnesses has been a concern for organizations for a long time. Likewise, quality control has emerged as a key focus.

One can easily argue that both safety and quality are important for the success of the business, but is one more important than the other? Should one be given priority over the other? It will be the contention here that safety and quality are not necessarily mutually exclusive performance goals. Working safely and producing a high-quality product or service are goals that organizations should view as compatible and complementary instead of competing. It has even been suggested that safety and health professionals should have a key role in a total quality management (TQM) system (Lark 1991; Manuele 1993; Vincoli 1991).

Ergo, this chapter will examine two main issues. First, it will discuss how safety performance management can parallel and even be an integral part of a comprehensive quality management effort. It will focus on how safety performance relates to the major TQM principles espoused by Deming (1986), Crosby (1979), and Juran (1989). It will also consider the criteria for the Malcolm Baldrige National Quality Award. Second, it will show how key TQM techniques can be incorporated with a successful total safety performance management program.

Before an adequate discussion can begin, two definitions need clarification. First, exactly what is TQM? Second, what is included in safety performance management?

As Dean and Bowen (1994) observed, despite the volumes of articles in the business and trade press, the concept of TQM remains ambiguous. While there may be some differences among the TQM gurus such as

Deming, Juran, and Crosby, the fundamentals may be synthesized. To be succinct, this section will focus on the consolidated list of principles presented by Bowen and Lawler (1992). These are somewhat generic or at least consistent with other recent reviews (Dean and Bowen 1994; Dean and Evans 1994). Bowen and Lawler (1992) summarize the TQM principles as follows:

1. Quality work the first time

2. Focus on the customer

3. Strategic, holistic approach to improvement

4. Continuous improvement as a way of life

5. Mutual respect and teamwork

It should be recognized that these principles may serve more to create the proper atmosphere and corporate culture necessary for organizational development rather than to specify plans of action. As Dean and Bowen (1994) point out, the principles can serve to drive practices and techniques commonly found in TQM efforts. Further, most of the principles are generic enough that one can make intuitive inferences with human resource management (HRM) issues. Certainly, HRM needs to be involved in TQM efforts. This chapter focuses on one specific HRM topic: safety performance.

Safety performance management refers to a comprehensive effort to reduce occupational injuries and illnesses. It should go beyond compliance with mandatory guidelines established by the Occupational Safety and Health Administration (OSHA) (including hazard communications), the Environmental Protection Agency (EPA), the Mine Safety and Health Administration, and other regulatory groups. Like TQM, safety performance management is concerned with the process involved (that is, preventing unsafe acts) as well as the end result (that is, fewer injuries and illnesses). This is especially true of behaviorally based safety programs (Chhokar and Wallin 1984; Duhon et al. 1989; Komaki, Barwick, and Scott 1978; Komaki, Heinzmann, and Lawson 1980; Krause, Hidley, and Hodson 1990; Reber and Wallin 1984).

Similar to TQM, safety performance management should be process oriented. For example, Heinrich's (1959) classic domino model of occupational injuries represents the injury process as a number of dominos that can fall into one another; the resulting cascade effect leads to an injury. The model reveals several areas where organizations may stop the domino from falling and thus interrupt the injury process. The first two dominoes indicate the antecedent part of the accident process since they keep the worker from performing an unsafe act. Maintaining a safe working environment and constantly improving machinery and equipment with human safety in mind is the first domino. For example, double-palm operating buttons and sensors that disable equipment if a light beam is interrupted are used to prevent hands and other body parts from being caught in machinery. Regulatory agencies such as OSHA have probably had their biggest impact in this area.

The second domino—human factors—dwells on issues such as personality, attitude, cultural norms, and physical or physiological factors. This domino may be eliminated or reduced from the chain of events through improved employee selection procedures. There is a dearth of well-documented selection tests validated for safety performance. One notable exception may be in the area of stress management focusing on the relationship between stress and work burnout. Tests such as the Hogan Personnel Selection Series (Hogan and Hogan 1985) or the Maslach Burnout Inventory (Maslach and Jackson 1981) have been correlated with stress-related occupational injuries and illnesses. More research, however, is needed in this area.

The third domino refers to unsafe behaviors or acts performed by workers. Developing behavioral measures of safety and consequently working to increase the frequency of safe acts (and concurrently reducing the frequency of unsafe acts) has provided one possible solution (Chhokar and Wallin 1984; Komaki, Barwick, and Scott 1978; Komaki, Heinzmann, and Lawson 1980; Krause, Hidley, and Hodson 1990; Reber and Wallin 1984).

THE ROLE OF SAFETY IN TQM

Quality Work the First Time

The premise for this principle is that it is more efficient for the company to do the job correctly once rather that rework defective parts or handle returns and complaints. Although the time it takes to provide a quality part or service may be initially lengthened, time should be saved in the long term. As Crosby (1979) stated, there is no such thing as the economics of quality; it is always cheaper to do the job right the first time.

Similarly, the safe performance of a job may take longer, yet it actually may be more efficient when long-term data are considered. I am reminded of a tragic accident that I once investigated as a safety consultant. One individual was killed and another severely injured when a suspended load fell on them. This incident is even more tragic when one considers that it could have been prevented had the employees and supervisors taken a negligible amount of time to properly secure the load. Instead, in a rush to perform a job, they failed to take the time to properly assess the hazards of the situation.

Even Deming (1986) warned that one of the seven deadly diseases that obstruct the search for quality is excessive medical costs that increase the final costs of goods and services. The costs associated with occupational injuries and illnesses could certainly be included in this category. As Pye (1993) reported, the costs of injuries and ill health at work can amount to 37 percent of the company's annual profit. It has already been documented that a successful safety program can save a company substantial sums (Reber and Wallin 1984; Duhon et al. 1989). For example, based on data collected from three companies over a three-year period, the average direct medical cost associated with a back injury was approximately $27,000. This figure should be viewed as being conservative as it does not included the many intangible costs associated with an injury or illness.

As Heinrich (1959) noted, companies often only compute the proverbial tip of the iceberg. Consider what happens to the production or service process when an employee is injured on the job. In many cases, work in at least the immediate area practically ceases as coworkers render assistance. The costs of this disruption and the impact to the morale of those who witnessed the incident are difficult to assess. There are direct costs attributed to the incident, such as medical expenses, workers' compensation, increased insurance rates, lost production, repairs, and (to Deming's disdain) legal fees. The costs, which are often overlooked yet are substantial, could include medical supplies; recruiting, hiring, and training replacement workers; supervisor time completing reports; employee time completing reports; product waste; coworkers' lost production; and the more evasive costs associated with decreased morale and damage to the company's image.

The hidden part of the iceberg increases when the costs associated with nonrecordable incidents are considered. These include the "near-misses" that might result in property damage or the minor first-aid injuries that are not reported on OSHA forms. Such unofficial accidents still disrupt production and could ultimately affect customers if damaged parts are undetected or shipments are delayed. In other words, all accidents, whether they result in a recordable injury/illness or not, affect the process of supplying a product or service. In terms of improving this process, reducing these incidences should enhance the efficiency of the operation.

Another "deadly disease," according to Deming (1986), is running the company on visible figures alone. Measurement is important to TQM, but the intangibles need to be considered too. Financial costs can be reduced with a successful safety program, but the human side must also be considered. It is difficult to put a precise dollar amount on the pain and suffering associated with an industrial injury or illness. The bottom line—both financially and ethically—is that a safe work operation is best for the company.

It is difficult to get managers and employees to view the long-term consequences of behaving safely. Granted, a safe way of performing an operation may not always be the fastest. As Krause, Hidley, and Hodson (1990) observed, employees may favor the more immediate consequences of saving time and effort by doing a job unsafely. The long-term consequences, however, of performing unsafe acts is that an accident will eventually result. When this occurs, the time initially gained will be lost as part of the aforementioned hidden costs of accidents.

In order to help correct this short-term orientation and encourage workers to focus on safe acts, rewards and recognition (another key feature of TQM) can be based on improving behavioral safety performance as well as reducing incidence rates. A common safety management practice is to award prizes to individuals or groups that achieve a milestone such as working a year without a lost-time accident. These rewards can also be used to reinforce the intrinsic satisfaction of achieving behavioral safety goals.

Focus on the Customer

For obvious reasons, it is understandable why customers are concerned with the quality service or products they receive from suppliers. Why, however, should customers worry about the internal operations of a company? Should customers consider a supplier's safety record when awarding contracts? Deming's (1986) fourth principle would suggest that companies should end the practice of awarding business based on price tag alone. Did he intend that human resource practices in general, and safety performance in particular, also be considered? Bowen and Lawler (1992) have suggested that human resource departments need to become more externally service oriented and less production oriented. The latter tends to focus more on internal technologies and employee needs than on satisfying customers per se.

One premise supporting this principle is that companies should focus on long-term relationships with suppliers. In developing this level of trust and loyalty, companies should expect suppliers to be able to deliver goods or services on a reliable basis. As noted, a safe operation is usually a more efficient one.

Thompson (1995) suggested that reducing production/service cycle time is an important part of the quality process. If things can be done more efficiently, then costs should be lower. In addition, the company should then be more responsive to customers since there is a focus on reducing unnecessary operations requiring unnecessary hours to do redundant work. Customers practicing such TQM techniques as just-in-time inventory in manufacturing need to know that a supplier can provide quality on a reliable basis. Since industrial injuries usually correlate with downtime, rework, and additional labor costs, then customers should appreciate a safe company. Thus, an effective safety program can be viewed as a containment action by companies to protect their customers from internal problems.

Admittedly, the role of safety performance management as it relates to the customer focus principle of TQM is indirect; however, some companies do consider a supplier's safety record when negotiating a relationship (Duhon et al. 1989). It has even been suggested (albeit undocumented in public literature) that companies such as DuPont consider adherence to safe procedures when awarding contracts for construction and other services.

A corollary issue to the customer-focus principle stems from the increased use of temporary employees and employee leasing agencies. There may be some confusion about who is responsible for employee safety. Is the temporary/leasing agency or the company where the work is performed? Since both organizations have a vested interest (ethically, financially, and perhaps legally) in preventing injuries/illnesses in the workplace, then both should also invest in safety training and management.

Strategic, Holistic Approach to Improvement

While Deming (1986) may have had producing quality products/services and customer satisfaction as the primary aims of a company, maintaining a safe working environment should also be listed. In fact, in the United States, the general duty clause of the Occupational Safety and Health Act of 1970 mandates this goal for most organizations. Just as focusing on quality should become ubiquitous, so should a concern for safety. Different jobs in a given company may have varying degrees of exposure to occupational injuries and illnesses. Yet it can also be stated that virtually everyone in a company has a chance of being injured. Therefore, everyone in an organization should be responsible for safety.

If managers are reluctant to support safety efforts for ethical reasons alone, then they can always turn to cost savings. One company president was heard saying that the safety program had produced one of the best returns on investment in the past two years. The company had reduced its direct medical costs associated with injuries from $330,000 per oil rig to less than $30,000 per unit. Another company spent approximately $80,000 on implementing a behavioral safety program, and saved more than $440,000 after one year. For bottom-line oriented companies, these figures should be convincing.

Continuous Improvement as a Way of Life

This principle probably has more application to safety performance management programs than vice-versa. In other words, just as companies need to constantly strive to improve their processes, reduce waste, and reduce cycle times, they also need to continuously focus on finding a safer way of doing their work. Again, this is easier said than done. All too often, companies seem to become concerned with safety performance usually only after an accident. Similarly, they only become concerned with quality after customer complaints. Total quality management and total safety management both advocate a proactive stance.

One obstacle to fulfilling this principle for safety purposes could be the type of measures and feedback workers receive on the job. When someone gets hurt on the job, there is an immediate, painful consequence usually due to an unsafe act (Krause, Hidley, and Hodson 1990; Reber and Wallin 1983, 1984; Reber, Wallin, and Duhon 1989). Such consequences, however, are often infrequent. As Heinrich (1959) estimated, a person may commit more than 300 unsafe acts before even experiencing an accident, let alone an injury. The perceived positive consequences associated with performing an unsafe operation may outweigh the perceived negative ones, especially in terms of probability.

Wearing safety glasses or goggles when operating a circular saw is a useful example. Complaints are sometimes made that the glasses or goggles are uncomfortable, that they fog up, distort one's vision, are hot, are inconvenient, and so on. Thus, not wearing them becomes negatively reinforcing since the probability of getting something painful in the eye is not extremely high. After all, do people wearing proper personal protective equipment stop to observe that they didn't get hurt as a result of the precaution? This is why safety *kaizen* is needed. A focus on continuous safety improvement keeps the negative and positive consequences in perspective. As will be discussed later, statistical control charts and other TQM techniques provide excellent feedback to reinforce safety efforts.

Mutual Respect and Teamwork

Deming (1986) talks about driving fear out the workplace and creating a climate of trust and innovation. Further, he says to remove barriers that rob people of pride of workmanship. Like the previous principle, total quality management and total safety management are parallels with respect to this concept. Empowering employees, if done properly, can facilitate the other principles of customer focus and continuous improvement. Concerning safety performance management, employees must be given the responsibility for maintaining a safe work environment. After all, they are the ones with the most at stake. By the same token, they must be allowed to take the initiative for their safety without fear of reprisal from managers overly concerned with production quotas.

A major source of frustration for employees is having them participate in meetings and training sessions on safety and/or quality control and then not allowing them to utilize the information on the job. Participative management ideas have been around for a long time, but all too often it appears to be mainly lip service. This participatory facade can destroy the level of trust needed to improve quality and safety (Peters and Waterman 1982; Reber, Wallin, and Duhon 1989). Perhaps this is why programs such as the Malcolm Baldrige National Quality Award and the ISO 9000 series standards list employee involvement among their criteria. On the safety side, OSHA strongly recommends continued safety training and employee participation. The caveat is that companies should truly empower employees and not just go through the formalities to appease an outside agency or customer.

One threat to the increased use of empowered safety or quality teams may be the recent National Labor Relations Board ruling known as the *Electromation* decision (King 1993; Tyson 1993). In this case, the board referred to Section 8(a)(2) of the National Labor Relations Act in holding that Electromation's "Action Committees" were "labor organizations" that had been unlawfully dominated by the employer. As King (1993) recommends, a committee may be unlawful if it addresses wages, fringe benefits, grievances, absenteeism, hours of work, labor disputes, or other working conditions. Although safety and/or quality committees are not mentioned per se, the question remains: Will these teams become unions that are controlled by the company? Given the longevity of the participation of employees on safety committees or teams, it is doubtful that this area will be challenged directly. Nevertheless, the decision does raise a concern that human resource, safety, and total quality professionals need to monitor. In 1996, legislation (H. R. 743, *Teamwork for Employees and Managers Act of 1995*) was considered to open the doors for more employee involvement systems, but it presents dangers as well.

SAFETY AND THE BALDRIGE AWARD

The importance of safety performance management to TQM may be evident when the Malcolm Baldrige National Quality Award is considered. According to the 1996 award examination criteria, 14 percent of the review is weighted by human resource utilization (National Institute of Standards and Technology 1996). The guidelines specifically address safety with subcriterion 4.4: Employee Well-Being and Satisfaction. Companies are evaluated on how well they maintain a safe work environment. This includes examining services, facilities, activities, and measures supporting the overall well-being of employees. As Blackburn and Rosen (1993) note, past Baldrige Award-winning companies monitor health and safety continuously and systematically. Companies such as Xerox, Westinghouse, and General Motors' Cadillac Division work to eliminate root causes of safety problems and not just mitigate the symptoms (Blackburn and Rosen 1993).

USING TQM TECHNIQUES IN SAFETY PERFORMANCE MANAGEMENT

The tools and techniques commonly used by TQM systems can vary widely as companies customize the tools to specific needs. This section focuses on the techniques that are amenable to safety and quality programs. In many respects, the term *quality* in TQM is being replaced with the word *safety* (that is, TSM). The techniques discussed include the following:

1. Deming cycle (plan, do, study, act)

2. Flowcharts

3. Check sheets, histograms, and Pareto diagrams

4. Fishbone or cause-and-effect diagrams

5. Control charts

These techniques are not really foreign to safety performance management. The literature provides several examples of each of them being applied to safety, albeit with slight variations or under different titles (Chhokar and Wallin 1984; Komaki, Barwick, and Scott 1978; Komaki, Heinzmann, and Lawson 1980; Krause, Hidley, and Hodson 1990; Reber and Wallin 1984; and Duhon et al. 1989).

Deming Cycle (Plan, Do, Study, Act)

As Dean and Evans (1994) summarize, the Deming (or Shewhart) cycle refers to utilizing engineering, operations, and management knowledge to make a process easier, faster, safer, less costly, and better suited to customer needs. Since the focus is on continuous improvement, it is a never-ending cycle. Duhon et al. (1989) observed the cycle in practice on mobile off-shore drilling units operating in the Gulf of Mexico. Each shift would begin with a 15–30 minute plan of action meeting. During this time the rig supervisor and the hands on duty would discuss the duties to be performed during that shift. Part of the discussion would focus on the applicable safety precautions. Then, they implemented the plans for the day (the "do" stage). The next time the workers met, they would briefly provide feedback on the previous day (thus the "study" phase). Necessary corrections were made, and the remaining part of the plan of action meeting focused on the shift to come. Of course, changes in the plans could be made during a shift if the situations dictated it.

Although the Deming cycle often involves a longer time frame and more detailed data collection (which also took place on the oil rigs), the basic elements of plan, do, study, and act were still present. These meetings also served to empower employees and foster teamwork as safety became everyone's concern. On a rotational basis, five to seven of the approximately 60 crew members formed a safety committee known as the Gold Hat Team (due to their gold hard hats). The team's role was to observe and correct any unsafe act or situation. Further, a safety suggestion system was implemented to allow input from anyone and at any time. Each suggestion essentially went through the Deming plan, do, study, act cycle. The planning took place when someone noticed a hazard or unsafe act. The do stage occurred when the suggestion was made, either verbally during meetings or in writing. The study part consisted of investigating the feasibility of making structural changes and/or instituting new standard safe operating procedures. The last phase, act, involved implementing the action and monitoring the results. A critical part of the process was keeping all employees informed of the various stages. One way to kill a suggestion system is to ask for input and then ignore it.

Flowcharts

Flowcharts provide a picture of a process that shows the sequence of steps performed (Dean and Bowen 1994; Dean and Evans 1994). This information can be used to identify exposure to hazards as well as quality problems and areas for improvement. As seen in Figure 5.1, the flowchart can facilitate a checklist of safe behaviors for each step in the process. At each step, questions such as the following should be asked: What personal protective equipment is needed? What is the safe way of handling the material? Do I have the proper tools or equipment for the job? Is it safe to perform the operation in the given location?

Check Sheets, Histograms, and Pareto Charts

These tools aid in the collection and organization of data to facilitate problem solving. Deming and others advocated building quality in rather than inspecting it out. A similar problem occurs with safety programs that rely on occupational injury and illness reports to assess safety performance. The analogy of closing the barn door after the horse has gotten out comes to mind. TQM focuses on the processes necessary for a quality product or service. Safety programs also need to follow suit and focus on the process of safe work and accident prevention.

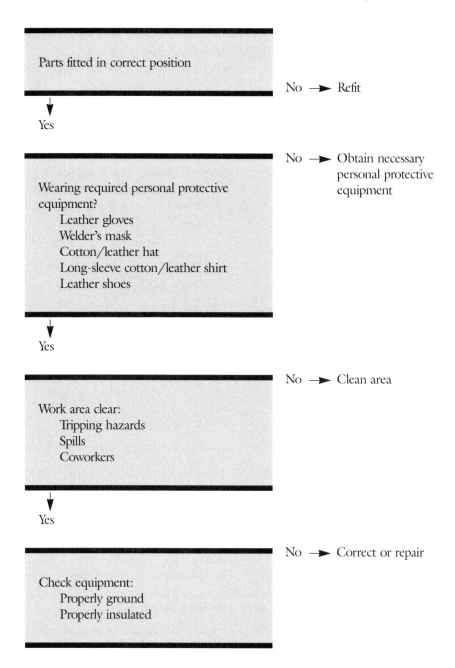

FIGURE 5.1. A safety performance management flowchart for welding tractor frames.

In developing behavioral measures of safety, a useful starting point is reviewing past injury/illness incident reports. A safety checklist, such as the one in Figure 5.2 (patterned from DuPont's Safety Training and Observation Program or S.T.O.P), can be used to collect data. When tabulated in check sheet form, the data can be used to identify what behavioral areas need attention.

The data presented in Figure 5.3 indicate that the vast majority of industrial accidents can be prevented as they relate to variables that can be controlled. (To provide anonymity, the data are based on a compilation of incident reports from three organizations.) Pareto charts or histograms could be developed further for each subarea by using the checklist in Figure 5.2.

Fishbone or Cause-and-Effect Diagram

These diagrams were originally introduced in Japan by Kaoru Ishikawa as an aid to sort and organize the many possible causes of quality problems. Although several studies have attributed the main cause of occupational injuries to human error, there is still room for further analysis. As seen in Figure 5.4, if a group brainstorms on the causes of an injury, several areas will deserve attention. Four of the five areas are still under human control with the lone exception being the environment. Even then, precautions can be taken to minimize the risks.

Control Charts

OSHA requires posting annual injury and illness data for all employees to see. The effects of this action remain to be seen. As Krause, Hidley and Hodson (1990) noted, there are more prevention-oriented measures of safety that a company can develop and report. The checklist in Figure 5.2, for example, can be used as part of an observation and reporting system. Safety inspectors (employees comprising a safety committee) can make unobtrusive and unannounced worker observations. They simply note whether all parties observed are following all of the behavioral safety rules applicable to the respective operation. If workers are in complete compliance, then they are considered working safely. Unlike TQM control charts that have upper and lower control limits, the all-or-none approach stems from the philosophy that if only one unsafe act is committed, then there is an increased probability of injury. In order to focus on the positive, the percentage of employees per department or other unit that is observed to be working safely can be charted on a form such as that shown in Figure 5.5.

One precaution to this system is that it should not be likened to a police officer trying to catch someone doing something wrong. One

SAFETY CHECK	SAFETY CHECK

SAFETY CHECK

Name _____

Dept ___*FA*___   Observer ___*RAR*___

Date ___*10-1-81*___   Time ___*AM*___

Activity _____*welding*_____

General safety
___ Horseplay
✔ Position of self
✔ Position of others
___ Other (specify below)

Personal protective equipment
✔ Eyes/face
✔ Hands/arms
✔ Clothing
✔ Other (specify below)
        welder's cap

Housekeeping
✔ Spills
✔ Equipment and tools
✔ Tripping hazards
___ Other (specify below)

Material handling
___ Lifting (manually)
___ Stacking/crating
✔ Secure material
___ Other (specify below)

Tool and equipment use
✔ Welding/cutting/fitting
___ Chipping/grinding
___ Cranes/hoists
___ Ladders/scaffolds
___ Paint/chemicals
___ Hand tools
___ Other (specify below)

COMMENTS _____
_____
_____
_____

**Example of completed form for
employee working safely.**

SAFETY CHECK

Name _____

Dept ___*SA*___   Observer ___*WH*___

Date ___*9-27-81*___   Time ___*PM*___

Activity _____*grinding*_____

General safety
___ Horseplay
✔ Position of self
✔ Position of others
___ Other (specify below)

Personal protective equipment
✔ Eyes/face
✔ Hands/arms
✔ Clothing
___ Other (specify below)

Housekeeping
✔ Spills
✔ Equipment and tools
✔ Tripping hazards
___ Other (specify below)

Material handling
___ Lifting (manually)
___ Stacking/crating
✔ Secure material
___ Other (specify below)

Tool and equipment use
___ Welding/cutting/fitting
✔ Chipping/grinding
___ Cranes/hoists
___ Ladders/scaffolds
___ Paint/chemicals
___ Hand tools
___ Other (specify below)

COMMENTS _____
_____
_____
_____

**Example of completed form for
employee working unsafely.**

FIGURE 5.2. Sample safety checklist for a heavy equipment manufacturer.

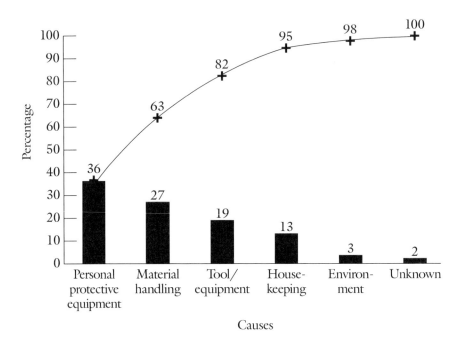

FIGURE 5.3. Pareto chart for causes of occupational injuries/illness.

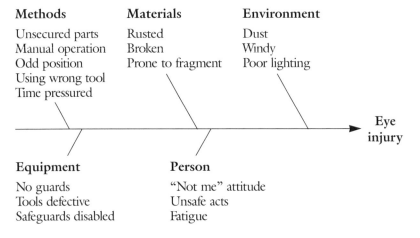

FIGURE 5.4. Fishbone/cause-and-effect diagram for an injury.

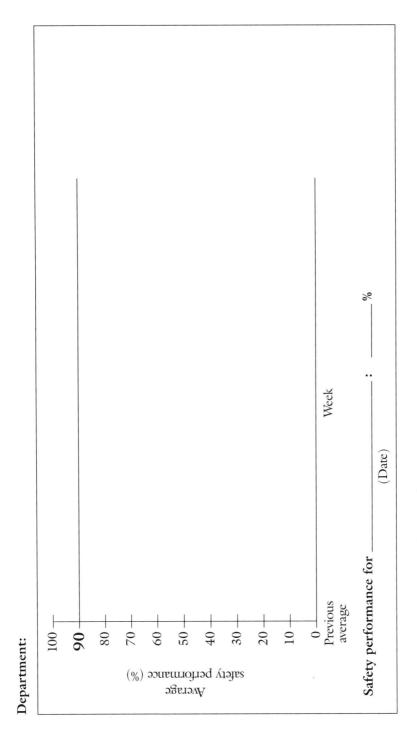

FIGURE 5.5. Safety control feedback form.

93

employee on an offshore oil rig once remarked that the previous safety supervisor for the company used the "seagull method of safety." He would fly in on a helicopter, crap on everybody, and then fly out. This is not the intent of the safety inspections conducted in conjunction with a total safety performance management system. Corrective feedback should be given when an unsafe act is observed by a safety inspector. This can be done in a constructive manner. The safety control chart should also serve to encourage self-correction and increase the frequency of safe behaviors. Further, by having employees rotate serving on the safety committee, everyone will have a chance to be an inspector.

CONCLUSIONS

Safety performance management and TQM have a lot in common. Performing a job safely is an integral part of the production or service process. A safe operation should enhance the overall efficiency of the company, thus enabling it to better serve customers. Similarly, several techniques popular with TQM can be adapted to improving safety. Both are worthy goals for virtually any organization. For benchmarking purposes, it would be beneficial to see more published information on what companies are specifically doing to improve safety and quality performance.

Perhaps the marriage of safety and quality efforts is best summed up by a commercially produced banner that was observed in several locations of a wire manufacturer. It was a large green and white banner that said, "Safety Protects People, Quality Protects Jobs."

REFERENCES

Blackburn, Richard, and Benson Rosen. 1993. Total quality and human resource management: Lessons learned from Baldrige Award-winning companies. *The Academy of Management Executive* 7, no. 3:49–66.

Bowen, David E., and Edward E. Lawler III. 1992. Total quality-oriented human resources management. *Organizational Dynamics* (spring): 29–41.

Chhokar, Jagdeep, and Jerry A. Wallin. 1984. Improving safety through applied behavior analysis. *Journal of Safety Research* 15, no. 2:141–151.

Crosby, Philip B. 1979. *Quality is free*. New York: McGraw-Hill.

Dean, James W., Jr., and David E. Bowen. 1994. Management theory and total quality: Improving research and practice through theory development. *The Academy of Management Review* (July): 392–418.

Dean, James W., Jr., and James R. Evans. 1994. *Total quality: Management, organization, and strategy.* Minneapolis/St Paul: West Publishing.

Deming, W. Edwards. 1986. *Out of the crisis.* Cambridge, Mass.: MIT Center for Advanced Engineering Study.

Duhon, David L., Stephen B. Knouse, Robert A. Reber, and Jerry A. Wallin. 1989. Improving oilfield safety performance by behavior modification techniques. Paper presented at the Annual Academy of Management Meeting, August, Washington, D.C.

Heinrich, H. W. 1959. *Industrial accident prevention: A scientific approach.* New York: McGraw-Hill.

Hogan, Robert, and Joyce Hogan. 1985. *Hogan personnel selection series.* Minneapolis: National Computer Systems.

Juran, J. M. 1989. *Juran on leadership for quality.* New York: Free Press.

King, G. Roger. 1993. Employee participation committees: Implications of electromation. *Society for Human Resource Management Legal Report* (spring): 5–8.

Komaki, J., K. D. Barwick, and L. R. Scott. 1978. A behavioral approach to occupational safety: Pinpointing and reinforcing safe performance in a food manufacturing plant. *Journal of Applied Psychology* 63, no. 4:434–445.

Komaki, J., A. T. Heinzmann, and L. Lawson. 1980. Effect of training and feedback: Component analysis of a behavioral safety program. *Journal of Applied Psychology* 65, no. 3:261–270.

Krause, Thomas R., John H. Hidley, and Stanley J. Hodson. 1990. *The behavior-based safety process.* New York: Van Nostrand Reinhold.

Lark, James. 1991. *Leadership in safety.* Professional Safety (March): 33–35.

Manuele, Fred A. 1993. Make quality the watchword of your safety program. *Safety & Health* (October): 106–109.

Maslach, Christina, and Susan E. Jackson. 1981. *Maslach burnout inventory.* Palo Alto, Calif.: Consulting Psychologists Press.

National Institute of Standards and Technology. 1996. *Malcolm Baldrige National Quality Award criteria.* Gaithersburg, Md.: National Institute of Standards and Technology.

Peters, Thomas J., and Robert H. Waterman Jr. 1982. *In search of excellence.* New York: Harper & Row.

Pye, Andy. 1993. True costs of health and safety. *Engineering* (January): 27.

Reber, Robert A., and Jerry A. Wallin. 1983. Validation of a behavioral measure of occupational safety. *Journal of Organizational Behavior Management* 5, no. 2:69–77.

Reber, Robert A., and Jerry A. Wallin. 1984. The effects of training, goal setting, and knowledge of results on safe behavior: A component analysis. *The Academy of Management Journal* 27, no. 3:544–560.

Reber, Robert A., Jerry A. Wallin, and David L. Duhon. 1989. Safety programs that work. *Personnel Administrator* (September): 66–70.

Thompson, Kenneth R. 1995. *Total quality management: Implications for managing today's organizations.* Module prepared for Virtual OB Primus database. New York: McGraw-Hill.

Tyson, Patrick R. 1993. Are safety committees illegal? *Safety & Health* (October): 47–50.

Vincoli, Jeffrey W. 1991. Total quality management and the safety and health professional. *Professional Safety* (June): 27–32.

Chapter 6

Barriers and Facilitators of TQM: A Human Resources Perspective*

Richard S. Blackburn and Benson Rosen

BACKGROUND

Staunch total quality management (TQM) advocates would have managers believe that a TQM approach to doing business is fully applicable to all organizations and would nearly always provide desirable results. This "main effects" approach to the predicted impact of TQM is represented by Jablonski's (1991) assertion that "those implementing TQM will realize increased productivity, increased customer satisfaction, reduced costs, enhanced quality of work life, and improved competitive position" (p. xvii). This near-religious fervor regarding the efficacy of TQM has won many converts. Indeed, Malcolm Baldrige National Quality Award winners provide substantial evidence of the positive impacts that a TQM approach can have on an organization. For a discussion of the positive impact on a stock portfolio composed of Baldrige Award winners see Helton (1995).

On the other hand, thoughtful readers of the TQM literature are also aware of numerous organizations whose TQM implementation efforts have been less effective than desired. The well-known problems associated with Florida Power and Light and Wallace Company are two of the more startling examples of the dark side of TQM. In summarizing the literature regarding TQM "failures," Larson and Sinha (1995) cite studies suggesting that between 60 percent and 70 percent of TQM programs analyzed were considered failures.

While it is not always clear what constituted failure in these studies, or from whose perspective failure was defined, the fact remains that some

*This research was funded by a grant from the Society for Human Resource Management Foundation. The interpretations, conclusions, and recommendations, however, are those of the authors, and do not necessarily represent those of the Foundation.

97

firms have been less successful than others at implementing TQM programs. These differential results suggest the existence of a set of contingency factors that influence the likely success of TQM efforts. Recent literature has examined some generic obstacles to less successful TQM efforts including cognitive inertia (Reger et al. 1994); confusion between implementing total quality control and/or total quality learning programs (Sitkin, Sutcliffe, and Schroeder 1994); lack of integration of TQM efforts with an organization's values (Reid 1994); too much training (Chaudron 1992); and trying to make too many changes at once (Goodden 1994; Shaffer and Thomson 1992).

Fortunately, it is also possible to identify a general set of facilitating factors, the presence of which tends to increase the probability of successful TQM implementation. These facilitating factors include the following:

- Top management commitment to TQM (Dobbins 1995)

- A holistic, systemic approach to the implementation of TQM (Blackburn and Rosen 1993)

- An appreciation of TQM as a way of doing business, not merely as a set of tools or tactics (Butz 1995)

- The alignment of the other organizational systems with the demands of the TQM strategy/culture (Blackburn and Rosen 1993; Olian and Rynes 1991)

STRATEGIC HUMAN RESOURCE MANAGEMENT AND TQM

The importance of system alignment as a TQM facilitator suggests a place to look for a specific set of factors that may act as either barriers to or facilitators of TQM, depending on their presence or absence during implementation. This set of contingencies is related to a firm's human resource management (HRM) practices during a TQM change effort and the extent to which those practices support the ability and motivational requirements of a TQM strategy/culture. Appreciation of the role of HRM in successful organization change efforts of any type has grown out of a strategic perspective on HRM (Lengnick-Hall and Lengnick-Hall 1988; Schuler and Jackson 1987; Wright and McMahan 1992). In particular, a strategic human resource management (SHRM) approach argues for the importance of the human resource (HR) function and supportive HRM practices in the development and successful implementation of any organizational strategy and attendant actions. From an SHRM perspective, HRM practices must be aligned with an organization's strategy for it to be effective. That is, there must be a vertical alignment between strategy and practice.

Just as important, however, the HRM practices must also align internally, in a mutually supportive framework reflecting a horizontal alignment. To the extent that alignment exists in both directions, strategic change efforts in general and TQM change efforts in particular, should be facilitated (Wright and McMahan 1992).

Given this strategic perspective, the authors propose a model that links HRM practices and important organizational outcomes (Blackburn and Rosen 1996) (see Figure 6.1). An integration and expansion of models proposed by Wright and McMahan (1992) and Olian and Rynes (1991), this framework illustrates how certain HRM practices, as well as other organizational characteristics, can inhibit or encourage the development of a TQM strategy or culture and influence other important performance outcomes.

For instance, the ability of a firm to undertake certain strategies will be influenced by the available HR resources found in the HR capital pool as well as the institutional and political forces found in the firm's external environment. Should the firm choose TQM as a strategy or TQM as a complementary or supplementary program for a different strategy, then there are a variety of supporting processes necessary if these TQM efforts are to be successful. These would include outcome measures to assess the extent to which TQM behaviors are being supported, stakeholder support at all levels within the firm, and a set of HRM practices that support the development

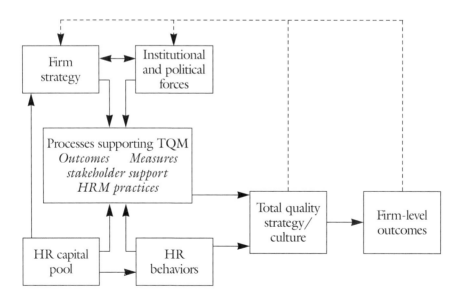

FIGURE 6.1. Combined model impact of firm processes on TQM efforts.

Source: Blackburn and Rosen 1996. By permission of JAI Press.

of a TQM strategy/culture. (This last measure will be discussed in this chapter.) Hopefully, the successful introduction of such a strategy/culture should lead to the desired levels of important firm outcomes. The extent to which these outcomes are—or are not—achieved will influence the previous elements in the model through a series of feedback loops.

Blackburn and Rosen (1996) offer empirical support for this particular framework by illustrating how changes in HRM practices (referred to as high-performance or high-involvement work practices by Lawler, Mohrman, and Ledford (1992) and Ernst & Young (1992)) facilitate the successful adoption of a TQM strategy or culture. High-involvement HRM practices have also been linked to "objective" measures of organizational performance (Huselid 1994, 1995).

The cited literature has examined potential barriers and facilitators of TQM efforts in rather general ways, or has been based on anecdotal, single-case analyses. See Hackman and Wageman (1995) for a discussion of the problems associated with this type of report. There appears, however, to have been little systematic, empirical research across organizations aimed at better understanding specific barriers and facilitators of TQM.

It would be beneficial to organizational members in general, and to HR managers in particular, to better understand, in detail, both the potential obstacles and the factors that encourage successful TQM change efforts. Lewin's (1951) force-field approach to change suggests that his three-step change process (unfreeze-change-refreeze) would be most successful relative to TQM, to the extent that organizations remove the barriers to TQM implementation or encourage the facilitators of TQM implementation, or—in the ideal—do both. If this can occur, then TQM implementation has a far higher probability of success, and the firm as a whole should perform more efficiently and more effectively.

BARRIERS TO AND FACILITATORS OF TQM

As part of a comprehensive investigation of TQM effectiveness, HR managers were asked to assess the extent to which they believed certain organizational characteristics might act as barriers to, or facilitators of, TQM efforts. Indirect evidence of additional barriers or facilitators were also gathered in two ways. First, respondents were invited to rate the relative importance (or the implicit facilitative value) of a variety of HRM programs, such as selection, job design, and performance evaluation, in establishing a TQM strategy or culture. Second, respondents were asked about any changes their firms had made within the management of the respondent's HRM function.

In particular, survey respondents were asked to what extent their HRM function had adopted aspects of TQM (statistical process control, benchmarking, and so on) *within* the function itself. The hypothesis was that those organizations reporting greater levels of success with their TQM efforts would also report that their HR functions incorporated more of the basic TQM precepts. Indirectly, then, the authors hoped to argue that one facilitator of TQM efforts is for the HR function to adopt the basics of TQM and to act as a role model for the remainder of the organization.

METHODS

Sample and Data Collection

As part of a larger study, a sample of HR managers was surveyed to directly and indirectly assess the barriers and facilitators these professionals see to their firms' efforts to implement a TQM strategy/culture. Five thousand members of the Society for Human Resource Management were randomly selected from the Society's membership roster. Each received a copy of the study survey, a cover letter introducing the study, and a stamped, self-addressed return envelope. The 14-page survey was pretested for face and content validity and for ease of completion with a number of academic colleagues and HR professionals in the local business community. The pretest revealed that the survey items reflected adequate face and content validity and could likely be completed in a reasonable period of time.

Responses were received from 346 organizational representatives, with usable surveys received from 245 individuals. Nearly one-third of the 346 respondents (101) indicated that their organizations did not have TQM programs in place at the time they received the survey. Fifty-five uncompleted surveys were returned for a variety of reasons including an inability to reach the addressee or the respondents' belief that they were not an appropriate part of the sample.

The response rate for this research was low, although the rate seems to be in line with that reported in a study by Delaney, Lewin, and Ichniowski (1989). These authors sent a 29-page survey concerning HRM activities to 7765 business units and received 495 responses, a response rate of 6.37 percent. Similarly, Ostroff (1995) reported a 12.4 percent response rate in a survey of 3000 Society for Human Resource Management members, the same group as this study surveyed. Usable survey and performance data were only available for 8.7 percent of those originally surveyed. Despite the low response rate in the current study, the demographic profile of the organizations in this sample is quite similar to the profile of the general SHRM membership, reflecting the nationwide composition of the membership.

Survey Instrument

Items included in the survey were designed to both directly and indirectly assess potential barriers to, and facilitators of, TQM implementation. A set of 12 possible barriers and 9 possible facilitators was developed based on TQM literature and discussions with HR and line managers involved in TQM implementation efforts. The set of HRM practices, hypothesized to be important to a successful TQM program, was developed in the same way. Similarly, the set of TQM principles that might be adopted by the HR function was developed from a review of TQM literature. Five-point, Likert-type response scales were used for all of the measures, with higher item and scale scores reflecting a greater barrier to, facilitator of, or importance to the successful implementation of a TQM strategy or culture.

In addition, efforts were made to assess the extent to which respondents believed their organizations were committed to TQM as well as an assessment of how effective the TQM efforts had been to date. The authors wanted to determine if perceptions of TQM commitment and/or effectiveness colored a respondent's view of the magnitude of possible barriers or facilitators.

To determine the relative success of TQM efforts in the organizations in the sample, respondents were asked to complete two multi-item scales. In particular, respondents were asked how committed their organizations were to TQM as well as how effectively their TQM programs were working. These TQM-commitment and TQM-effectiveness measures were determined using 10-item and 11-item scales, respectively. To facilitate comparative analyses, scores on these two measures were combined to serve as a third criterion variable, TQM-success. Specific items used in each scale are presented in the chapter appendix.

RESULTS

Factor analyses and internal consistency reliability assessments indicated that all of the multi-item scales were psychometrically sound. Scale scores for each set of variables were developed by summing individual item scores and averaging over the number of items in each scale. Means, variances, ranges, and correlations for the scale scores are presented in Table 6.1. Cronbach's alpha values appear in the diagonal of the correlation matrix.

Before examining results for the specific barriers and the different measures of possible facilitators of TQM programs, it would be helpful to describe the sample in terms of commitment to, and effectiveness of, the organizations' TQM change efforts. If the sample reflects only firms that had very good or very bad experiences with TQM change, then the responses with regard to possible barriers and facilitators might be biased in

TABLE 6.1. Means, standard deviations, ranges, and correlations for all study variables.

Variables	Mean	Standard deviation	Range	Commitment	Effectiveness	Success	Barriers	Facilitators	HR system importance	HR adoption of TQM precepts
Commitment	3.06	.91	1–5	(.93)						
Effectiveness	2.62	.84	1–5	.76	(.95)					
Success	5.72	1.62	2–10	.94	.93	(na)				
Barriers	2.37	.77	1–5	–.66	–.59	–.66	(.80)			
Facilitators	2.50	.76	1–5	.59	.58	.62	–.54	(.76)		
HR system importance	4.07	.74	1–5	.05	.01	.01	–.03	.02	(.94)	
HR adoption of TQM precepts	2.96	1.00	1–5	.49	.46	.53	–.40	.43	–.03	(.92)

Notes: All correlations are significant at $p < .0001$, *except* those involving HR system importance. None of those correlations are significant. Cronbach's alpha is a measure of internal consistency of the individual items comprising a scale. The value can range from 0 (indicating no consistency in responses by individual survey participants to the items in a scale) to 1.0 (indicating perfect agreement in responses by individual survey respondents to the items in a scale). Generally, alpha values above .70 are considered acceptable in this type of research (Nunnally 1978).

103

some way. Those associated with less successful efforts may be overly critical of factors that inhibited their change attempts. Those associated with
successful efforts may not see any factors as particularly bothersome or
troubling.

TQM commitment. Respondents were asked to rate 10 statements
regarding the extent to which their firms were committed to quality as an
important priority. A complete list of scale items is presented in the chapter
appendix. A few sample questions are as follows:

- To what extent is TQM a top priority in your organization?
- To what extent is there a strong commitment to building a TQM
  culture in your organization?
- To what extent is each (unit) evaluated against quality goals and
  objectives?

Responses were made on a five-point, Likert-type response set ranging
from "little or no extent (1)" through "moderate extent (3)" to "very
great extent (5)."

Organizations represented in the sample were moderately committed
to TQM. When individual responses to the 10 items were summed and
averaged, the average commitment score for the full sample was 3.06, the
midpoint of the response scale. Forty percent of the sample had a commitment score of less than 3.0, while 15 percent reported a scale score of 4.0
or greater. Fifty-five percent of the sample indicated that their firms pursued
each of the 10 indicators of TQM commitment to a moderate or greater
extent. More than 80 percent of respondents agreed, at least to a moderate
extent, that TQM is a "top priority" in the firm and that there is a strong
commitment to a TQM culture in the firm. While the majority of firms in
the sample were committed to TQM at least to a moderate extent, there
does seem to be sufficient variation on the scale score to reduce the likelihood of sample bias.

TQM effectiveness. While TQM commitment is an important determi-
nant of TQM success, respondent perceptions regarding how effective
their firms' TQM efforts had been were also assessed. Eleven questions
were asked regarding the effectiveness of TQM efforts in a number of different areas. A complete list of scale items appears in the chapter appendix,
while a few sample questions are as follows:

- How successful has your organization been in implementing a TQM
  program?
- How successful has your TQM program been at engendering higher
  morale among your employees?

- How successful has your TQM program been at reducing cost overruns?

Responses were made on a five-point, Likert-type response set ranging from "little or no success (1)" through "moderate success (3)" to "very great success (5)."

Respondents indicated that their TQM efforts had been somewhat successful. When individual responses were summed and averaged, the average effectiveness scale score was 2.62. Forty percent of the sample had a scale score of less than 3.0 while only 5.5 percent reported a scale score of 4.0 or greater. In this sample, reported effectiveness of TQM was marginally lower than reported commitment to TQM. In seven of the areas where the survey asked for a TQM effectiveness evaluation, 55 percent or more of the sample indicated that quality efforts had been at least moderately effective. These areas included improved product quality, service quality, and quality reputation, as well as reduced cycle times. Areas where TQM had not been as effective included morale (53 percent reported little or no effectiveness in improving morale); missed deadlines (47 percent reported little or no effectiveness in reducing the number of missed deadlines); cost overruns (54 percent reported little or no effectiveness in reducing cost overruns); and absenteeism and turnover (68 percent reported little or no success in reducing employee absenteeism and turnover).

These results suggest that the organizations represented in the sample reflect a sufficiently wide range with regard to reported commitment to, and effectiveness of, TQM efforts. This would suggest that bias in terms of rating barriers and facilitators should be minimized. Such a range of commitment and effectiveness responses also means that differential ratings of barriers and facilitators as a function of such perceptions of success could also be examined.

TQM success. Another issue measured in the survey was the extent to which reported barriers and facilitators of the TQM effort might be colored by perceptions of TQM success. To investigate this issue, some way of classifying the relative success of TQM efforts was needed. The substantial correlation between TQM commitment and TQM effectiveness ($r = .76$, $p < .01$) suggested that these scales could be combined to simplify further analyses. This new variable (the sum of commitment and effectiveness scores), dubbed TQM-success, reflects perceptions of both an attitudinal measure of TQM success (commitment) as well as an activity-based measure of TQM success (effectiveness evaluations of important outcomes for the organization). Scores on the TQM-success variable could range from 2 to 10.

The resulting TQM-success scale scores were arrayed from lowest to highest. The resulting array was divided into groups reflecting low ($n = 60$), medium ($n = 73$), and high ($n = 74$) levels of TQM success. These scores became the basis for categorizing sample organizations to further examine the impact of success perceptions on perceptions of barriers and facilitators to TQM.

Barriers to TQM

With regard to possible barriers to TQM efforts as perceived by HR professionals, the survey measured their reactions to 12 organizational factors previously associated with less successful TQM efforts. (A complete list of these barriers appears in the chapter appendix.) Respondents rated the extent to which they felt each of these factors could or did interfere with the successful development of a TQM strategy/culture in their organization. The second column in Table 6.2 presents the sample means for each possible barrier. The mean value for the aggregated barriers scale for the sample was 2.36, suggesting that the full sample viewed this set of characteristics as creating barriers to successful TQM efforts to less than a moderate extent. In general, for this sample of organizations, the collective set of barriers was not viewed as particularly troubling.

According to the sample, three individual factors surfaced as the most bothersome for TQM efforts. Short-term performance pressure (mean response = 3.38) was cited as a barrier to TQM to a moderate or greater extent by 74 percent of the sample. Nearly 60 percent (58.5 percent) of the sample indicated that a lack of coordination of TQM programs with other company systems (mean = 2.92) was a barrier to a moderate or greater extent; while 56.7 percent of the sample responded in similar fashion when asked about overly centralized managerial authority (or conversely, an inability or unwillingness on the part of top management to decentralize authority and control) (mean = 2.82). Obviously, these three factors are related. Short-term performance pressures may lead managers to maintain as much control as possible in the frequently mistaken belief that this will ensure improved performance levels. In responding in such a way, these same managers may fail to appreciate the interactions of TQM program requirements with other organizational activities, and be unable or unwilling to coordinate TQM activities with other organizational systems (Senge 1990).

Past research suggests that the failure to integrate HRM systems with TQM efforts represents an obstacle to the overall success of the TQM program (Blackburn and Rosen 1996; Ernst & Young 1992). Slightly less that 50 percent (49.6 percent) of the sample indicated that unclear TQM program objectives (mean = 2.63) were barriers to TQM to a moderate or greater extent.

TABLE 6.2. Barriers to TQM efforts.

Barriers	Full sample results	Low TQM-success	Medium TQM-success	High TQM-success
TQM-success score	5.72	3.74	5.74	7.46
Barriers— scale score	**2.36**	**2.92**	**2.34**	**1.81**
Short-term performance pressures	3.38	3.88	3.25	3.02
Lack of coordination with other systems	2.92	3.53	2.92	2.28
Centralized authority	2.82	3.22	2.78	2.46
Unclear TQM objectives	2.63	3.69	2.53	1.65
Lack of tangible improvements	2.35	2.86	2.33	1.94
Lack of long-term strategy	2.31	3.01	2.46	1.47
Lack of TQM champion	2.30	3.06	2.27	1.55
Worsened business conditions	2.12	2.28	2.27	1.82
Lack of top management support	2.06	2.86	2.06	1.24
Management opposition	1.81	2.33	1.80	1.31
Unionized workforce	1.63	1.47	1.86	1.54
Top management turnover	1.57	1.91	1.46	1.35

Note: All group differences are significant at p < .001, *except* those that are *shaded*.

Three factors were cited as barriers to TQM to a moderate or greater extent by slightly less than 40 percent of the sample. In particular, lack of a long-term TQM strategy was cited by 39.2 percent (mean = 2.31); a lack of tangible improvements from TQM efforts was cited by 37.4 percent (mean = 2.35); and a lack of a TQM champion was cited by 37.8 percent (mean = 2.30). These three characteristics apparently represent important elements of TQM programs that are missing before (strategy), during (TQM champion), and after (tangible improvements) TQM change efforts.

Two of the factors listed were cited slightly less than one-third of the time as moderate or greater barriers to the TQM change effort. Worsening business conditions was cited by 31.4 percent of the sample (mean = 2.12) and lack of top management support for TQM was cited as a moderate or greater barrier to TQM by 27.4 percent (mean = 2.06). These possible barriers are also not independent. That is, if business conditions start to worsen, management's attention may be directed at quick fixes for the bottom line. This may divert managerial support away from TQM efforts, which frequently provide returns only in the long run.

Finally, three of the factors listed as possible barriers to TQM were described as occurring to a moderate of greater extent by less than 20 percent of the sample. General management opposition to TQM was cited by 19.3 percent (mean = 1.81); top management turnover was cited by 15.4 percent (mean = 1.57); and among those organizations with unions, a unionized workforce was cited by 15.4 percent (mean = 1.63).

This final result is somewhat surprising. The business press might lead readers to believe that unions and collective bargaining agreements are major obstacles to TQM efforts. Those respondents from unionized firms indicated, however, that among the potential barriers listed, their unionized workforce represented the least problematic barrier to their TQM implementation efforts.

Note that in Table 6.1 the correlation between the scale score for this set of barriers and scores on the TQM-success scale are significant and negative. The greater the level of TQM-success reported by the respondents, the less problematic respondents viewed the full set of possible barriers. The mean scores for the barriers scale decreased significantly ($p < .01$) as a function of TQM-success scores. The overall barriers scale score was 2.92 for low TQM-success firms, 2.34 for medium TQM-success firms, and 1.81 for high TQM-success firms (Table 6.2).

The most substantial barriers reported by the low TQM-success firms included, in rank order, (1) short-term performance pressures, (2) unclear TQM objectives, and (3) lack of TQM coordination with other company systems. Least substantive barriers for this subgroup included the presence of a unionized workforce and top management turnover.

At the opposite end of the TQM-success measure, respondents reporting high levels of TQM-success listed short-term performance pressures, centralized authority, and lack of TQM coordination with other company systems as most problematic in terms of their role in TQM efforts.

When categorized by the TQM-success level, the overall ratings of the 12 barriers were not significantly different (Kendall's coefficient of concordance* was $W = .86$ with $p < .01$.) Within each of three categories, respondents believed the potential barriers were generally problematic in the same order; however, the perceived magnitude of each barrier was greatest among those respondents who rated their firms as least successful in implementing TQM.

Facilitators of TQM-Direct Measures

Given the discussion so far, it could be argued that to facilitate TQM, firms need only reduce or eliminate the most problematic of these barriers. While this may be a useful recommendation, information was also sought from the respondents as to the extent to which they saw nine organizational factors as explicit facilitators of their organization's TQM efforts. (A complete list of these facilitators is presented in the chapter appendix.) On a five-point scale ranging from "little or no extent (1)" through "moderate extent (3)" to "very great extent (5)," respondents indicated the extent to which they believed each characteristic was or would be a TQM facilitator in their firm.

Top, middle, and first-line management support and resource availability were seen as the most useful facilitators of TQM efforts. Seventy percent of the sample indicated that to a moderate or greater extent top management support was facilitative of their TQM efforts (mean response = 3.33). Sixty-seven percent felt that way about middle management support (mean = 3.01), and 54 percent indicated similar beliefs relative to first-line management support (mean = 2.74). In addition, nearly 60 percent of those responding indicated that the availability of resources (money, personnel, time, and so on) for TQM activities facilitated TQM efforts to a moderate or greater extent (mean = 2.85) (see Table 6.3).

Of the remaining possible facilitators, only 12.5 percent of those in unionized settings indicated that unions were facilitative of TQM efforts to a moderate or greater extent (mean = 1.43). Combined with the other

---

*Kendall's coefficient of concordance provides a test of the agreement among three or more sets of rankings (Kendall 1948). It can range from 0 (indicating no agreement among the rankings) to 1.0 (indicating complete agreement among the rankings).

TABLE 6.3. Facilitators of TQM efforts.

Facilitators	Full sample results	Low TQM-success	Medium TQM-success	High TQM-success
Facilitators— scale scores	**2.50**	**2.05**	**2.42**	**3.03**
Top management support	3.33	2.51	3.24	4.24
Middle management support	3.01	2.25	2.95	3.84
Availability of resources	2.85	2.43	2.82	3.34
First-line management support	2.74	2.05	2.66	3.48
Decentralized decision making	2.30	1.91	2.26	2.74
Third-party consultant	2.17	2.19	2.06	2.28
Employment security	2.17	1.89	2.13	2.48
Monetary rewards	1.86	1.31	1.88	2.33
Unionized workforce	1.43	1.38	1.34	1.57

Note: All group differences are significant at p < .001, *except* those that are *shaded.* The full model for employment security was significant at *p* < .01. The low and medium group means were not significantly different and the medium and high group means were not significantly different for this item.

result that only 15 percent of the sample believed that unions were barriers to TQM efforts to any great extent, this suggests that unions are viewed as neither particularly helpful nor hurtful of TQM efforts.

For those facilitators that applied to all respondents (not just those with a union presence), monetary rewards for TQM activities were seen as the least facilitative, and were used by less than 25 percent of the sample to a moderate or greater extent to advance their TQM efforts (mean = 1.86). One-third of the sample believed external consultants were facilitative of TQM efforts to a moderate or greater extent (mean = 2.17). Somewhat surprising was the fact that only 35.4 percent of respondents believed that employment security was a facilitator of TQM to a moderate or greater extent (mean = 2.17).

Finally, despite the responses indicating that centralized authority was viewed as a barrier to TQM by nearly 60 percent of the sample, only 38.5 percent of those responding viewed decentralized authority as particularly facilitative of TQM to a moderate or greater extent (mean = 2.30).

The authors would have assumed that if perceptions had been consistent, then closer to 60 percent of the sample should have responded that decentralization was facilitative. For this sample, perceptions of the locus of authority for decisions as a barrier or facilitator are apparently not complementary.

When these nine facilitators are considered as a set, the sample viewed the entire set as currently being facilitative in their organizations to less than a moderate extent. The mean response for the full set of possible facilitators was 2.50. Correlations between the facilitator scale score and TQM commitment and effectiveness scores were both positive and significant. Respondents who saw their TQM efforts as engendering commitment and being effective were more likely to describe this set of possible organizational conditions as being more facilitative of those efforts than did respondents whose TQM efforts had been less successful.

The mean score for the facilitators scale increased significantly ($p < .01$) as a function of TQM-success scores. The overall facilitators scale score was 2.05 for low TQM-success firms, 2.42 for medium TQM-success firms, and 3.03 for high TQM-success firms. The most substantial facilitators reported by the low TQM-success firms included top management support, availability of resources, and middle management support. At the opposite end of the TQM-success measure, respondents reporting high levels of TQM-success listed top, middle, and first-level management support as most facilitative, with availability of resources as the fourth most facilitative.

The overall ratings of the nine facilitators when categorized by the three TQM-success levels were not significantly different. (Kendall's coefficient of concordance was $W = .91$ with $p < .01$.) Within each of three categories, respondents believed the facilitators were relatively beneficial in the same order, but the perceived magnitude for each facilitator was greatest among those respondents indicating their firms had been most successful in implementing TQM.

Facilitators—Impact of HR Systems on TQM Efforts

Respondents were asked to indicate how important each of 10 HRM systems would be to a successful TQM effort. In the context of the larger survey, these systems represented activities that others have described as high-performance work practices (Lawler, Mohrman, and Ledford 1992;

Ernst & Young 1992; Huselid 1995). These practices have been hypothesized to facilitate commitment-based cultures as opposed to command-and-control cultures. Thus, these systems represent another possible set of TQM facilitators related to HR practices. A listing of these 10 systems is provided in the appendix. Respondents were asked to indicate their beliefs relative to system importance on a Likert-type scale ranging from "not important at all (1)" through "neither unimportant nor important (3)" to "very important (5)." Perhaps not so surprisingly, every HRM system was rated to be important or very important by at least 69 percent of those responding (see Table 6.4).

For the full sample, three systems clustered together at the top of the importance rankings. (See column 2 in Table 6.4.) Eighty-six percent of the sample indicated that performance appraisal systems were important or very important to successful TQM efforts (mean = 4.23), closely followed by downward and upward communication systems (85 percent each; means = 4.23, 4.22 respectively).

TABLE 6.4. Relative importance of HRM practices in support of TQM efforts.

HRM practices	Full sample results	Low TQM-success	Medium TQM-success	High TQM-success
HRM practices— scale scores	**4.07**	**4.03**	**4.11**	**4.08**
Downward communication	4.23	4.07	4.38	4.30
Performance appraisals	4.23	4.32	4.12	4.25
Upward communication	4.22	4.06	4.40	4.24
Training and development systems	4.16	4.10	4.29	4.08
Recognition	4.12	4.09	4.20	4.12
Compensation	4.10	4.04	4.17	4.07
Promotion	4.05	4.03	4.03	4.10
Career development	3.97	3.90	4.02	4.00
Selection	3.90	3.89	3.94	3.88
Job design	3.76	3.71	3.71	3.89

Note: None of the differences are significant.

A second group of four systems clustered behind these in terms of their perceived importance to successful TQM efforts. Training and development systems were viewed as important or very important to TQM efforts by 83 percent of the sample (mean = 4.16). Compensation systems were viewed as important or very important by 83 percent of the sample (mean = 4.10); noncompensation recognition systems by 82 percent (mean = 4.12); and promotion systems by 81 percent (mean = 4.05).

Finally, career development systems were viewed as important or very important by 78 percent of the sample (mean = 3.97); selection systems by 74 percent (mean = 3.90); and job (re)design systems by 69 percent (mean = 3.76).

From these results it should be clear that respondents generally believed that all of these systems have important implications for the success of a firm's TQM efforts. In particular, treating the 10 systems as a set of HRM practices, the average rating for the full set of responses was 4.07. Unlike most of the scales examined in this analysis, reported commitment to or effectiveness of TQM was *not* significantly associated with the scale score for these importance levels. All of the correlations between this scale and the measures of commitment and effectiveness were nonsignificant, indicating that the relative importance of these 10 systems was appreciated by all members of the sample regardless of judgments of TQM commitment or effectiveness.

This is also true when the commitment and effectiveness measures were combined into TQM-success scores. The mean scale scores for the low, medium, and high TQM-success categories were 4.03, 4.11, and 4.08, respectively. These were not significantly different from each other. Similarly, as illustrated in Table 6.4, there were no systematic or significant differences in the importance of individual HRM systems as a function of TQM success. All respondents seemed to view each of these systems as relatively important to the successful implementation of TQM in any organization.

Facilitators—The HRM Function as Facilitative Example

As has been shown elsewhere, the HR function plays a key role in building a TQM organizational culture (Blackburn and Rosen 1993; Olian and Rynes 1991). In some organizations, HR managers champion the TQM philosophy by sponsoring TQM educational initiatives, bringing in outside consultants to redesign work processes, and communicating TQM successes. In other organizations, the HR function takes a more direct role in TQM implementation by developing and delivering leadership training and team-building training programs to managers and employees throughout the organization. Thus, in some organizations, HR managers seek to be the key facilitators in the development of a TQM strategy or culture.

For all of the HR function's efforts to champion and support TQM throughout an organization, an issue of interest is whether or not the HR function itself integrates TQM principles into the unit's own activities. That is, does the HR function serve as a role model to facilitate the spread of TQM to the remainder of the organization by following basic TQM precepts? To the extent such occurs, this should facilitate the TQM change efforts.

Survey participants were asked to evaluate the extent to which their HR function had applied the following seven TQM principles taken from the TQM literature.

1. Sees other departments as internal customers

2. Assesses satisfaction of other departments with HR activities

3. Benchmarks HR practices against best-in-class

4. Uses quality tools (SPC, feedback, and so on) to improve HR services

5. Establishes cross-functional teams (within HR and between HR and line units) to resolve quality problems with HR services

6. Reduces cycle/response time associated with HR services

7. Sets specific quality improvement objectives relative to HR services

On a five-point, Likert-type scale ranging from "little or no extent (1)" through "moderate extent (3)" to "very great extent (5)," respondents indicated the extent to which each of these practices was used in their own HR function.

Findings relative to these responses are summarized in Table 6.5. They provide a good barometer of the extent to which adoption of TQM precepts has changed the internal operations of the sample's HR functions.

From Table 6.5, it should be clear that although many firms have adopted several aspects of TQM, a majority of HR functions in the sample have implemented only one aspect of the TQM philosophy to any great extent in the HR department; that is, "other departments are our customers" (mean = 3.87).

On the other hand, few HR functions have translated any other aspects of the TQM philosophy into specific actions. For instance, less than one-third of the HR functions benchmark their activities against best practices elsewhere (mean = 2.55); use quality tools to track performance improvement (mean = 2.65); address internal quality issues with cross-functional quality teams (2.73); set specific goals for quality improvements (mean = 2.87); or attempt to reduce cycle time for the delivery of HR services (mean = 2.92). When it comes to HR functions walking the TQM

TABLE 6.5. HR function adopting TQM precepts as a function of TQM-success.

TQM principles	Full sample results	Low TQM-success	Medium TQM-success	High TQM-success
TQM principles in HRM— scale scores	**2.98**	**2.44**	**2.89**	**3.60**
View departments as internal customers	3.87	3.53	3.77	4.32
Assess firm satisfaction with HR activities	3.16	2.69	3.12	3.67
Set quality improvement objectives	2.87	2.24	2.68	3.66
Attempt reduced cycle time for providing services	2.92	2.36	2.89	3.50
Establish cross-functional work teams to resolve HR problems	2.73	2.14	2.62	3.46
Use quality tools	2.65	2.1	2.45	3.37
Benchmark HR practices	2.55	1.92	2.49	3.23

Note: All group differences are significant at $p < .001$, *except* those that are *shaded*.

talk, in the sample, HR appears to be taking only a tentative first step of the TQM journey.

To examine these results in additional detail, consider first the correlations between measures of TQM effectiveness, commitment, and success, and the scale score reflecting the summation of TQM practices in the HR function (see Table 6.1). As scores for effectiveness and commitment increase, so do scores for the HR function's use of the seven TQM principles included in the survey. When the sample was divided according to levels of TQM success, a strong positive and significant ($p < .01$) relationship between TQM success and implementation of TQM principles within the HR function was found (Table 6.5). Respondents reporting the highest levels of TQM success also reported that their HR functions had gone the farthest toward implementing these TQM principles.

In low TQM-success firms, the only TQM principle that is practiced to even a moderate extent by the HR function is viewing other internal departments as customers (mean = 3.53). The mean scores for the other six principles do not exceed the midpoint of the five-point response scale for this less successful group of organizations. Medium TQM-success firms collectively view other internal departments as customers to nearly a great extent (mean = 3.77) and to a lesser extent attempt to assess their customers' satisfaction with the HR services offered (mean = 3.12).

In contrast to these results, in high TQM-success firms, each of the seven TQM principles is applied to nearly a great extent. HR functions in these organizations view internal departments as their customers to a great extent.

Despite the mean differences in the extent to which various HR units apply this set of TQM principles, the relative order of the extent to which these principles have been applied is nearly identical across the three different categories of TQM success. (Kendall's coefficient of concordance was $W = .94$ with $p < .01$.) In all three TQM-success categories, HR functions viewed "internal departments as customers" and "assessing customer satisfaction with services delivered" as the two most-often-implemented principles. Similarly, in all three categories, firms were relatively less likely to establish cross-functional teams, use quality tools, or benchmark their practices against the best HR practices in the industry.

DISCUSSION

Even without these empirical results related specifically to TQM change efforts, the general change literature suggests that barriers or facilitators of any organizational transformation would also apply to TQM-related changes. Resisting forces like threats to individual power, high risk, potential losses, and lack of a felt need for change frequently act as resistors in firms attempting to implement TQM. Supportive forces in other firms might include the need for survival, competitor actions, potential gains, and a felt need for change. As Hackman and Wageman (1995, 336) note,

> Changes may be so ambitious . . . that for all their potential merit, the organization cannot accommodate to them. . . . [or] changes may be more window-dressing than real. . . . Implementation is easy, but the old organizational structures and systems remain untouched and continue to generate the same behavioral dynamics as before.

The research results presented here have attempted to move the understanding of the potential barriers to and facilitators of TQM beyond anecdotal evidence and generic admonitions to a broader set of data—the perceptions of a national sample of 245 HR managers.

Summarizing the results of this research suggests that the biggest barriers to successful TQM efforts are short-term performance pressures. These appear to dominate an investment perspective toward TQM. While some managers are able to view TQM as a long-term investment, others are unable to think beyond the next quarterly report. This latter group will find successful TQM implementation an elusive goal.

The inability of some senior managers to appreciate the systemic requirements of TQM means they fail to coordinate supporting systems with TQM demands. This is especially true with regard to financial evaluation and HRM systems. In any organization, what gets evaluated and rewarded is what gets done. Management can talk about TQM, but if it still evaluates and rewards financial outcomes, the TQM change effort will have a difficult time succeeding.

Since TQM has historically been viewed as a top-down management program, it is interesting that respondents viewed centralized authority as a barrier to TQM. It may be that HR practitioners were responding to overly autocratic attempts at TQM implementation where top management's introduction of TQM to the organization was of the form, "Do TQM my way or hit the highway."

Finally, unclear TQM objectives were viewed as barriers to TQM. This suggests that communication and focus are needed to overcome the view that TQM is simply another flavor-of-the-month. As Butz (1995, 107) suggests, "TQM is a philosophy; it is not something an organization does but the way an organization does everything." Creating and communicating both a vivid vision and broad, concrete goals can provide the direction needed to focus employee actions (Bohan 1995).

Not surprisingly, these barriers are more problematic to those who have yet to overcome them. In the survey sample, firms reporting greater levels of TQM success also reported that these barriers generally become less of a concern. They apparently have been able to overcome most of these obstacles.

The absence of a barrier is not necessarily a facilitator. Thus, while centralized authority was viewed by respondents as a barrier to TQM, decentralized authority was not viewed as a particularly strong facilitator of TQM. Simply reducing or eliminating barriers, while important, is not enough. The results suggest the need to take actions that will likely be directly supportive of TQM.

Management support, at the top, middle, and first levels, was seen as the most facilitative activity by survey respondents. The desire for this support does not equate with the desire for centralized authority. In fact, the other most frequently cited facilitator of TQM was the availability of adequate resources to allow low-level employees to undertake quality-related actions without centralized direction. The provision of appropriate resources is also an example of managerial support. The literature on TQM suggests that while top management is responsible for communicating the TQM vision and strategy, middle managers implement the appropriate tactics. First-level managers use the resources made available to implement the necessary TQM actions.

All levels of management must work with, and within, a set of HRM practices, the presence or absence of which can act as barriers or facilitators of TQM. Regardless of perceptions of TQM success, the survey sample indicated that communication, performance appraisal, training and development, and reward systems were all viewed as facilitative of TQM. These HRM practices should be especially supportive if the actions that comprise them have moved in the direction of high-performance work practices. In conjunction with the explicit facilitators discussed, these results suggest that management support for TQM can be conveyed by judicious use of both upward and downward communication systems. Multidirectional communication is necessary to clarify TQM objectives. Previously, ambiguous objectives were identified as major barriers to TQM success. Management support can also be evidenced by the development of appropriate appraisal, training, and reward systems. Such efforts will require making available the needed resources.

To better coordinate TQM actions with other organizational systems, these results indicate which of the HRM systems require the most significant coordination efforts by top management. It should not be overlooked, however, that respondents suggested that all of the traditional HRM practices were very important to successful TQM implementation. Blackburn and Rosen (1996) found that when these systems are defined by explicit HRM activities (specific types of pay systems, specific elements in appraisals, and so on), then communication, training and development, and job design systems significantly discriminated between the various TQM-success categories. Those firms that had implemented intensive communication systems, training and development programs designed to serve specific line unit needs, and increased levels of individual employee empowerment and team-based job design, were also reported to have been more successful in their TQM efforts.

Finally, the results suggest that HR functions that undergird their own operations with basic TQM tactics are more likely to be found in organizations that have more successful TQM programs. Encouraging the HR function to "walk the TQM talk" appears to be facilitative of TQM efforts (Blackburn and Rosen 1995). To the extent that HR activities will become decentralized in the future (Caudron 1994), HR representatives will likely find themselves partnering with line managers and dealing with their internal customers on an increasingly intimate basis. Line units will likely be employing TQM precepts, and HR employees must do likewise if they are to have any credibility in these partnerships.

Based on the results of this research, the ideal context for maximizing the success of a TQM implementation effort would be one in which there are few short-term pressures for performance on top management. Top managers must be willing and able to communicate clear, focused TQM objectives while resisting the urge to direct the program from on high. Managerial support at all levels will be important, as will an appreciation of the systemic effects that such transformational change may have on other organizational systems.

One set of important systems are those managed by the HR function. To maximize the likelihood of a successful TQM implementation effort, all key HRM practices need to be adapted to support the necessary TQM behaviors. Communication, appraisal, training, and reward systems are key in this regard. And, as HRM practices change, the practices within the HR function should also change to reflect the acceptance of basic TQM precepts by a staff unit in support of important line activities. To the extent these changes can be made, the probability of a successful TQM program will increase.

LIMITATIONS

As with all empirical research, the authors would be remiss if the limitations associated with this work were not identified. Hopefully, the efforts made during the course of the preparation, delivery, analysis, and interpretation of the survey results would mitigate the effects of these limitations on the interpretations of results.

Since the response rate was low, the sample may have underrepresented firms in the population with little or no explicit commitment to TQM but who, nevertheless, had different views on possible barriers or facilitators of TQM. While the response rate was low, the sample size was still substantial for this type of survey research, and the sample demographics did approximate the overall demographics of the survey population. The sample size was certainly larger than the single organizational case study that has dominated much TQM research.

Both independent and dependent variables were collected in the same manner from the same source, suggesting possible concern about common method error. The broader survey was designed to collect additional information about a variety of TQM-related issues. The measures of the criterion variables were purposely placed before the measures of TQM barriers and facilitators to reduce the possibility of such method error. Differing response formats were used for each of the scales. Factor analyses suggest that common method variance should not have been a substantial problem in this research.

When developing new measures, validity and reliability are always a concern. The authors believe that the measures developed were sufficiently complete to tap most of the important aspects of commitment to TQM, effectiveness of TQM, and possible barriers and facilitators of TQM. Based on reading TQM literature, interviews with HRM managers, and pretests with practicing managers, these measures appeared to be comprehensive, reliable, and high in face validity.

That said, it is still possible that a sufficiently complete set of possible barriers or facilitators was not provided. Open-ended prompts allowing respondents to provide their own listing of other barriers or facilitators not included in the measure resulted in some additional factors, but these were neither large in number nor consistent in their frequency. In addition, the dependent variables in this study were not accounting or market-based variables. They were perceptions of commitment to and effectiveness of TQM efforts in the respondents' organizations. It was not possible to determine the financial or market performance of the firms classified as low, medium, or high on the TQM-success variable. Perhaps barriers and facilitators of TQM commitment and effectiveness are different than those that allow TQM to generate desirable financial and market results.

HR managers provided all of the data for this study. The burden was on a single HR manager to evaluate overall organizational commitment to and effectiveness of his or her firm's TQM efforts. While multiple assessments of these variables would have been preferred, logistics prevented such triangulation of the variables. Similarly, the survey asked for that same individual's perception of factors that might support or resist TQM implementation efforts. While this may have been a difficult task, it is not certain that others' perceptions might not have been different. Line managers, senior executives, and customers might have reported different perceptions of commitment to or the effectiveness of TQM efforts in the sample organizations, as well as differing reactions to which of the factors in the survey might encourage or discourage TQM.

The data represent a snapshot of TQM commitment and effectiveness perceptions and of important barriers and facilitators of TQM. The research design made it impossible to determine if these barriers and facilitators might change over time as TQM becomes an accepted part of the organization's culture or as TQM efforts begin to flounder.

FUTURE RESEARCH

Additional work that takes into account these theoretical and method-ological limitations should be high on the priority list. In particular, mul-tiple assessments of TQM barriers and facilitators (from employees, HR managers, line managers, and executives) and multiple assessments of TQM outcomes (from internal evaluators and external customers) would be beneficial. Objective measures of organizational performance (includ-ing financial measures) might also prove useful. These changes could reduce possible respondent bias.

In addition to these methodological suggestions, there are certainly a number of content-based issues that remain unresolved in this area of research. For instance, possible moderators of the barriers or facilitators of TQM were not considered. Do the factors that inhibit or encourage TQM differ as a function of organizational size, extent of unionization, or the position of the firm in its business life cycle? It seems logical that what might encourage TQM development in new, small firms may be different than what inhibits such development in traditional, large firms.

A complete set of barriers and facilitators must be developed. And per-haps the context in which these factors might arise needs to be considered. For instance, are the barriers to developing TQM as a philosophy or under-pinning for a corporate culture different from those that might impede developing TQM as a set of tools and tactics? Do certain profiles or port-folios of barriers and/or facilitators have differential effects on the success of TQM programs? How do the various supportive or resistive factors inter-act with each other? Might one extremely important facilitator be able to overcome a number of smaller barriers?

Finally, Dean and Goodman (1993, 1) consider the processes by which firms move beyond total quality implementation and institutional-ization to total quality integration, wherein TQM becomes "as common and unremarkable as any other aspect of the organization." Future research should seek to determine not only the barriers and facilitators of TQM implementation, but also the environmental and organizational factors that influence successful TQM integration.

CONCLUSIONS

Many previous discussions of this topic have simply enumerated possible barriers and facilitators to TQM based on single-case evaluations. No extant research was found that presented an empirical basis for identifying key HRM barriers and facilitators to TQM. Survey evidence of a set of potential barriers to and facilitators of TQM efforts in U.S. organizations has been presented. Factors that appear to be related to successful TQM programs have been identified. Those HRM practices that should be most supportive of TQM have been suggested, as well as which TQM precepts when applied to HR operations should facilitate TQM success.

In a recent review and commentary on the state of TQM in research and practice, Hackman and Wageman (1995, 338) offered "a relatively gloomy projection about the future of total quality management." Their concern is a function of three trends they see with regard to TQM (pp. 338–339).

1. Rhetoric is winning out over substance.

2. Change programs, regardless of their genesis, are routinely (and mistakenly) "herded under the TQM banner."

3. Research is not providing the corrective function for TQM that it could and should.

They close their piece with the following admonition (p. 339).

> If TQM is to prosper, . . . rhetorical excesses will have to be kept in better check than they are at present, and researchers will have to do a better job of illuminating the mechanisms though which TQM practices realize their effects. For only if the continuous improvement idea comes to apply to TQM itself will this provocative philosophy have a chance of sustaining itself over time.

The authors trust that these efforts at the continued improvement of understanding TQM will move the field beyond story and anecdote to specific guidance about those environmental, organizational, and HR actions that should support TQM. They further trust that this information will be of use to both academicians and practitioners interested in the effective implementation of TQM in organizations.

APPENDIX

Individual Survey Items

TQM Commitment
With regards to total quality management, to what extent . . .

1. Is TQM a top priority in your organization?

2. Is there a strong commitment to building a TQM culture in your organization?

3. Does top management regularly communicate with the remainder of the organization about the company's commitment to TQM?

4. Has a comprehensive TQM plan been created and communicated throughout the organization?

5. Are quality goals and policies understood and accepted throughout the organization?

6. Have department heads accepted responsibility for quality improvement?

7. Is each division evaluated against quality goals and objectives?

8. Does your organization work with suppliers to improve their processes, products, and services?

9. Does your organization solicit feedback from customers about the quality of its products and services?

10. Does your organization use quality techniques such as statistical process control to monitor and improve quality?

TQM Effectiveness
With regards to total quality management, how successful . . .

1. Has your organization been in implementing a TQM program?

2. (Relative to your competitors) has your TQM program been in improving the quality of your *products*?

3. (Relative to your competitors) has your TQM program been in improving the quality of your *services*?

4. Has your TQM program been at engendering higher morale among your employees?

5. Has your TQM program been at reducing cycle times for your products or services?

6. Has your TQM program been at enhancing your organization's reputation for quality?

7. Has your TQM program been at improving the overall effectiveness of your organization?

8. Has your TQM program been at reducing the number of customer complaints received?

9. Has your TQM program been at reducing the number of missed deadlines?

10. Has your TQM program been at reducing cost overruns?

11. Has your TQM program been at reducing employee absenteeism and turnover?

Barriers to TQM

To what extent is each of the following factors a barrier to the TQM effort in your organization or work unit?

1. Lack of coordination of TQM programs with other company systems
2. Short-term performance pressures
3. Centralized authority
4. Top management turnover
5. Lack of long-term strategy
6. Lack of tangible improvements (for example, dollar savings)
7. Unclear TQM objectives
8. Management opposition to TQM
9. Unionized workforce
10. Lack of top management support
11. Lack of a TQM champion
12. Worsened business conditions

Facilitators of TQM

To what extent is each of the following factors a facilitator of the TQM effort in your organization or work unit?

1. Top management support
2. Middle management support
3. First-line management support
4. Third-party consultation
5. Availability of resources (money, personnel, and so on) for TQM activities
6. Monetary rewards for TQM activities
7. Unionized workforce
8. Decentralization of decision-making authority
9. Employment security

Importance of HR systems to support TQM

How important do you believe each of these systems is to support TQM objectives?

1. Training and development systems
2. Job design systems

3. Selection systems

4. Promotion systems

5. Career development systems

6. Communication systems (downward)

7. Communication systems (upward)

8. Compensation systems

9. Noncompensation recognition systems

10. Performance appraisal systems

The Role of TQM in the Human Resource Management Function
With regards to the role of TQM in the operations of the human resource management function, to what extent has the HR department . . .

1. Adopted the philosophy that other departments are internal customers?

2. Attempted to assess the level of satisfaction with HR activities throughout the organization?

3. Benchmarked its practices against the best practices in the industry?

4. Used quality tools (such as statistical controls, feedback, and so on) to improve the quality of its products and services?

5. Established cross-functional work teams (both within HR and across the organization) to resolve quality problems with HR services?

6. Attempted to reduce cycle times in providing services to other units?

7. Set specific quality improvement objectives?

REFERENCES

Blackburn, Richard, and Rosen Benson. 1993. Total quality and human resources management: Lessons learned from Baldrige Award-winning companies. *Academy of Management Executive* (August): 49–66.

———. 1995. Does HRM walk the TQM talk? Paper presented at the annual Society of Industrial Organizational Psychology meetings, May, Orlando, Florida.

———. 1996. Human resource management practices and total quality management. In *Research in quality management*, edited by D. Fedor and S. Ghosh. Greenwich, Conn.: JAI Press.

Bohan, George. 1995. Focus the strategy to achieve results. *Quality Progress* (July): 89–92.

Butz, H., Jr., 1995. Strategic planning: The missing link in TQM. *Quality Progress* (July): 105–108.

Caudron, Shari. 1994. HR leaders brainstorm the professional future. *Personnel Journal* (August): 54–60.

Chaudron, D. 1992. HR and TQM: All aboard! *HR Focus* (November): 1, 6.

Dean, James, and Paul Goodman. 1993. Toward a theory of total quality integration. Unpublished manuscript.

Delaney, J., D. Lewin, and C. Ichniowski. 1989. *Human resource policies and practices in American firms*. Washington, DC: U.S. Government Printing Office.

Dobbins, Richard. 1995. A failure of methods, not philosophy. *Quality Progress* (July): 31–34.

Ernst & Young. 1992. *International quality study: Best practices report*. New York: American Quality Foundation.

Goodden, R. 1994. The error in TQM. *Quality Digest* (May): 73–76.

Hackman, Richard, and R. Wageman. 1995. Total quality management: Empirical, conceptual, and practical issues. *Administrative Science Quarterly* (June): 309–342.

Helton, B. Ray. 1995. The Baldie play. *Quality Progress* (February): 43–46.

Huselid, Mark A. 1994. Documenting HR's effects on company performance. *HRMagazine* 39, no. 1:79–85.

———. 1995. The impact of human resource management practices on turnover, productivity, and corporate financial performance. *Academy of Management Journal* (June): 635–672.

Jablonski, J. R. 1991. *Implementing total quality management*. Albuquerque, N. M.: Technical Management Consortium.

Kendall, M. 1948. *Rank correlation methods*. London: Griffin.

Larson, Paul D., and Ashish Sinha. 1995. The TQM impact: A study of quality managers' perceptions. *Quality Management Journal* (spring): 53–66.

Lawler, Edward, Susan Mohrman, and Gerald Ledford. 1992. *Employee involvement and total quality management: Practices and results in Fortune 1000 companies*. San Francisco: Jossey-Bass.

Lengnick-Hall, Cynthia A., and Mark L. Lengnick-Hall. 1988. Strategic human resource management: A review of the literature and a proposed typology. *Academy of Management Review* 13, no. 3:454–470.

Lewin, Kurt. 1951. *Field theory in social science.* New York: Harper & Row.

Nunnally, Jum. 1978. *Psychometric theory.* 2d ed. New York: McGraw-Hill.

Olian, J., and Sara Rynes. 1991. Making total quality work: Aligning organizational processes, performance, measures, and stakeholders. *Human Resource Management* (fall): 303–333.

Ostroff, C. 1995. Human resources management: Issues and trends in personnel. *Human Resources Management,* 1995 Society for Human Resources Management/Commerce Clearinghouse Survey. Chicago: CCH Incorporated. Issue no. 356, Part 2.

Reger, Rhonda K., Loren T. Gustafson, Samuel M. DeMarie, and John V. Mullane. 1994. Reframing the organization: Why implementing total quality is easier said than done. *Academy of Management Review* (June): 565–584.

Reid, R. P. 1994. There's more to quality management than TQM. *Quality Digest* (May): 67–72.

Schuler, Randall J., and Susan E. Jackson. 1987. Linking competitive strategies with human resource management practices. *Academy of Management Executive* 1, no. 3:207–219.

Senge, P. 1990. *The fifth discipline.* New York: Doubleday/Currency.

Shaffer, R., and H. Thomson. 1992. Successful change programs begin with results. *Harvard Business Review* (January/February): 80–91.

Sitkin, Sim B., Kathleen M. Sutcliffe, and Roger D. Schroeder. 1994. Distinguishing control from learning in total quality management: A contingency perspective. *Academy of Management Review* (June): 537–566.

Wright, Patrick M., and Gary C. McMahan. 1992. Theoretical perspectives for strategic human resource management. *Journal of Management* (summer): 295–320.

Part II

Human Resources Management and TQM in Various Sectors

Chapter 7

Quality-Based Human Resource Practices at Granite Rock Company

Laura Junod

Granite Rock Company is a construction material supplier serving the Northern California area. Established in 1900, the company currently has 15 branch locations with its corporate headquarters located in Watsonville, California. The company is family-owned and employs approximately 400 people, two-thirds of whom work under collective bargaining agreements.

In 1992, Granite Rock received the Malcolm Baldrige National Quality Award in the small business category, and as such was the first company in the construction industry to achieve this honor. In 1994, Granite Rock also received the Governor's Golden State Quality Award in California.

Throughout its history, Granite Rock Company has maintained a strong commitment to the people who work within the organization. This belief is particularly reflected in one of the company's nine corporate objectives. The objective concerning people is stated as follows:

> To provide an environment in which each person in the organization gains a sense of satisfaction and accomplishment from personal achievements, to recognize individual and team accomplishments, and to reward individuals based upon their contributions and job performance.

This chapter will discuss two elements of the company's human resource practices, the Individual Professional Development Plan (IPDP) and the Team Interviewing process. Both of these programs have proven to have a positive and dramatic impact on the organization and its people.*

THE INDIVIDUAL PROFESSIONAL DEVELOPMENT PLAN

Granite Rock has always believed that in order to ensure its competitive advantage in the marketplace and remain a leader in the construction industry, there must be continual investment in the education of its people. Supporting and encouraging people to continually develop themselves is also a crucial ingredient in maintaining and improving job satisfaction and connection with the company. Despite the severe economic recession experienced in California from early 1991 though late 1994, which significantly impacted the construction industry, Granite Rock continued to fully support its training programs. Table 7.1 details the level of that support. As Bruce W. Woolpert, co-president and CEO of Granite Rock stated, "The only way we'll become a better company is if our people become more knowledgeable. When our people invest in their own future, they invest in the company's future as well."

The IPDP was established at Granite Rock Company in 1987. It is the foundation of the company's training and development program.

The IPDP process begins when a manager and an individual meet to discuss and formulate a developmental plan for the upcoming 12-month

TABLE 7.1. Granite Rock training support.

Year	Average amount spent on training per person	Average hours of training per person
1991	$1697	37 hours
1992	$1855	32 hours
1993	$2369	40 hours
1994	$2406	40 hours

*The IPDP program was primarily developed and refined through collaborative efforts between co-president and CEO, Bruce W. Woolpert, corporate psychologist, Philip E. Berghausen, Jr., Ph.D., and director of human resource services, Shirley Ow. Dr. Berghausen was also influential in the design and implementation of the team interviewing process at Granite Rock Company.

period. The manager and the individual generally have independent ideas of proposed developmental objectives to discuss. The plan should not be the product merely of the individual or the manager, but a blending of ideas and thoughts to produce a consensus document.

The plan itself is based on a four-page form (see Figure 7.1). It consists of a summary of the individual's major job responsibilities, a summary of the previous year's developmental plan, the individual's exceptional job strengths, the actual developmental plan for the upcoming 12 months, and a summary of the progress made throughout the year on a quarterly basis.

How the IPDP Works

The first part of the form (Section A) documents the individual's major job responsibilities. Though this information might seem fairly straightforward, sometimes individuals and their managers have differing opinions as to what these major responsibilities are. Completing this section of the IPDP results in the two parties coming to agreement and stating the job responsibilities in a clear and succinct manner. New or modified responsibilities may be added as a result of an accomplished developmental objective.

The next part (Section B) is a summary of the accomplishments made as a result of last year's developmental plan. Each result is documented, and if the objective has been achieved then an *A* (achieved) is listed alongside the objective statement. The other designations are *AM* (achieved modified), *AP* (achieved partially), *NAM* (not achieved modified or excused), or *NA* (not achieved). This coding system allows the company to monitor if objectives are actually being met and track the percentage of goals achieved on a yearly basis. Also, in this section, an individual and manager document any additional developmental accomplishments achieved during the year that were above and beyond the scope of the IPDP.

The strengths on the job portion of the IPDP (Section C) is an opportunity for the individual and manager to discuss and document the individual's clearly exceptional strengths. Through this discussion, the individual receives the manager's recognition of the areas in which he or she excels. Sometimes new strengths emerge as a result of the previous year's IPDP goals. If a new strength has emerged, it is highlighted on the form with an asterisk. Conversely, if the same strength has appeared on the IPDP for several years, it might be time to take the strength for granted and delete it from the list.

The heart of the IPDP is Sections D and E, which document the major developmental objectives and the developmental plan for the upcoming 12 months.

Under the major developmental objectives heading, individuals are encouraged to think of means to improve their knowledge or skills to

Graniterock

Individual Professional Development Plan

Name: _____   IPDP Plan Year: ___ / ___ to ___ / ___

Position: _____   Branch/Location: _____

Hire Date: _____   Time in Current Position: _____

A. Major Job Responsibilities: Include major responsibilities; new responsibilities made possible by last year's development (star these with *).

B. Summary of 19____ IPDP Results: Include items from Section E, Column 2 of last year's IPDP, using same numbering. Precede each item with A, AM, AP, NAM or NA. Also, list other special accomplishments (star these with *).

FIGURE 7.1. Form used for the Individual Professional Development Plan.

Source: Reprinted by permission of Granite Rock Company

C. Strengths on the Job: Include clearly exceptional strengths that are displayed consistently and new strengths added this year (star these new strengths with *).

D. Major Developmental Objectives: Describe what you want to learn to do in the next twelve months. Include new skill development that can enhance job performance quality, job satisfaction, and general professional growth. Also, you may want to include new skill development that could lead to interesting new challenges. Use format: "Learn _____ so that I can _____."

FIGURE 7.1. *(continued)*.

E. Developmental Plan for the Period Beginning ___ / ___ and
   Ending ___ / ___ .

Column 1—Planned Experiences/Activities:	Column 2—Observable Measures:
Include *how* skills will be learned, with at least one learning activity/experience per objective in Section D. Number items so as to correspond to Section D.	Include criteria which will demonstrate that the planned activities/experiences from Column 1 have been completed *and* that each objective in Section D has been met. Include target dates.

Sign below on final form after Roundtable discussion:)

_____   _____
Manager/Supervisor   Date

_____   _____
Individual   Date

FIGURE 7.1. *(continued).*

F. Quarterly Review of Progress

1st Quarter

Achievements:

Modifications to Developmental Plan:

Date Completed: _____

2nd Quarter

Achievements:

Modifications to Developmental Plan:

Date Completed: _____

3rd Quarter

Achievements:

Modifications to Developmental Plan:

Date Completed: _____

This Individual Professional Development Plan is intended to encourage investment in people skills and knowledge growth. It is intended to support your developmental and career objectives. As a development planning and tracking method, it does *not* assess job performance.

FIGURE 7.1. *(continued)*.

develop themselves further in either their personal or professional lives. An example of a goal an individual might list is to learn more about Granite Rock and its various products in order to have a better understanding of the company and to provide better customer service. This would be accomplished by arranging a time to visit another branch location. Or the objective might involve benchmarking with another company to learn more about that organization and its processes, and thus bring new ideas to Granite Rock. The objective might be an educational goal such as to attend an in-house seminar, a course at a local college, or perhaps to complete an undergraduate degree. The costs of attending courses or completing developmental objectives are fully paid by Granite Rock.

Granite Rock people have also utilized the IPDP to achieve personal developmental goals. For example, some people have documented goals to improve their overall health through an exercise program or a smoking cessation program. Successfully achieving this type of goal will likely have a positive impact on the individual's professional life as well.

It is expected that developmental objectives should not simply involve the accomplishment of a task to benefit the company. The objective should have learning involved that causes the individual to develop in some way. If learning is not involved, then it is not an appropriate objective.

Individuals are encouraged to write the objective statements in such a way that they include a *so that* or *in order to* phrase. This is to emphasize that the learning involved should help the individual in his or her job. For example, the objective might stated as "Learn more about word processing so that I can produce my own reports and documents."

Column 1 of Section E states how each developmental objective will be accomplished. The adjacent Column 2 provides objective criteria to determine whether the objective has been achieved. The fact that the IPDP contains actual target dates for completion is very important. Even more crucial, however, is that the importance is not just placed on the date of completion but the application of the new skills or learned behavior. For example, the individual has not only completed the computer course, but what can that person now do that he or she was not able to do before?

The quarterly review of progress provides for ongoing discussions throughout the year between the individual and manager. It is important to understand that the IPDP is a living document; it is not meant to be filed in a drawer and not touched or seen until the end of the plan year. Quite the contrary, there should be ongoing communication about the progress of the individual toward completing his or her goals. Often, goals are no longer appropriate due to changing circumstances, and may need to be modified or even deleted, with another goal inserted in their place.

Granite Rock encourages these discussions to occur at least on a quarterly basis, and this section is used to document these discussions.

The Roundtable

Once the individual and manager have met to develop this consensus document, then the plan is presented by the manager to the company's roundtable. The roundtable consists of the company's senior management including the president. Typically, the roundtable meeting also includes peer-level managers from other departments or other parts of the company who are also presenting their people's IPDPs.

The role of the roundtable is to review each IPDP and offer advice or suggestions as to how the IPDPs might be improved or modified. The roundtable members are used as consultants to the manager who may need input on how to improve the plan or offer advice about working with a particular individual.

The advantages of having the IPDPs reviewed by the roundtable are numerous. Besides offering helpful suggestions to the manager, roundtable members learn about particularly talented people within the company and those who have set and achieved particularly ambitious goals. The managers at the roundtable also learn more about the various positions, job duties, responsibilities, and skill levels of many people within the company. The discussions that occur during the roundtable session help to develop coaching and leadership skills in managers as well. For the individuals, the opportunity to have their IPDP reviewed and discussed by the company's president and senior management is a form of recognition itself. The time and effort given by the roundtable members to review each and every IPDP within the company is another indication to Granite Rock people that the company cares about its people and wants to help improve their lives.

Once the IPDP has been reviewed by the roundtable, the manager's role is to return to the individual to relay any feedback or suggestions. It is important that this be done as soon as possible because the individual is often quite eager to hear the results of the discussion. Use of the roundtable's input by the manager is voluntary.

A final IPDP form is then developed and signed by both the manager and the individual. Each keeps a copy with the original being returned to the human resources department. The original document is retained separately from the personnel file because the IPDP is not used to address performance problems. Both compensation and performance issues are addressed separately from the IPDP process. When performance problems do exist, IPDP involvement is suspended until the individual's performance has improved.

Advantages of the IPDP

Since the implementation of the process, Granite Rock has seen the IPDP program truly become an important part of the company's culture. Participation in the program is voluntary; however, as of the 1995 IPDP plan year, the participation rate stood at an impressive 83 percent.

The benefits to Granite Rock and to the people in the organization from the IPDP program are somewhat hard to objectively measure. It is believed, however, that the IPDP program is at least partially responsible for the following benefits.

Loyalty One of the ways in which Granite Rock proves its commitment to its people is through the IPDP program. When Granite Rock people take advantage of this opportunity and experience the rewards that it offers, the result is a deep respect and gratitude toward the organization.

Reduced turnover and absenteeism People who have been treated differently by other employers realize the uniqueness of their opportunities at Granite Rock. This very favorably impacts their attitude about their employer. Granite Rock Company's turnover and absenteeism rates are remarkably low as compared to national standards. The turnover rate in 1994 stood at 6.1 percent; the absenteeism rate for 1994 averaged one day per year.*

Promotion from within People who have improved their skills, abilities, and self-confidence are versatile and are well positioned for promotions and job changes within the company. Granite Rock people are encouraged to seek new job opportunities within the company and to challenge themselves by taking risks with new positions. People who have been successful in their own positions appreciate the opportunity to be seriously considered for new job opportunities within the company.

Safety Granite Rock is very serious about ensuring a safe working environment. The company has maintained an impressive safety record that consistently comes in at almost twice that of its competitors. Granite Rock people are encouraged to continually look for ways in which to do their jobs more safely. Often, ideas for safety-related improvements come from benchmarking trips to other companies or from classes taken where these topics are discussed. Additionally, one could make the assessment that people who are satisfied with their jobs and with their employer would tend to be alert and content and, therefore, less likely to be involved in a work-related injury. All of these factors translate into a safe working environment and decreased workers' compensation costs for the company.

---

*The Bureau of National Affairs cited the absenteeism rate in 1994 at 3.5 days per year. The turnover rate in 1994 was documented at 13.2 percent.

Customer satisfaction and service If Granite Rock people are satisfied with their jobs and the company, this will most certainly be reflected in their dealings with customers. A high level of customer service is also offered when people are given the opportunity to learn new ideas and then implement them. Continuing education can also encourage increased independent thinking and decision-making abilities, which are crucial in an environment where people are asked to creatively offer ideas to improve customer service and solve customer-related problems.

Granite Rock believes it has survived the recession in a stronger fashion than its competitors because of its commitment to total quality management (TQM). This management style includes the commitment to its people through the promotion of lifelong learning. When the quality of the organization's products and services is continually improved, greater customer loyalty is generated.

Productivity With people growing in job responsibility and improving their abilities to do their job, productivity (revenue per employee) increases. Also, through training, errors are eliminated so less time is spent fixing problems and upsetting customers.

The impact on people from implementing such a training and development program is difficult to fully comprehend without real-life examples. Granite Rock's IPDP program has been strengthened due to some inspirational success stories. Three people in the company, who are good examples of the program's influence, are Paul, Danny, and Laura. All three had struggled through school as children and were generally viewed by teachers as lazy. Their teachers, however, were not aware they were dyslexic.

Even as functional illiterates in the adult world, each was highly proficient in their job. Through hard work and intelligence, they were able to get by and hide the real truth. Their lives changed, however, when they had the courage to confront their learning disabilities and become involved in the IPDP program. As a result, Granite Rock arranged for them to work with a private tutor who specializes in teaching people with dyslexia.

Paul, Danny, and Laura are also special because they openly spoke about their experiences and encouraged others who needed help to come forward. Paul was one of 15 Granite Rock people to travel to Washington, D.C. in February 1993 to participate in the Quest for Excellence Conference. At the conference, more than 1200 people attended to listen to and learn from the 1992 Baldrige Award winners. Paul was able to read his speech about how the IPDP program and Granite Rock helped him to read and write. This was quite a moment for Paul because his speech received a standing ovation and brought tears to the eyes of many in the audience. Paul also focused attention on the importance of addressing literacy issues in the workplace.

The benefits derived from implementing a development program such as the IPDP are many. Granite Rock people are fortunate that the company has made a true commitment of resources to ensure the success of the program. This commitment, however, is not an easy one to adhere to on a sustained basis.

IPDP Challenges

To make the IPDP program successful, a great deal of managerial time is necessary. For example, if a manager has 30 people reporting to him or her, the implementation of the IPDP process is more complex than if there are only five people in the department. So, the process takes a significant amount of time from already busy schedules. Additionally, there is a great commitment of time necessary from the people on the roundtable, because their function involves reviewing every individual's IPDP. This is accomplished through scheduling many meetings throughout a six-month period. In a company of 400 people, this is still a manageable number of meetings; however, in organizations much larger than Granite Rock, the orchestration of this process would become much more complex. The commitment of a manager's time is certainly easier when he or she truly believes in the process and experiences first hand the benefits the process can yield.

As noted, Granite Rock has maintained its commitment of financial resources to the program. If this were discontinued, then the program's success of the program would most likely diminish. For people to gain maximum value from the program and achieve their objectives, it seems important for the employer to support the costs associated with education and training.

Though the IPDP was introduced to Granite Rock's salaried payroll people in 1987, it was not offered to the remaining collective bargaining people in the company until 1991. (Introduction of the IPDP to salaried people was used to test and fine-tune the concept before expanding it companywide.) As with any new program, the IPDP took time for people to understand. At first, some people were skeptical and participation among those working under collective bargaining agreements was low. As people saw that the program was not meant to just benefit Granite Rock and was truly a benefit to individuals, then acceptance of the process rose dramatically. The program is now firmly implanted in the language and culture of the company. The people who truly take advantage of its benefits gain a tremendous amount of satisfaction from personal and professional achievement and continued growth.

THE TEAM INTERVIEWING PROCESS

In 1992, Granite Rock implemented a new and innovative approach to its hiring process. Instead of relying only on an individual manager to make a hiring decision based solely on his or her best judgment, the company decided it was important to bring the opinions of colleagues into that decision-making process through the formation of interview teams. This was a substantial change in philosophy for the company. Since its implementation, much has been learned and gained. Improvements and refinements continue to be made and certainly more will be learned.

The team interviewing process will first be explained in detail. Then the benefits and challenges that Granite Rock has encountered will be described.

The role of the interview team is advisory, which means that the team does not make the hiring decision. Rather, the team provides information to the hiring manager to assist in the decision.

How the Process Works

The process begins when a position becomes available and an employment requisition is posted throughout the company. The requisition details the job duties, minimum qualifications, and other information. Also included on the requisition are the names of the people who will be participating on the interview team. Typically, the team consists of four to six individuals identified by the hiring manager with input from the human resources department. The team typically consists of people from the department or branch where the position exists, along with a representative from the human resources department. Team members might also include someone who has previously held the position, who holds a similar position in the company, or who would work closely with the new hire. The team does not include the hiring manager.

Once the hiring manager has determined the candidates that should be interviewed, then the interview date is finalized. Candidates must meet the minimum qualifications.

The day of the interviews begins with a training session, led by a member of the human resources department, which the hiring manager is invited to attend. This session lasts approximately 1 to $1\frac{1}{2}$ hours and includes a discussion of the concept of team interviewing, the company's hiring philosophy (described later), the importance of confidentiality, and legal guidelines regarding interviewing. This training session also includes a discussion of the traits and characteristics that the team and hiring manager believe to be crucial in order for the individual to be successful in the position. Some of these success traits are required of every Granite Rock person. They are honesty, integrity, commitment to lifelong learning, job ownership, customer service, and a safety-minded approach to work.

From the list of desired traits, the team then develops a list of interview questions to help assess if the candidates possess these necessary qualities. The team is encouraged to ask open-ended, thought-provoking questions that require the candidates to do most of the talking. As much as possible, the team tries to center questions around real-life challenges where the candidates need to explain how they would handle a situation.

Once the list of questions is developed, the team divides into two groups and is ready to begin interviewing. One group interviews the first candidate while the other team interviews the second candidate. Then the two groups change candidates and the process continues until all the candidates have been interviewed by both groups. Interviews by each group are typically 30–45 minutes.

The list of questions is also divided into two, so that one group will consistently ask the same questions to each candidate, while the other group asks the other set of questions. The group hears the response to the same question by each candidate.

It is beneficial for the interview team to divide into two groups because this allows each group to gather information independent of the other. Sometimes one group will form a different impression of a candidate than the other group, and this leads to a complete discussion and evaluation of the candidates as a whole.

Granite Rock's hiring philosophy is centered around analyzing the talent, experience, and chemistry factors of each candidate (referred to as TEC).* Talent includes such traits as aptitude, intelligence, achievement orientation, persistence, and motivation. Experience includes the specific technical skills and knowledge required for satisfactory job performance. Chemistry involves compatibility between an individual and the company's values and overall fit with the company.

This TEC method of interviewing emphasizes the importance of an individual's talent and chemistry factors as opposed to primarily focusing on the experience that he or she would bring to the position. Granite Rock's belief is that an individual hired solely based on experience will most likely be successful in a position only on a short-term basis. If the individual does not possess the necessary talent to learn new skills and adapt well to changing conditions, and if he or she lacks the chemistry factors to mesh well with the culture of Granite Rock, this person will probably not be successful in his or her position in the long run. Therefore,

---

*The TEC method of interviewing was introduced to Granite Rock Company through Marketing Personnel Research, Inc., 6035 N. Northwest Highway, Chicago, IL 60631. The process was subsequently modified to meet Granite Rock's needs.

when the team evaluates each candidate, his or her experiences are discussed, but greater weight is placed on the talent and chemistry factors.

After the interviewing is completed, the team immediately meets to discuss each candidate in order to provide feedback to the hiring manager. The team might recommend that one or more candidates be eliminated from further consideration due to knock-out factors. These factors might be a conflict with a required chemistry trait, such as honesty, or just an obvious problem from a talent standpoint. Generally, teams will provide a ranking of the candidates for the hiring manager. This, however, is not required. Instead, the team may give broad feedback regarding the top candidates and may identify strengths (areas of good fit) and weaknesses (areas of concern). With this information, the hiring manager then conducts further interviews of the top candidate(s).

It is important to recognize the value of the human resource professional's involvement throughout the team interviewing process. This individual's role is not only to ensure that team members receive proper training regarding interviewing guidelines and the company's hiring philosophy. He or she must also act as a facilitator to ensure that fairness and impartiality are maintained. If team members present personal biases, the human resources person will identify them as such and bring this to the attention of the team to maintain the integrity of the process.

Advantages of the Team Interviewing Process

Granite Rock Company has found the team interviewing process to benefit the organization in a number of ways. The advantages to using such a process for team members, job candidates, the hiring manager, and the organization as a whole are described as follows:

Team members

1. Interview team members often consist of a cross section of people who hold different positions and work in different parts of the company. Because Granite Rock has 15 locations, people on an interview team may meet for the first time. This meeting produces a great respect and understanding of the type of work each does and the diversity of expertise and experiences each brings to the table.

2. Team members who have never interviewed before are sometimes nervous about participating in the process. After receiving coaching and training and then successfully interviewing the candidates, the experience can produce a high level of self-confidence.

3. Through their participation on the interview team, members have an opportunity to influence an important decision. Their work life will be

greatly enhanced if the newly hired person has the right chemistry and talent features to be a productive part of a team.

4. After participating on the team, members understand the value of asking open-ended questions and actively listening to responses. These skills are applicable in a wide variety of situations, such as everyday communications with customers, coworkers, and family members.

5. As a result of being involved on an interview team, members gain a better understanding of the characteristics that are necessary for people to succeed in the company. This knowledge will be of value in their own careers.

6. It is easy to criticize a hiring decision when one does not understand the difficulty of making such a decision. Those people who participate on an interview team have a much better understanding of the complexity of the hiring process and the challenges facing the hiring manager. They receive practice in making a difficult decision.

Candidate

1. Being interviewed by a group of people can be intimidating; however, candidates can also grow professionally and develop confidence through this experience. Candidates are given practice in thinking quickly and communicating clearly and succinctly. As one candidate stated on a team interview process survey distributed in 1994, "I found that I had more confidence and knowledge from previous jobs that I didn't really ever think about."

2. Candidates learn about the qualities and traits which are important to the company from the types of questions asked. For example, if a team member asks, "What job-related improvements have you recently made of which you are particularly proud?" each candidate realizes that continuous improvement is important at Granite Rock. If the individual is already employed at Granite Rock, this knowledge will be a valuable reinforcement whether or not he or she is hired for the position.

Candidates can also learn from participating in this process if they are not a good match with Granite Rock. Therefore, they may choose to remove themselves from the process and withdraw their candidacy.

3. If the candidate is hired for the position, the opportunity to meet some of his or her future coworkers is helpful. The candidate also knows that coworkers were involved in the decision-making process, and this will help build confidence upon entering the new position.

4. Because the hiring decision is influenced by more than one person, all candidates benefit from the opportunity for a fair, consensus-based decision.

Hiring manager

1. The hiring manager participates in the training session and discussion of desired traits for the position. He or she benefits from the training about proper interviewing techniques and legal guidelines. The hiring manager also gains a deep understanding of the type of person needed for the position from the group's input and knowledge of the position's responsibilities.

2. The hiring manager receives a wealth of written and oral information from the team about the candidates. The team often provides an actual ranking of the candidates that includes both the strengths and potential weaknesses the individual would bring to the position. Information with this depth would be difficult for the hiring manager to obtain on his or her own. This information allows the hiring manager to conduct more thorough subsequent interviews and reference checks than would have otherwise been possible.

3. Because the team can bring additional support, the selected candidate may very well have an improved chance of being successful in the position. The hiring manager benefits from reduced turnover, lower training costs, and less general frustration. For example, when Granite Rock hired a new manager for its accounting department, there was a ground swell of support for this new person well before his first day on the job. Because of department members' involvement in helping select their new manager, they very much wanted to make sure he was successful in his new position. Instead of being leery and apprehensive of their new manager, there was an abundance of positive feelings and support.

The organization as a whole

1. Granite Rock believes that the efforts of a team of people will be more successful than a decision based on one person's judgment. The interview team truly understands the challenges of the position and the kind of person who can meet these challenges. Therefore, team interviewing can lead to successful hiring, which dramatically benefits the company.

2. Through the amount of time and energy devoted to the team interviewing process, a message is sent to the community that Granite Rock is a unique place to work. And because the process is rigorous for candidates, they understand that it is difficult to become part of the organization. Those who accept new positions with Granite Rock are likely to appreciate what they have achieved. These factors enhance the company's image and reputation in local communities.

3. Because the team interviewing process is utilized throughout the company in a consistent manner, Granite Rock is protected from possible

legal problems due to allegations of unfair hiring practices. Granite Rock can document the training each team receives in proper interviewing procedures (such as the review of the protected classifications and unacceptable interview questions). The team's written summary of the candidates is retained in the human resources department and clearly documents the basis for each decision. These records could be used in the event of an audit from state or federal authorities. The company can, without question, prove that hiring decisions are fair and not based on discriminatory factors. Since settlements and jury verdicts for unlawful hiring or promotion practices can range in the millions of dollars, this is prudent protection for any business.

4. Combining efforts between the interview team and the hiring manager works to diminish barriers that may exist between management and nonmanagement people. As noted, the interview team is often a mix of people who have very different positions in the company. Involvement in the process is a reminder of the contributions everyone makes to the success of the organization.

Challenges of the Team Interviewing Process

As with any new program, team interviewing has produced several interesting and challenging situations from which the company has learned. It has made changes to continuously improve the process.

One of the ongoing challenges faced is the difficulty presented when internal candidates (those already employed with the company) are interviewed for an open position. Often, those on the interview team know the candidates quite well. Being placed in a situation where the team member is asked to judge the capabilities of a friend or coworker can create a conflict of interest and be quite awkward. One way Granite Rock deals with this issue is to have the hiring manager or a member of the human resources department ask prospective team members if they feel they can be a fair, unbiased member of the team, similar to being on a jury. If individuals do not feel they can do this, then they are not placed on the team.

At the early stages of implementing the team interview process, some people felt it was not valid because of preselection or favoritism used by some managers. (This was reflected in a companywide opinion survey conducted in 1993.) In part, this could have been due to hiring managers giving people the impression of favoring one candidate over another, perhaps through subtle comments or casual conversation. These perceptions can have a seriously detrimental impact on the entire process. Through hiring managers' training, this has largely been avoided.

Also, as the process developed, there were situations where some Granite Rock people assumed that a particular internal candidate was certain to be offered the position. But when interview teams made recommendations contrary to what was "expected," this helped to prove the validity of the process.

Another issue with team interviewing is the importance of confidentiality. It is important to explain to members that the team's discussions during the interview process must remain confidential. In other words, it is not acceptable to return to the work site and discuss the applicants and the team recommendations with coworkers. When this occurred at Granite Rock, it created difficulty because the hiring manager had not yet had time to make any decision. Often, inaccurate information was relayed to applicants. Granite Rock now includes a written statement in the training session, which emphasizes that the applicants should only receive feedback about the interview from the hiring manager, rather than through the "grapevine." As a result of this training, problems surrounding confidentiality have been largely avoided.

Granite Rock has found that the success of the interview team is dependent on the quality of the team members. If they are not comfortable evaluating others, or are not comfortable actively participating in such a process, then their presence is of little value. Therefore, it is prudent for the hiring manager and the human resources department to be selective of who is asked to be on the team and consider this decision carefully.

As noted, participation on a team involves training on the company's hiring philosophy, which emphasizes talent and chemistry traits over experience. This philosophy has taken some time to be learned and accepted throughout the organization. This ideology is really in conflict with the concept of seniority, which is associated with collective bargaining agreements. The greater the number of years a person has been with an organization, the higher the person is on the seniority list. This list dictates the order and how often people will be asked to work. In effect, this system reinforces the belief that years of experience correlates to greater success in an organization.

Thus, with the TEC model, Granite Rock introduced a change in perspective for many people in the company. It is not always easy to convince team members or hiring managers that the candidate with three years' experience might be a better choice than the candidate with 25 years of experience. From the formation of each team and from discussions during each training session, the TEC concept is reintroduced and traditional thinking is continually challenged.

CONCLUSION

The IPDP and the team interviewing process have made significant contributions to Granite Rock Company. Both programs help to support an environment where people have the opportunity to improve themselves and are given respect and dignity for the contributions they make to the organization. Each program necessitates a commitment of time and resources, but the rewards reaped by the company and its people are truly far reaching and significant.

Chapter 8

Human Resource Management and TQM in the Medical Sector

Paula Phillips Carson, Kerry D. Carson,
and C. William Roe

AN OVERVIEW OF THE MEDICAL SECTOR'S QUALITY IMPROVEMENT EFFORTS

Unarguably, the medical sector is unique. There are few other industries that provide life-saving interventions, that are demanded by human beings worldwide, and that have such limited acceptable substitutes. As a result, societal perceptions hold that health care institutions should operate for purposes that extend beyond economic prosperity. Health care services dramatically affect both the physiological and social-psychological well-being of patients. Indeed, evidence suggests that satisfaction with medical treatment ultimately affects life satisfaction (Sirgy, Hansen, and Littlefield 1994). It is predictable then that attention to quality has been important throughout medical history.

Efforts to ensure high-quality health care date back to 1800 B.C., when Hammurabi required physicians to lose a hand if a noble patient died or lost sight as a result of surgery. Less intimidating quality initiatives were attempted by Florence Nightingale during her service as a nurse in the Crimean War (1854–1856). Nightingale focused on issues such as sanitation, nutrition, and infection control (Stiles and Mick 1994).

The relative emphasis afforded to quality issues in the health care industry has, however, cyclically waxed and waned. Social, economic, and political pressures exerted during some eras diverted attention away from quality to other health-related issues such as accessibility and cost. In the 1980s, for example, cost containment became the focal point. This was spurred by the U.S. federal government's introduction of the diagnostic-related group (DRG) fixed reimbursement system (McFaul and Lyons 1995) and concerns about annual medical expenditures spiraling upwards toward the $1 trillion mark (Bard 1994). But under the threat of impending health care reform in the mid-1990s, it appears that the focus on quality improvement is an issue at the forefront.

The (Resisted) Quality Improvement Efforts of the JCAHO

History demonstrates that internal improvement is often spurred by threats of external reform. Faced with such risks, industries proactively attempt to demonstrate their capacity to effectively self-govern, hoping to avert the imposition of restrictive mandates. This is contemporarily the case in the health care industry (Schoenbaum 1995).

The agency that is spearheading the movement for the health care industry to "heal thyself" is the Joint Commission on the Accreditation of Healthcare Organizations (JCAHO). The JCAHO was formed in 1951 under the collaborative sponsorship of the following organizations. Each holds seats on JCAHO's 28-member board.

- American Hospital Association (AHA)—seven seats
- American Medical Association (AMA)—seven seats
- American College of Surgeons—three seats
- American College of Physicians—three seats
- American Dental Association—one seat

In addition, six seats are held by members of the public and one is held by a nursing representative. The JCAHO accredits about 11,000 health care institutions per year, including about 5300 hospitals.

In 1992, the JCAHO introduced a major paradigm shift. Specifically, it revamped all its standards to center on the total quality management (TQM) or continuous quality improvement (CQI) philosophy. As the JCAHO's 1995 *Comprehensive Accreditation Manual* states, "The standards do not require adoption of any particular management style, subscription to any specific 'school' of CQI or TQM, use of any specific quality improvement tools, or adherence to any specific process for improvement" (p. 221). But the standards do "incorporate several core concepts of CQI and TQM" (p. 220). To prove its dedication to this revolutionary management ideology, the JCAHO successfully implemented quality improvement efforts to reduce variability in its inspection processes and to minimize its response time. Using CQI, the JCAHO reduced the number of days it took to return an inspection report from 137 in 1990 to 75 in 1991.

But among the JCAHO's consumers—organizations that provide health care services—reactions to this paradigm shift were mixed. Some viewed it positively, arguing that in the contemporary medical environment, where prices are relatively fixed, competition will inevitably be based on quality (Duval 1995). Others, though, viewed the changes with less enthusiasm.

In fact, in late 1994, two of the JCAHO's most prominent sponsors— the AHA and the AMA—threatened to withdraw their support from the commission. Independently, the AHA and the AMA announced plans to investigate the availability and/or creation of alternate certification agencies. This could be devastating to the JCAHO, a not-for-profit organization, as these two professional associations contribute about $280,000 annually to the Joint Commission (Burda and Morrissey 1994).

Several justifications are offered for the AHA and AMA's dissatisfaction with the JCAHO. For example, it is argued that TQM/CQI is a fledgling philosophy, characterized by ambiguous and conflicting tenets (Hart and Schlesinger 1991). As a result, it is perceived that the JCAHO's standards are unattainable moving targets (Morrissey 1995). Another argument is related to the cost-benefit ratio of adopting the new TQM/CQI standards. For example, in one large-scale study, only 19 percent of radiologists reported CQI was cost beneficial (Deitch et al. 1994). Such research reinforces skepticism about TQM/CQI.

But perhaps the threatened deathblow occurred for the JCAHO with its 1995 plans to introduce the IMSystem. This would allow public access, at a cost of about $30, to 28 quality performance indicators from each health care institution surveyed (Davidson 1994; O'Leary 1995). Despite empirical studies suggesting that negative "report cards" do stimulate improvement in quality service delivery (Thomas 1995), health care organizations do not appear ready to publicize their weaknesses.

WHY QUALITY IMPROVEMENT IS RESISTED IN THE MEDICAL SECTOR

There is little debate that the health care industry has historically been plagued by inefficiency, excessive paperwork, and duplication/rework. In fact, nearly one-third of a health care provider's day is wasted on such non–value-added tasks (Bard 1994). Given the pragmatic necessity as well as the external pressures spurring quality improvement initiatives, many health care organizations have attempted implementation of TQM/CQI.

According to Ryan (1994), 94 percent of all hospitals report to have introduced some quality improvement programs. Domains where such initiatives have been successful include discharge planning (Quick 1994a, 1994b), improving patient iron levels (Quick 1994a), pharmaceutical research and development (Gentry and Sites 1994), trauma care (Eastes 1994), anesthesia administration (Posner et al. 1994), and intravenous therapy (Dunavin, Lane, and Parker 1994). There is a myriad of additional evidence of success in support services departments (Sepic and McNabb 1994), such as dietary (Latort and Boudreaux 1994).

But the medical literature also provides many examples of failed quality improvement efforts. This growing body of literature will be discussed in the following sections, where TQM/CQI principles are reviewed, and reasons why these principles may not fit within the health care culture are explored (Clinton, Williamson, and Bethke 1994).

Principle 1: Measurement Is Essential to Quality Improvement

As knowledge about medical service delivery has evolved, so have perceptions about what constitutes quality health care. During the 1800s, a patient with a limb infection equated quality health care with rapid service delivery. Expert surgeons of that day could perform amputations in less than a minute. In the absence of anaesthesia and other technological assisters, a quick operation was the most effective. Today, perceptions of quality are significantly more sophisticated and multidimensional. But with this sophistication comes conflict. Very little consensus exists regarding what factors embody quality care.

Regulatory agencies have attempted to track a variety of surrogate quality indicators, such as malpractice suits, morbidity, and mortality. But each has limitations and risks. For example, reliance on mortality statistics may encourage refusal of treatment for seriously ill patients or even patient dumping.

With the advent of the TQM/CQI philosophy, which suggests that quality is what consumers perceive it to be, recent attempts have been made to measure patients' perceptions of quality. But many providers argue that patients do not possess the technical expertise necessary to judge the quality of health care services (Mitra 1993). For example, some protesters cite research demonstrating that patients' quality assessments are influenced by factors beyond providers' control, such as the severity of the diagnosis (Light, Solheim, and Hunter 1976).

Factors identified as important to the quality of hospital-based health care services must also be considered. These factors include the following (Thomas 1995):

- Physicians respect patients' preferences.
- Care is well-coordinated.
- Providers communicate the long-term implications of illnesses.
- Pain is promptly relieved.

- Staff is emotionally supportive.
- Family and friends are involved in decisions.
- Patients are prepared for discharge.

Most of these criteria relate to interpersonal rather than technical quality.

Related investigations show that patients are more strongly influenced by interpersonal than by technical factors (Koenig and Kleinsorge 1994). For example, patients admitted into teaching hospitals report greater dissatisfaction than those in nonteaching hospitals—despite evidence that teaching hospitals are technologically superior and employ highly trained and specialized staff. The explanation for the anomaly appears to be based on perceptions that teaching hospitals are more oriented toward student education than toward patient healing. Thus, the bedside manner of providers is more clinical and less interpersonal (Fleming 1981).

Despite reservations about measuring and responding to patient quality indicators, such a focus is critical, because "whether or not you believe the public is able to judge quality, it is important to keep in mind that they do" (Ware 1995, JS27). And patient judgments translate into the bottom-line health of the organization. Ware and his colleagues have conducted extensive research into this relationship and have concluded that 80 percent to 90 percent of patients who rate their medical care as excellent would recommend their health services to another. For very good care, this figure drops to 50 percent, and it decreases to less than 10 percent for good care.

Hence, it is imperative to examine which aspects of the health care delivery process are deemed relevant to patients' evaluations of excellence. Research investigating this issue in the medical domain is summarized in Table 8.1. For more information, see Bowers, Swan, and Koehler (1994).

As indicated in Table 8.1, patients consider interpersonal factors as much as they do competency factors. In contrast, the JCAHO's defined quality performance indicators are generally technical in nature. Such an exclusion of interpersonal considerations can, however, jeopardize technical quality outcomes. For example, research demonstrates that positive interpersonal relations contribute to patient compliance with physician orders (Korsch 1984). And since compliance typically results in improved technical outcomes, perhaps the industry needs to more closely examine how quality is assessed.

Principle 2: TQM/CQI Demands a Focus on Satisfying Customers' Needs

Until very recently, health care organizations generally believed that physicians were their primary customers, as they were seen as the stakeholders most influential in increasing the profitability of the institution. But recent

TABLE 8.1. A comparison of JCAHO's and patients' perceptions of factors contributing to high-quality health care service delivery.

Performance dimension	Definition
JCAHO	
Doing things right	
Efficacy	Treatment achieved desired outcome
Appropriateness	Treatment relevant to patient needs
Doing the right things well	
Availability	Treatment accessible when needed
Timeliness	Treatment provided at most beneficial time
Effectiveness	Treatment provided in the correct manner
Continuity	Treatment coordinated among practitioners
Safety	Risk minimized during treatment
Efficiency	Treatment outcomes versus resources utilized
Respect/caring	Patient involved in treatment decisions
Patient perspective	
The art of medicine	
Responsiveness	Willingness to promptly provide care
Courtesy	Politeness, respect, and friendliness
Communication	Patient kept informed about treatment
Security	Freedom from danger, risk, or doubt
Caring	Caregivers personally concerned about patient
Understanding	Patients' individualized needs considered
The science of medicine	
Credibility	Caregivers are trustworthy and believable
Competence	Caregivers possess skills and knowledge
Reliability	Treatment provided dependably and accurately
Other	
Tangibles	Physical features/appearance of personnel
Access	Approachability/ease of contact

environmental destabilizers, such as the introduction of DRGs, increased industry competition, and the TQM/CQI movement, have forced a broader conceptualization of just who are the health care organizations' customers. According to a 1990 *Hospitals* article (Williams 1992),

> The consumer receives, but doesn't pay. The provider gives to the consumer, but receives from the intermediary. The intermediary pays, but doesn't receive. None of them buys. The physician-buyer buys, but neither pays nor receives.

Figure 8.1 depicts the expanded view of the customer base currently ascribed to by most health care institutions. But recognition of these diverse constituents highlights the fact that the conflicting needs and desires of each of these parties cannot possibly be satisfied. Consider the expectations of the following customer groups.

Patients. Recipients of health care services typically desire utilization of the latest and most expensive technology and don't mind duplication of service if it is perceived to enhance diagnosis accuracy. Patients are often insulated from expense issues and historically have had little regard for cost.

Patients' support networks. Supporters, which include the patients' family and friends, desire to be kept as well informed as the patients. And, they can often be more difficult to satisfy than the patient (Schweikhart, Strasser, and Kennedy 1993). The support network expects to receive counseling and training as part of the health service delivery package. This expectation has prompted some health care institutions to regard support network members as surrogate patients—an insightful stance since networks influence patients' quality perceptions.

Staff members. Hands-on providers desire to preserve their clinical autonomy through insulation from external cost-containment pressures. Among professional staff, adherence to occupational codes of conduct is perceived to be more important than adherence to institutional demands. Techniques such as economic credentialing pose a threat to occupational codes. Economic credentialing focuses on identifying physicians most likely to make money for their employing organizations. This process is being imposed because physicians control variable health care costs, which can amount to as much as 60 percent of total medical service expenditures (Thompson 1994). While many staff members believe such techniques are inconsistent with quality health care service delivery, others believe "while

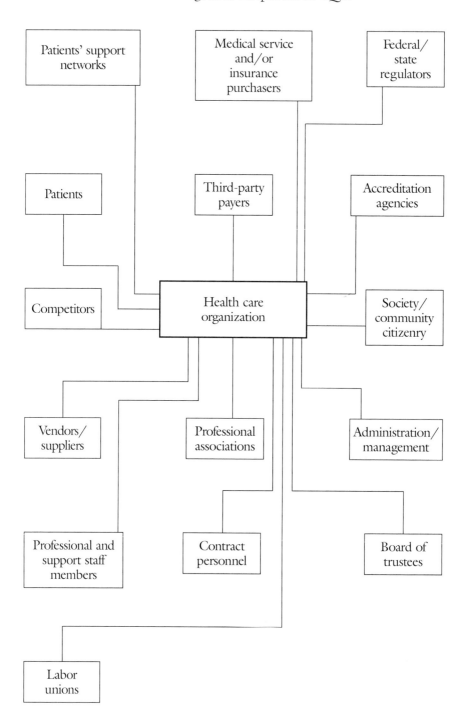

FIGURE 8.1. A schematic of the multiple customers involved in the health care service delivery process.

we might like to cloak ourselves in righteous language, we have generally done little to evaluate, improve, and monitor the practice of our peers" (Povar 1995). This is true in terms of both quality and cost.

Purchasers and third-party payers. Medical service/insurance purchasers and reimbursement entities are primarily concerned with the provision of cost-beneficial services. To payers, quality is equated with value. They adhere to the assumption that it is not appropriate in a world of scarce resources to permit physicians to do whatever benefits the patient no matter what the costs (Veatch 1995), notwithstanding the Hippocratic oath that has been the moral mantra of medical ethics for over 2000 years (Povar 1995).

In summary, evaluation of these customer groups reveals that each has its own unique expectation concerning the level and type of quality demanded. The ultimate result of these divergent perspectives is customer gridlock—when a health care institution attempts to satisfy the needs of one group, others will, de facto, be dissatisfied.

Principle 3: Create an Environment Conducive to Continuous Improvement

TQM/CQI requires an organizational structure that facilitates empowerment and decentralized decision making (Bounds et al. 1994). But such a structure is difficult to achieve in the medical sector, as most health care enterprises are organized as "professional bureaucracies" (Koumoutzis 1994). In professional bureaucracies, the nucleus of power rests not with administrators, not with low-level employees, but with a specific occupational group. In the case of health care institutions, this group is the physicians (Mitra 1993). Overcoming the traditional power stratification structure, as explicated in the following passage, is often met with resistance.

> The doctor knows best, the nurse was his "handmaiden," and the patient followed orders rather than participated in care. Trustees felt they handled the business matters, and often thought of themselves as beholden to the institution, rather than to the constituents the institution serves. Managers thought of themselves as the third leg of a wobbly three-legged stool with the physicians and trustees. (Griffith 1994, 456)

TQM/CQI requires a more enlightened and democratic approach. But to be successfully implemented, quality improvement efforts in the medical sector must have the endorsement of physicians. Doctors, however, have generally been uninvolved in TQM/CQI processes (Duval 1995), and they remain resistant even when they move to administrative positions (Babka 1994). Several suggestions have been offered for engaging physicians in the quality improvement effort, including the following:

- Using familiar metaphors such as *pain* when communicating about the effects of poor quality (Coffey et al. 1993)

- Providing credible statistical data about the cost–benefit of improvement (Nathanson 1994)

- Indoctrinating them into TQM/CQI while in medical school (Headrick et al. 1995)

But perhaps the most expedient suggestion is to genuinely solicit caretakers' involvement in the process. Evidence indicates many health care organizations have not encouraged clinical participation in quality programming. For example, one study showed that only 15 percent of caretakers were familiar with the mission statement of their employing institution and 75 percent did not know its origin (Richman and Wright 1994).

Another structural impediment to the implementation of TQM/CQI is the necessity of teams. Cross-functional teams are very difficult to organize and coordinate in the medical sector given established power differentials, incompatible vocational orientations and value systems, and the tendency to seek interaction only with members of the same professional group (McKenzie 1994). In fact, in the health care setting, "affinity group" interaction involving members of the same occupational cohort appears to be more desirable than cross-functional team interaction (Van Aken, Monetta, and Sink 1994).

Cross-functional training is another challenge in health care organizations. Increased specialization, strict licensure requirements, and lengthy formal educational standards make cross training nearly impossible in the clinical environment. For example, potential team members such as pharmacists, radiologic technicians, chaplains, nurses, discharge planners, and nutritionists all complete occupation-specific training and cannot easily substitute for each other. While 42 percent of hospitals have created team manager positions (Pierson and Williams 1994), there is little evidence that much else has been done in the health care industry to perpetuate a team orientation.

An additional hindrance is the continual downsizing, deployment, and reengineering occurring in the health care environment (Lumsdon 1994). Cost cutting and declining inpatient admissions have forced many hospitals to reduce their staffs. Retained providers complain about overwork and excessive demands, feeling that little time is left to devote to seemingly extra-role issues such as quality improvement. In addition, an environment that is plagued with concerns about job insecurity promotes fear and resistance to any type of change (Bergman 1994a).

Principle 4: Do It Right the First Time by Focusing on Process Improvement and Problem Prevention Rather Than Inspection

The health care industry has historically been more oriented toward problem detection and correction than prevention (Eagle, Davies, and Pagenkopf 1994). This orientation has been institutionally reinforced through industrywide quality assurance (QA) efforts (D'Aquilla, Habegger, and Willwerth 1994). Differences between the TQM/CQI philosophy and the reactive QA approach are outlined in Table 8.2 (Darr 1991).

Another concern about the prevention focus of TQM/CQI is that it fails to address actions that should be taken when quality breakdowns occur. And in all service environments, where consumers are influential in determining the success or failure of outcomes, breakdowns inevitably occur. Zero defections, then, is an unattainable goal—unless attention is afforded to recovering from breakdowns (Zemke 1994).

Health care providers object to the lack of discussion about recovery. They reject the implication that, if breakdowns are addressed, a self-fulfilling prophecy will become operative and actually encourage reduced quality

TABLE 8.2. A comparison of quality assurance (QA) and continuous quality improvement (CQI).

QA	CQI
Focuses on detecting post-occurrence clinical errors	Focuses on prevention of clinical/administrative breakdowns
Measures outcomes	Measures processes
Searches for individual(s) to blame	Searches for how defective processes can be improved
Is the sole responsibility of one department	Is diffused throughout the organization
Does not attempt to eliminate the root causes of recurrent problems	Directs efforts toward identifying and eliminating root causes of problems
Induces fear through individual blame	Induces optimism through team efforts to improve
Assumes quality breakdowns will occur	Assumes quality breakdowns can be prevented

(Harding 1994). And they propose that, since medicine is still an inexact science, leading patients to expect perfection will inevitably promote dissatisfaction (Kelley and Davis 1994).

Medical institutions cannot afford to concentrate all their energies on prevention to the exclusion of recovery. Research indicates the conservative value of recapturing a patient who has defected after a service breakdown to be between $25,000 and $40,000 (Roselli, Moss, and Luecke 1989).

Hence, health care providers regret that the TQM/CQI philosophy largely ignores the growing body of literature available on service recovery. This relates to how an organization goes about "doing it right the second time" (Zemke and Bell 1990), or how the organization uses its "second chance to make a first impression" (Rondeau 1994). There is overwhelming consensus among theorists about the types of restitutional actions customers expect when breakdowns occur (Bell 1994; Zemke 1994). These actions have been categorized by the authors in their CARE model of service recovery (Carson, Carson, and Roe 1995). CARE is an acronym for compensation, apology, reparation, and empathy. These tactics, as well as related research from the literature on service recovery, are summarized in Table 8.3.

CHALLENGES TO TQHRM IN THE MEDICAL SECTOR

Despite the structural, interpersonal, and cultural barriers impeding implementation of TQM/CQI in the medical sector, the JCAHO has placed some of the responsibility for successful administration of quality improvement programs on the human resources (HR) department. One of these responsibilities involves implementation of total quality human resource management (TQHRM). This, in itself, is challenging since HR customers are internal to the organization (Carter 1993), and internal customers can be more difficult to serve than external customers (Chaston 1994).

No single department can be solely responsible for TQM/CQI implementation. But questions arise as to which department should take the lead. While some support and others debate the contention that the HR department should pilot quality initiatives (Schneider and Bowen 1993), this much is known—employee attitudes about HR practices are strongly correlated with external customers' satisfaction and perceptions of quality. In essence, a mirror effect is operative, in which customers' attitudes reflect staff members' attitudes.

Recognizing this relationship and realizing that, in the health care environment, "HR professionals must become consultants, coproducers, and collaborators in the creation and improvement of organizational systems" (Bounds et al. 1994, 468), the JCAHO took action. For the first time in 1995, its accreditation manual included a chapter on management

TABLE 8.3. A typology of service recovery tactics.

Tactic	Example	Research findings on tactic effectiveness
Compensation	• Reduce/eliminate charges • Offer complimentary gift, such as flowers or fruit basket	Following breakdown, consumers expect to be offered some value-added atonement. The amount expected varies depending upon contingencies such as (1) the degree of customer loyalty and attachment to the enterprise; (2) pre-transaction service expectations; (3) the availability of alternative services; and (4) the perceived cost-benefit ratio of the service (Kelley and Davis 1994). Interestingly, research has shown that compensatory recovery techniques may effectively prevent subsequent liability lawsuits (Dinell 1994). Many organizations fear, however, that overempowerment in the domain of compensatory service recovery may induce providers to "give away the store" (Hart, Heskett, and Sasser 1990).
Apology	• Say "I'm sorry" after breakdown • Call patient after discharge to express regret	Offering an apology is one of the most cost-effective service recovery techniques. In instances where a customer complains, however, only 48 percent of organizations are forthcoming with an apology. This seems paradoxical given its potential value and marginal expense. Some legal experts warn that an apology may be equated with an admission of guilt, and that may ultimately create a legal liability (Schweikhart, Sasser, and Kennedy 1993). Also notable is that an apology is often insufficient to make restitution (Hart, Heskett, and Sasser 1990) and is most effective when accompanied by another service recovery strategy.

Continues on next page

TABLE 8.3. *(continued)*.

Tactic	Example	Research findings on tactic effectiveness
Reparation	• Correct, replace, or repeat service to the level originally expected by patient	Reparation requires provision of the service that was initially expected by the consumer. Aggrieved customers want to be offered a fair and expedient fix for their problem that may take the form of correction, replacement, or repeating the service delivery transaction. Research suggests that customers whose complaints are satisfied expediently are more likely to continue patronizing the accused organization than are customers who have no complaints at all. Also, effective reparation enhances consumer trust in an organization's competence as well as the reputation of other goods and services offered by the enterprise.
Empathy	• Demonstrate understanding about the inconvenience, aggravation, or suffering caused by the breakdown	Empathy is manifested when consumers are treated in a manner that demonstrates the organization understands the inconvenience/distress caused by the service breakdown. Unlike the compensation and reparation recovery strategies, empathy deals more with "process" than with "outcomes" (Zemke 1991). Research indicates that while consumers don't necessarily expect perfection, they do desire recognition that a snafu is burdensome and annoying. While some service providers tend to be innately empathetic, others may need to practice sincerity (Rondeau 1994).

of human resources (JCAHO 1995). Whereas previous editions of the manual only dealt with the human resource management of the nursing staff, the newly formulated standards now apply to all personnel.

The JCAHO standards address three general areas: (1) establishment of and adherence to staffing strategies derived from the organization's mission; (2) selection of qualified and competent staff members; and (3) assessment, maintenance, and improvement of staff performance. The JCAHO standards relating to management of HR are summarized in Table 8.4.

DIAGNOSING RESISTANCE TO QUALITY IMPROVEMENT BY EXAMINING HUMAN RESOURCE MANAGEMENT PRACTICES

Through its influencial position, the JCAHO has attempted to mandate that health care organizations implement TQM/CQI. Publicized reactions to this institutionalized pressure range from enthusiastic conformity to outright defiance. But even professed compliance may not always translate into tangible changes in organizational functioning. To truly ascertain the degree to which health care organizations are instituting TQM/CQI, it is necessary to go beyond their rhetoric and examine their operations.

The extent to which health care organizations are, in fact, complying with the spirit and not just the letter of the JCAHO mandate can be diagnosed by an examination of a health care organization's human resource management (HRM) practices. A framework for assisting such a diagnosis is provided in Table 8.5.

This table incorporates Oliver's (1991) taxonomy of resistance to institutional pressures, which has been previously used to analyze the behavior of organizations in the health care industry (Bigelow and Stone 1995). Oliver (1991) identified five possible strategic responses to external pressures, such as those compelling the implementation of TQM/CQI in the medical sector. These responses are summarized as follows.

• *Acquiescence* occurs when organizations accede to pressures to conform, such as when health care providers pursue continuous quality improvement. This strategy is most likely when (1) the health care organization will benefit from compliance through increased patient load, more rapid and simplified reimbursement, and improved public image; or (2) widespread diffusion of continuous quality improvement infects other organizations through a contagion of legitimacy.

• *Compromise* results in qualified conformity and is most likely when the health care organization is dependent on multiple constituents with differing reactions to the mandate. Compromise is manifested when the

TABLE 8.4. A summary of the JCAHO standards relating to management of human resources.

Number	Standard	Evidence/intent	Scoring
HR.1 Human resource planning	The organization's leaders define for their respective areas the qualifications and job expectations of staff, and a system to evaluate how well the expectations are met.	This reflects an organization's ability to satisfy patient needs.	Percent of staff members who have defined qualifications and a system for performance measurement
HR.2 Human resource planning	The organization provides an adequate number of staff whose qualifications are commensurate with defined job responsibilities and applicable licensure, law and regulation, and/ or certification.	Evidence of appropriate licensure, ensuring requisite knowledge is possessed, is verified.	Percent of staff meeting JCAHO requirements and evidence there is an adequate number of staff
HR.3 Human resource planning	Processes are designed to ensure that the competence of all staff members is assessed, maintained, demonstrated, and improved on an ongoing basis.	Continuous educational activities at the organization, department, and individual levels is available.	Compliance with HR.3.1–HR.3
HR.3.1 Human resource planning	The organization has established methods and practices that encourage self-development and learning for all staff.	Performance is the result of (a) competence and b) the nature of the work setting.	The degree to which the organization has developed *and* implemented methods and practices for self-development and learning for all staff
HR.3.2 Orient, train, and educate staff	A staff orientation process provides initial job training and information, including an assessment of an individual's capability to perform specified responsibilities.	The health care organization offers an orientation designed to familiarize staff members with their obligations and job environment.	Percent of staff that have completed orientation designed to promote safe and effective job performance

Continues on next page

TABLE 8.4. *(continued).*

Number	Standard	Evidence/intent	Scoring
HR.3.3 Orient, train, and educate staff	Ongoing, in-service and/or other education and training to maintain and improve staff competence is available.	Programs should be appropriate to the patient's age and developmental needs.	Percent of staff that have attended at least one program in the past 12 months
HR.3.4 Orient, train, and educate staff	The organization collects aggregate data, on an ongoing basis, regarding staff competence patterns and trends to identify and respond to staff learning needs.	The governing body should be kept aware of staff developmental efforts.	Aggregate data collected and analyzed, and used to determine training needs and shared annually with the governing board
HR.4 Assess competence	The organization assesses an individual's ability to achieve job expectations as stated in his or her job description.	Formal performance evaluations are required.	Percent of staff that has received performance evaluations
HR.5 Self-rights mechanism	The organization has established policies and mechanisms to address a request by a staff member not to participate in any aspect of patient care, including treatment. These policies and mechanisms address HR.5.1 and HR.5.2:	Providers' cultural values, ethics, and religious beliefs are respected whenever possible (examples: do-not-resuscitate orders, withholding life support, and abortions).	The establishment of policies that describe the process of requesting not to participate
HR.5.1 Self-rights mechanism	(1) which specific aspects of patient care or treatment are included in those situations where there is a perceived conflict with the staff member's cultural values or religious beliefs; and	Inform providers, on a pre-employment basis, which potential conflictual aspects of care may be required.	Mechanisms in place for resolving conflicts of interest
HR.5.2 Self-rights mechanism	(2) how the organization will ensure that a patient's care (including treatment) will not be negatively affected if the request is granted.	Develop a staffing plan for allowing a provider to refuse to participate in certain aspects of care.	Mechanisms to ensure when a staff member will not participate, so that patient care is not compromised

TABLE 8.5. Health care organization responses to pressures forcing implementation of total quality management.

HRM functions											
Strategic responses to TQM		Job descriptions	Recruitment	Selection	Orientation/ socialization	Performance appraisal	Training	Career management	Discipline	Compensation	Labor relations
Acquiesce Accede to pressures and conform	*Habit* Unconscious adherence to expectations *Imitate* (Un)conscious mimicry of conformers *Comply* Conscious obedience to expectations	Team-based, very flexible, and centered around patient care. Used to determine if team performance standards are achieved.	Realistic job previews conducted. Pre-employment counseling to ensure applicants will fit within the TQM/CQI culture.	Once legal certification is verified, focus on factors such as ability to work in teams and problem-solving skills.	Extensive period of socialization at the organization, department, and job level to reinforce the values and culture of the organization.	Continuous process of developmental evaluations that are team based. Appraisals are solicited from peers, from incumbents themselves, and from internal and external customers.	All instruction is preceded by a needs analysis. Education in areas such as statistical process control and interpersonal skills as well as job skills.	Encourage horizontal or lateral career moves. Provide cross training when possible. Develop and distribute succession plans.	Monitored and administered by teams when possible. No-fault policies developed. Discipline is not fear invoking.	Combination of skill-based and team-based pay focusing on performance rather than job worth or seniority. Indirect pay is egalitarian; internal equity is emphasized; and salary data are openly shared.	Unions are considered equal partners in quality improvement efforts. TQM is not used to bust unions, and cooperation prevails.
Compromise Qualified conformity	*Balance* Accommodation of multiple stakeholders *Pacify* Appeasing or placating expectation *Bargain* Active effort to exact concessions	Flexible team-based descriptions supplemented with rigid and structured individual descriptions.	Advertise and promote TQM opportunistically as an inducement encouraging organization membership.	Equal emphasis on traditional factors (such as experience) and skills needed to operate in a culture of continuous quality improvement.	Realistic job preview on a post-employment basis, which includes an explanation of requirements necessary to quality improvement initiatives.	Professional staff members' performance is peer reviewed. Others receive only supervisory evaluations. Appraisals may be both team and individual based.	Some education on the TQM philosophy, but little on process improvement. Most training is job specific.	Some horizontal career paths available. Also, some opportunity to pursue clinical career ladders. But linear career orientation most reinforced.	Team provided with some latitude in areas such as absence control. But positive discipline is not always adhered to.	Compensation has a tenure/seniority component and is individually based with some provision for organizationwide incentive. Wide discrepancy between administrative and low-level salaries.	Union input is sought in areas of quality improvement. But suggestions not typically implemented TQM may be promoted to discourage union membership.

168

TABLE 8.5. (*continued*).

HRM functions / Strategic responses to TQM	Job descriptions	Recruitment	Selection	Orientation/ socialization	Performance appraisal	Training	Career management	Discipline	Compensation	Labor relations
Avoid Preclude necessity of conformance										
Conceal Disguising nonconformity with a facade	Traditional individual descriptions, which are rigid and highly structured.	TQM/CQI not addressed during recruitment process.	Traditional focus on job skills.	No TQM orientation. Very little orientation into organization. Focus on department and job.	Appraisals are individual based and conducted primarily by supervisors.	Emphasis on job skills instruction.	Career paths are linear, requiring providers to advance out of their specialties into administration.	Discipline often viewed as punitive and unjust.	Pay based on job worth and seniority. Emphasis on base pay rather than pay-for-performance.	Adversarial relations with union.
Buffer Avoiding scrutiny, inspection, or evaluation										
Escape Exiting domain where pressure is exerted										
Defy Actively resist conformance										
Dismiss Ignoring pressure or expectations										
Challenge Active departure from expectations										
Attack Assaulting, blaming, or denoucing pressure forces										

Continues on next page

169

TABLE 8.5. (*continued*).

Strategic responses to TQM		Job descriptions	Recruitment	Selection	Orientation/ socialization	Performance appraisal	Training	Career management	Discipline	Compensation	Labor relations
HRM functions											
Manipulate Eliminate forces for conformance	*Co-opt* Persuading pressure force to join side	Traditional individual descriptions, which are highly structured. Rigidity defended by stated need to comply with laws such as the Americans with Disabilities Act (1990).	Recruiting efforts primarily emphasize factors external to the institution, such as desirable location or the external equity of pay.	Criteria focus on efficiency and individual skills.	Newcomers encouraged to avoid pursuit of "fads" such as TQM. Problems of TQM emphasized. Focus is on how well the organization has historically operated.	Traditional, individual-based evaluations by supervisors.	On-the-job training that emphasizes cost control.	Emphasize traditional linear progression, which is based on seniority as well as some measure of performance.	Process emphasizes legal and practical need for traditional, punitive discipline. Focus is on punishing rather than improving staff performance.	Promote pay based on individual position. Little concern for internal equity. Components such as key contributor plans included.	Seek alliance with union against implementing TQM or other improvement programs.
	Influence Lobbying to minimize pressure										
	Control Creating power or dominance over pressure										

170

organization selectively incorporates some aspects of TQM/CQI while ignoring other aspects of the philosophy.

• *Avoidance* is manifested when an organization attempts to preclude the need for conformity. Avoidant reactions are most likely when (1) a health care organization can be accredited by alternate bodies that do not require TQM/CQI; or (2) TQM/CQI will not have a positive cost-benefit impact on operations. For example, avoidance occurs when organizations laboriously study the effects of TQM/CQI or when organizations attempt to delay inspections by the JCAHO.

• *Defiance* occurs when organizations actively resist conformity. Defiance is most likely when (1) the chance of getting caught under non-compliance is low; or (2) an organization's autonomy and/or values are jeopardized by the mandated change. Defiance occurs when organizations flatly refuse to comply with pressures to implement TQM/CQI. For the purposes of the analysis presented in Table 8.5, the avoidance and defiance strategies are combined. It is predicted that HR practices will look very similar in organizations that are pursuing either of these strategies.

• *Manipulation* is manifested when organizations attempt to eliminate forces for compliance. As the most oppositional strategy, manipulation is likely when there is widespread support for eliminating forces for compliance. Examples include lobbying and building coalitional alignments to force an alteration in mandates.

In the remainder of this chapter, the HR interventions in Table 8.5 will be reviewed.

Job Descriptions

Health care organizations pursuing TQM/CQI develop team-based job descriptions that outline patient care expectations. The descriptions, however, avoid specific allocation of responsibilities, instead leaving decisions about work distribution to the team. Attainment of the objectives outlined in the description is then used to evaluate performance and determine compensation.

Somewhat inconsistent with TQM/CQI, the JCAHO mandates individual position descriptions. Hence, health care organizations may produce both individual and team descriptions. In contrast, organizations that resist TQM/CQI are likely to have rigid, structured individual descriptions that do not address team interaction requirements.

Resistance to the deformalization of job descriptions has also been advanced by health care institutions that believe in the descriptions' practical value. For example, while rigid job descriptions may hinder creativity, they simultaneously offer guidance for inexperienced staff members. Furthermore, as health care organizations experiment with alternative work arrangements, such as telecommuting (as did Bergen Mercy Medical Center in Omaha, Nebraska with its project specialist position), some are finding job descriptions critical to high-quality performance (Yancer and Moe 1995).

Recruitment

Many health care organizations actively promote their TQM/CQI programs during recruitment (Denburg and Kleiner 1994). But the motivation to do so varies. Some organizations simply advertise quality improvement initiatives to attract a large pool of applicants (Neuhs 1994). Alternatively, acquiescing organizations engage in open dialogue about TQM/CQI to ensure a candidate's willingness to be employed in a continuously improving environment.

According to the tenets of quality improvement, a specific person-job match should be considered less important than the applicant's desire to work in a TQM environment (Heneman and Heneman 1994). To ensure a fit within the TQM culture, a realistic job preview (RJP) should be offered.

RJPs require an organizational agent to present a balanced view of the work setting. This includes highlighting not just the positives, but also forewarning of the negatives. RJPs are most effective at reducing voluntary turnover when conducted on a prehire basis (Hom, Griffeth, and Carson 1995). This is because applicants enter the organization aware of the potential downside of life in their new work setting. RJPs are, in essence, a cost-effective way to reduce recruiting costs, which average over $450,000 per year for nursing positions alone in a medium-sized hospital (Moseley, Krepper, and Morris 1994).

Selection

In all selection decisions in the medical sector, verification of requisite licensures and certifications must be a priority. But acquiescing organizations go far beyond this confirmation in their attempt to acquire appropriate personnel. Given that fit within a TQM culture is critical to retention of medical personnel, the selection battery should include assessment center evaluations or ability tests that measure skills such as the ability to understand patient needs (Bounds et al. 1994). Issues such as applicant willingness to be compensated on a team basis should also be assessed during selection.

Orientation/Socialization

To effectively communicate a health care organization's commitment to quality improvement, the socialization process for newcomers must be carefully engineered and must be initiated immediately upon hiring. It is during orientation that newcomers are first exposed to the institution's priorities. Failure to accomplish this can result in staff member withdrawal. In fact, up to 10 percent of turnover in major medical facilities can be attributed directly to inadequate orientation (Fottler et al. 1995).

Orientation programs should be comprehensive and long term, and should be conducted at both the organizational and departmental levels. Rather than focusing only on contractual issues, such as completing required paperwork, orientation sessions should emphasize the organization's culture and values. Most importantly, dedication to TQM/CQI should not only be verbalized, but must also be reinforced through interactions with newcomers.

Performance Appraisal

In an organization pursuing continuous improvement, performance feedback must be collected from a variety of nontraditional sources. Team-based evaluations must incorporate both peer and self-appraisals. When possible, input from patients should be solicited 14 to 30 days after treatment, as research indicates patients are most accurate in their assessments of staff member performance during that time period (Bergman 1994b).

Appraisals should also be an ongoing process rather than an annual event. And the focus should be on improvement. To deter intra-organizational competition, staff member performance should always be compared to standards rather than to other employees' performance (Bowen and Lawler 1992).

Training

In a TQM/CQI environment, training initiatives should always be preceded by an individual needs analysis (Schultz 1995). But to ensure that staff members will honestly reveal their deficiencies, needs assessment information should only be used for developmental purposes. If information collected during needs assessment is used to penalize employees, trust in the training process will be undermined. Training content areas typically covered by organizations pursuing quality improvement include the following (Clinton, Williamson, and Bethke 1994):

- Review of the philosophy of TQM/CQI
- Introduction to statistical process control tools
- Team-building exercises
- Enhancement of interpersonal skills

For staff members that seek an in-depth, academic perspective on TQM/CQI, university training is increasingly being offered as part of health care institution training initiatives. Tuition reimbursements are seen as prudent investments by most hospital chief executive officers (CEOs). In fact, 75 percent of CEOs prefer that all clinical administrators have some collegiate management education (Weisman et al. 1995).

Organizations pursuing TQM/CQI must realize that the results of training interventions—either internal or external—may not be immediately noticeable. In fact, the acquisition of new skills requires approximately 2000 repetitions. Only after such repeated practice will responses become automatic (Barrett 1994). Despite this, pre- and postinstructional assessments should attempt to measure the degree of knowledge acquisition, retention, and transfer. Inquiring about affective reactions to training programs may also reveal opportunities for improvement in instructional programming.

Career Management

In a TQM/CQI environment, traditional linear promotions should be deemphasized and lateral moves encouraged. Horizontal transfers promote workforce flexibility and enhance staff members' understanding of the operational system. Health care organizations should also encourage and support professional association and continuing education activities. Finally, succession plans should be developed and shared to promote individual responsibility for career development (Johnson et al. 1994).

One career development technique that has proven to be particularly successful in health care settings is the clinical ladder. It allows hands-on care providers to advance up through their specialty as opposed to being forced to seek hierarchical advancement through promotion to administrative positions (Corley et al. 1994). This creates staff member satisfaction because clinicians are not forced to assume positions in which their specialized training and talents atrophy.

Discipline

When disciplinary procedures promote fear, dysfunctional reactions are elicited. Staff members should always perceive that discipline is administered only for just cause; due process is adhered to; and the purpose of discipline is to encourage improvement rather than to penalize. Since TQM/CQI suggests that most performance problems are attributable to the system rather than to individuals, acquiescing health care organizations are beginning to implement no-fault policies. Under these, individuals are not personally blamed or penalized for substandard performance. Other organizations are allowing disciplinary violations of some rules and policies (such as absence policies) to be handled within teams or work groups (Schuler 1992).

More health care institutions are recognizing that many so-called discipline problems result from organizational ineffectiveness in the HR domain. For example, the American Nursing Association reports that weekly rotating shifts, while being most common in health care institutions, are far more detrimental to personal productivity and well-being than are either permanent shifts or rapid shift rotations (Alward and Monk 1994).

Compensation

Compensation administration in organizations pursuing TQM/CQI diverges from traditional job- and seniority-based pay systems. In TQM organizations, the growth of base salary is stagnating (Pierson and Williams 1994). The focus is instead on team-based merit and skill-based pay, which rewards individuals based on their potential to contribute to the organization by mastering a variety of skills (Laabs 1994). TQM organizations also rely heavily on suggestion incentives, rewarding improvements that save as little as $0.50 (Mulich 1994). Incentives are becoming increasingly popular in health care institutions. As evidence, more than 50 percent of all hospitals have instituted incentive-based rewards at levels below the executive ranks (Flynn 1994).

But organizations instituting incentive programs that reward quantity must beware of diverting attention away from quality (Kohn 1993). Other concerns about incentives include the following:

- Tending to overemphasize pay and underemphasize intrinsic rewards
- Perceiving the absence of an incentive as coercive
- Viewing incentives as manipulative or as a bribe
- Using incentives to undermine satisfaction with the work itself

In fact, studies show that the larger the reward, the more negatively a task was viewed.

Health care organizations resisting the implementation of quality management are likely to offer key contributor plans that overreward specific individuals. Such plans reinforce hierarchical segregation and power differentials (Pierson and Williams 1994). In these organizations, pay systems are also likely to favor those who make vertical rather than horizontal moves. Plans are likely to be very secretive, which induces competition (Bowen and Lawler 1992). Internal equity is not seen as a concern in these organizations, despite the fact that Schneider and Bowen (1993) found that internal equity was significantly correlated with "service passion" (r = .43), whereas external equity of compensation was not (r = .16).

In many health care institutions, internal equity doesn't seem to be emphasized, as evidenced by the large gender pay differential that exists in the medical sector. Recent studies find that, given the same educational backgrounds, female health care administrators earned an average of $50,839 per year while males earned $61,491 (Walsh and Borkowski 1995). Such inequity can serve to undermine any improvement initiative.

Labor Relations

Health care organizations pursuing both the acquiescence and the manipulation strategies are likely to encourage alignments with organized unions. But the aim of the alignments will be diametrically opposed. Under the acquiescence strategy, unions are involved as full partners in the implementation of TQM/CQI. With the manipulative approach, the organization seeks union involvement to the extent that the alliance will encourage avoidance of TQM/CQI initiatives. In this case, the organization attempts to demonstrate to the union that its power and membership will be eroded by such a program. Organizations pursuing the remaining strategies are likely to maintain traditional aggressive relations with unions.

CONCLUSION

The health care industry must simultaneously attend to three conflicting objectives: (1) cost-effectiveness, (2) access, and (3) quality. Cost-effectiveness is of concern to U.S. economists today, as the price of health care approaches the trillion dollar mark. Cost issues were, however, the primary focus in the 1980s as government, insurance companies, and businesses used different mechanisms to force health care institutions to limit how much they charged for services. Access has been dealt with through such approaches as the Medicare system but still remains a major political issue today as more than 35 million Americans lack health insurance. During the 1990s, however, it is the quality issue that is receiving the most attention.

The driving force behind quality initiatives in the medical sector is the JCAHO. In 1992 this accreditation agency adopted a TQM/CQI approach that touched off mixed reactions throughout the industry. While many agree with the philosophical principle of focusing on the patients as the ultimate customers, there is controversy over how accurately patients can access information about the industry. A particularly heated issue is whether patients can appropriately interpret quality performance indicators on health care providers. Health care professionals are not accustomed to public scrutiny; they are more comfortable with peer reviews. Thus, this new objective is being met with fear, anger, and resistance.

Indeed, professionals and patients do seem to evaluate quality from different standpoints. Professionals view quality from a technical perspective and are concerned with qualifications of providers, appropriateness of therapeutic procedures, and effectiveness of interventions. Patients perceive quality from an interpersonal standpoint focusing on caring, integrity, and impressions of competence.

The HR department has been assigned responsibility by the JCAHO for assisting organizations in overcoming such obstacles to TQM/CQI implementation. For example, the HR department can aid the health care staff in coming to grips with the different stakeholder perspectives through such functions as socialization and training. Also, to the extent that HR policies influence employee attitudes and behaviors, the HR department is critical to successful implementation of TQM/CQI in the health care industry.

Because this is such a labor-intensive industry, health care organizations cannot expect to effectively pursue quality improvement without the full support and cooperation of staff members. This requires the HR department to develop staffing strategies, select competent personnel, and assess and improve the performance of these internal customers so that they can meet the needs of the most important external customer—the patient.

REFERENCES

Alward, R. Ruth, and Timothy H. Monk. 1994. Supporting shift workers. *Journal of Nursing Administration* (May): 53–59.

Babka, John C. 1994. Physician executives strive for balance in their changing roles. *Healthcare Executive* (May/June): 20–21.

Bard, Mark R. 1994. Reinventing health care delivery. *Hospital & Health Services Administration* (fall): 397–402.

Barrett, Derm. 1994. *Fast focus on TQM: A concise guide to company-wide learning*. Portland, Oreg.: Productivity Press.

Banes, Stephen C. 1994. New age personnel: Quality service delivery in changing times. *Public Personnel Management* (summer): 181–185.

Bell, Chip R. 1994. Turning disappointment into customer delight. *Editor & Publisher*, 6 August, 48.

Bergman, Rhonda. 1994a. The trials of accreditation. *Hospital & Health Networks*, 5 September, 42–49.

———. 1994b. Are patients happy? Managed care plans want to know. *Hospital & Health Networks,* 5 December 5, 68.

Bigelow, Barbara, and Melissa Middleton Stone. 1995. Why don't they do what we want? An exploration of organizational responses to institutional pressures in community health centers. *Public Administration Review* (March/April): 183–192.

Bounds, Greg, Lyle York, Mel Adams, and Gipsie Ranney. 1994. *Beyond total quality management: Toward the emerging paradigm.* New York: McGraw-Hill.

Bowen, David E., and Edward E. Lawler III. 1992. Total quality-oriented human resource management. *Organizational Dynamics* (spring): 29–41.

Bowers, Michael R., John E. Swan, and William F. Koehler. 1994. What attributes determine quality and satisfaction with health care delivery? *Health Care Management Review* (fall): 49–55.

Burda, David, and John Morrissey. 1994. JCAHO hit with reform edicts. *Modern Healthcare,* 12 December, 2–3.

Carson, Paula Phillips, Kerry D. Carson, and C. William Roe. 1995. *Management of healthcare organizations: Cases and exercises.* Cincinnati, Ohio: South-Western College Publishing.

Carter, Carla C. 1993. *Human resource management and the total quality imperative.* New York: AMACOM.

Chaston, I. 1994. Internal customer management and service gaps within the National Health Service. *International Journal of Nursing Studies* (August): 380–390.

Clinton, Roy J., Stan Williamson, and Art L. Bethke. 1994. Implementing total quality management: The role of human resource management. *SAM Advanced Management Journal* (spring): 10–16.

Coffey, Richard J., Lauren Jones, Ann Kowalkowski, and James Browne. 1993. Asking effective questions: An important leadership role to support quality improvement. *Journal of Quality Improvement* (October): 454–464.

Corley, Mary C., Barbara Farley, Norma Geddes, Lauren Goodloe, and Paul Green. 1994. The clinical leader: Impact on nurse satisfaction and turnover. *Journal of Nursing Administration* (February): 42–48.

D'Aquilla, N. W., D. Habegger, and E. J. Willwerth. 1994. Converting a QA program to CQI. *Nursing Management* (October): 68–71.

Darr, Kurt. 1991. Quality improvement and quality assurance compared. *Hospital Topics* (summer): 4–8.

Davidson, Dick. 1994. Telling the quality story. *Hospitals & Health Networks,* 20 October, 8.

Deitch, C. H., W. C. Chan, J. H. Sunshine, M. D. Zinninger, P. N. Cascade, and S. T. Cochran. 1994. Quality assessment and improvement: What radiologists do and think. *American Journal of Roentgenology* (November): 1245–1254.

Denburg, Matthew D., and Brian H. Kleiner. 1994. How to provide excellent company customer service. *Leadership & Organizational Development* (December): 1–4.

Dinell, David. 1994. Hot-coffee suit stirs businesses to evaluate customer response. *Wichita Business Journal,* 9 September, A1.

Dunavin, M. K., C. Lane, and P. E. Parker. 1994. Principles of continuous quality improvement applied to intravenous therapy. *Journal of Intravenous Nursing* (September-October): 248–255.

Duval, Charles, P. 1995. How will physicians respond? *Medical Care* (January): JS31–JS36.

Eagle, C. J., J. M. Davies, and D. Pagenkopf. 1994. The cost of an established quality assurance programme: Is the cost worth it? *Canadian Journal of Anesthesiology* (September): 813–817.

Eastes, L. E. 1994. Toward continuous quality improvement in trauma care. *Critical Care Nursing Clinics of North America* (September): 451–461.

Fleming, G. V. 1981. Hospital structure and consumer satisfaction. *Health Sciences* (spring): 43–63.

Flynn, Gillian. 1994. Non-sales staffs respond to incentives. *Personnel Journal* (July): 33–38.

Fottler, Myron D., Myra A. Crawford, Jose B. Quintana, and John B. White. 1995. Evaluating nurse turnover: Comparing attitude surveys and exit interviews. *Hospital & Health Services Administration* (summer): 278–295.

Gentry, P. E., and D. L. Sites. 1994. Using measures to guide the continuous improvement journey: A partnership between quality assurance and toxicology. *Quality Assurance* (March): 71–74.

Griffith, John R. 1994. Reengineering health care: Management systems for survivors. *Hospital & Health Service Administration* (winter): 451–470.

Harding, Michael. 1994. What material people need to know about quality. *Hospital Material Management* (August): 10–14.

Hart, Christopher W., James L. Heskett, and W. Earl Sasser, Jr. 1990. The profitable art of service recovery. *Harvard Business Review* (July/August): 148–156.

Hart, Christopher, and Leonard Schlesinger. 1991. Total quality management and the human resource professional: Applying the Baldrige framework to human resources. *Human Resource Management* (winter): 433–454.

Headrick, L. A., D. Neuhauser, P. Schwab, and D. P. Stevens. 1995. Continuous quality improvement and the education of the generalist physician. *Academic Medicine* (January): S104–S109.

Heneman, Herbert G., and Robert L. Heneman. 1994. *Staffing organizations.* Middleton, Wis.: Mendota House.

Hom, Peter W., Rodger W. Griffeth, and Paula Phillips Carson. 1995. Turnover of personnel. In *Book of public personnel administration*, edited by Jack Rabin, Thomas Vocino, W. Bartley Hildreth, and Gerald J. Miller. New York: Marcel Dekker.

Johnson, Joyce E., Linda L. Costa, Sandra B. Marshall, Mary Jo Moran, and Carol Sue Henderson. 1994. Succession management: A model for developing nursing leaders. *Nursing Management* (June): 50–55.

Joint Commission on Accreditation of Healthcare Organizations. 1995. *1995 accreditation manual for hospitals.* Oakbrook Terrace, Ill.: JCAHO.

Kelley, Scott W., and Mark A. Davis. 1994. Antecedents to customer expectations for service recovery. *Journal of Academy of Marketing Sciences* (winter): 5261.

Koenig, Harold F., and Ilene K. Kleinsorge. 1994. Perceptual measures of quality: A tool to improve nursing home systems. *Hospital & Health Service Administration* (winter): 487–503.

Kohn, Alfie. 1993. Why incentive plans cannot work. *Harvard Business Review* (September-October): 54–63.

Korsch, B. M. 1984. What do patients and parents want to know? What do they need to know? *Pediatrics* (November): 917–919.

Koumoutzis, Nick. 1994. Make behavioral considerations your first priority in quality improvements. *Industrial Engineering* (December): 63–65.

Laabs, Jennifer J. 1994a. Specialized pay programs link employees' TQM efforts to rewards. *Personnel Journal* (January): 17.

Latort, N. R., and J. Boudreaux. 1994. Incorporation of continuous quality improvement in a hospital dietary department's quality management program. *Journal of the American Dietary Association* (December): 1404–1408.

Light, H. K., J. S. Solheim, and G. W. Hunter. 1976. Satisfaction with medical care during pregnancy and delivery. *American Journal of Obstetrics and Gynecology* (July): 827–831.

Lumsdon, Kevin. 1994. Want to Save Millions? *Hospitals & Health Networks,* 5 November, 24–32.

McFaul, William J., and Diana M. Lyons. 1995. Vendors develop concepts for providers to offer high-quality service at lowest cost. *Hospital Materials Management* (January): 9–10.

McKenzie, Leon. 1994. Cross-functional teams in health care organizations. *Health Care Supervisor* (March): 1–10.

Mitra, Amitava. 1993. *Fundamentals of quality control and improvement.* New York: Macmillan Publishing Company.

Morrissey, John. 1995. JCAHO goal: Satisfied customers. *Modern Healthcare,* 23 January, 3–4.

Moseley, Kelley, Rebecca C. Krepper, and Mary Morris. 1994. Controlling the cost of nurse recruitment: An administrator's challenge. *Hospital Topics* (winter): 14–18.

Mulich, Joe. 1994. Wainwright acts on market's cue: Listening leads to Baldrige. *Business Marketing* (November): 3.

Nathanson, Philip. 1994. Influencing physician practice patterns. *Topics in Health Care Financing* (summer): 16–25.

Neuhs, H. P. 1994. TQM/CQI: Providing a steady supply of nurses for the future. *Nursing Forum* (October–December): 24–29.

O'Leary, Dennis. 1995. A silent majority backs JCAHO's change agenda. *Modern Healthcare,* 23 January, 27.

Oliver, Christine. 1991. Strategic responses to institutional processes. *Academy of Management Review* (January): 145–179.

Pierson, David A., and James B. Williams. 1994. Compensation via integration: New Hay survey sees integration efforts enhancing links between pay and performance. *Hospital & Health Networks,* 5 September, 28–38.

Posner, K. L., D. Kendall-Gallagher, I. H. Wright, B. Glosten, W. M. Gild, and F. W. Cheney, Jr. 1994. Linking process and outcome of care in a continuous quality improvement program for anesthesia services. *American Journal of Medical Quality* (fall): 129–137.

Povar, Gail. 1995. Profiling and performance measures: What are the ethical issues? *Medical Care* (January): JS60–JS68.

Quick, Barbara P. 1994a. CQI in action: Benefiting our patients. *ANNA Journal* (October): 341–345.

―――. 1994b. Integrating case management and utilization management. *Nursing Management* (November): 52–56.

Richman, Joel, and Pam Wright. 1994. Mission impossible or paradise regained? *Personnel Review* 23, no. 3:61–67.

Rondeau, Kent V. 1994. Getting a second chance to make a first impression. *Medical Laboratory Observer* (January): 22–25.

Roselli V. R., J. M. Moss, and R. W. Luecke., 1989. Improved customer service boosts bottom line. *Healthcare Financial Management* (December): 20–28.

Ryan, John. 1994. Alternate routes on the quality journey. *Quality Progress* (December): 37–39.

Schneider, Benjamin, and David E. Bowen. 1993. The service organization: Human resources management is crucial. *Organizational Dynamics* (spring): 39–52.

Schoenbaum, Stephen C. 1995. Health care reform and its implications for quality of care. *Medical Care* (January): JS37–JS40.

Schuler, Randall S.. 1992. Strategic human resource management: Linking the people with the strategic needs of business. *Organizational Dynamics* (summer): 30.

Schultz, James R. 1995. Align HR to serve the customer. *Personnel Journal* (January): 61–64.

Schweikhart, Sharon B., Stephen Strasser, and Melissa R. Kennedy. 1993. Service recovery in health services organizations. *Hospital & Health Services Management* (spring): 3–21.

Sepic, Thomas, and David McNabb. 1994. Applying TQM's golden rule to your support services. *Journal for Quality & Participation* (June): 44–49.

Sirgy, M. Joseph, David E. Hansen, and James E. Littlefield. 1994. Does hospital satisfaction affect life satisfaction? *Journal of Macromarketing* (fall): 36–46.

Stiles, Renee A., and Stephen S. Mick. 1994. Classifying quality initiatives: A conceptual paradigm for literature review and policy analysis. *Hospital & Health Services Administration* (fall): 309–326.

Thomas, Patricia. 1995. Quality of care: Getting the best. *Harvard Health Letter* (January): SS9–SS12.

Thompson, Richard E. 1994. Physician/hospital relations must include cost concerns. *Modern Healthcare,* 17 October, 34.

Van Aken, Eileen M., Dominic J. Monetta, and D. Scott Sink. 1994. Affinity groups: The missing link in employee involvement. *Organizational Dynamics* (spring): 38–54.

Veatch, Robert M. 1995. The role of ethics in quality and accountability initiatives. *Medical Care* (January): JS69–JS76.

Walsh, Anne, and Susan C. Borkowski. 1995. Gender differences in factors affecting health care administration career development. *Hospital & Health Services Administration* (summer): 263–277.

Ware, John E. 1995. What information do consumers want and how will they use it? *Medical Care* (January): JS25–JS30.

Weisman, Carol S., Ann F. Minnick, Jacqueline A. Dienemann, and Sandra D. Cassard. 1995. Management education for nurses: Hospital executives' opinions and hiring practices. *Hospital & Health Services Administration* (summer): 296–308.

Williams, William. 1992. The pitfalls of free enterprise health care. *Hospitals,* 20 July, 64.

Yancer, Deborah A., and Julie Klausen Moe. 1995. Telecommuters: The work force of the future. *Journal of Nursing Administration* (July/August): 52–59.

Zemke, Ron. 1991. Service recovery: A key to customer retention. *Franchising World* (May/June): 32–34.

———. 1994. Customer complaints. *Executive Excellence* (September): 17–18.

Zemke, Ron, and Chip Bell. 1990. Service recovery: Doing it right the second time. *Training* (June): 42–48.

Chapter 9

Human Resource Management and TQM at Oregon State University

Nancy Howard and Jacquelyn T. Rudolph

Oregon State University (OSU) began exploring total quality management (TQM) in 1989. Ten pilot teams were formed in 1990 in various administrative units. Early experiences and results have been well documented (Coate 1990, 1992). From the outset, the department of human resources (DHR) has had an integral role in leading OSU's quality efforts. In this chapter, the role of human resource professionals in leading universitywide implementation strategies will be discussed. Also, experiences in implementing TQM within a human resource department will be shared. Finally, some of the issues confronted and the lessons learned on the quality journey will be presented.

DHR AND OSU'S IMPLEMENTATION OF TQM

DHR's involvement in OSU's overall TQM implementation dates back to the university's first exploratory steps in 1989. The president and the vice president for finance and administration were OSU's early TQM advocates. Their enthusiasm sparked initial interest in exploring the applicability of quality concepts in an academic enterprise. Early on, they enlisted help and support from DHR. They asked the director of human resources and the staff development manager to work with them in a quasi-steering committee capacity. The four proceeded to identify preliminary reading materials and formulate early implementation strategies. This serendipitous beginning has led to a long-term collaborative partnership between TQM advocates and DHR.

After several months of learning about TQM and meeting with its advocates, including W. Edwards Deming, the vice president for finance and administration was eager to form process improvement teams in his division. As plans unfolded for pilot team implementation, it was difficult to find appropriate training for team participants. Available presenters and materials were geared toward manufacturing and other private enterprises. Yet using a consultant appeared to be the most expedient way to obtain training and launch pilot teams. In early 1990, a consultant was engaged and 10 teams commenced studying a variety of processes (Coate 1991).

Several months into the teams' work, a survey of team members revealed the need for more in-depth training. The teams were successful, but members felt they could have been even more productive with additional training. Further, participants wanted training specifically created for a university setting (Coate 1990). DHR, already responsible for employee training and development, segued into TQM training.

DHR was asked to design a workshop to provide TQM knowledge and skills to team leaders and facilitators. Over the next few months, the staff development manager worked with an administrative fellow to design the workshop and all related materials. Once the materials were complete, DHR assumed responsibility for providing TQM training for all OSU employees.

Continued success prompted formation of more teams. Interest expanded from finance and administration to other areas of the university. More of the staff development manager's time was spent providing TQM training, leaving little time to fulfill other employee training needs. Therefore, the director of human resources proposed creating a full-time position of TQM coordinator. The staff development manager returned to providing comprehensive employee training, and a new position, quality manager, was established to conduct TQM training and coordination. The quality manager was housed in DHR, reporting to the director (Howard 1993). At the same time, the director assumed more responsibility for managing the quality function. The vice president for finance and administration, director of human resources, and quality manager met regularly to assess campuswide implementation activities and training outcomes, and to strategize and troubleshoot.

The scope of TQM implementation continued to broaden. At the same time, OSU's president engaged a consulting firm to conduct an organizational audit. The auditors suggested that the quality function be relocated to report directly to the president. The auditors believed such a move would communicate leadership's strong commitment to the quality function and, therefore, encourage all areas of the university to utilize quality principles.

In June 1993, the office of quality and continuous improvement was created. The role of the quality manager was expanded to include increased responsibility leading and directing quality efforts. DHR helped establish the new office and continued to work closely with the quality manager. The director of DHR and the quality manager continued to coordinate all TQM-related training and co-present team leader and facilitator training for OSU employees and nonemployees. Further, DHR incorporated TQM-related concepts in other employee training courses. Employees could take workshops on team building and communication styles. And they found themselves discussing TQM in new employee orientation, hiring smart workshops, and other seminars offered by DHR.

The vice president for finance and administration, director of human resources, and quality manager had continued to meet as a mini steering committee. As long as the majority of implementation efforts were concentrated in administration, this was effective. A change was required, however, as OSU moved to universitywide participation focusing on academic implementation. Shortly after establishing the quality office, OSU formed a quality council to broaden interest and participation in TQM. It was decided that the president, the provost, the chief business officer (formerly titled vice president for finance and administration), and the quality manager would serve in ex-officio capacities. Other members would include quality champions from academic administration, faculty, staff, the student body, and business corporations. Membership on the council would require a demonstrated commitment to OSU's quality mission (Howard 1993). The director of human resources was asked to serve as a charter member of the council.

OSU's implementation of TQM continues to evolve. And DHR continues to work closely with TQM advocates.

IMPLEMENTING TQM IN DHR

Like all other finance and administration units, DHR participated in the pilot team phase of implementation. DHR's pilot team studied staff benefits. This was an area plagued by complaints about busy telephone lines and slow response. A survey of customers and a two-week collection of telephone call data revealed a quick, human response to phoned-in questions occurred only 58 percent of the time. The TQM team set out to increase the speed of initial response in the information dissemination process.

As it worked through the TQM problem-solving process, the team discovered its departmental processes and procedures shunted callers to the automated answering system. In addition, staff members were frequently engaged in other telephone calls or assisting walk-in customers.

Team members identified and implemented several solutions.

- Changing telephone configuration by adding lines and another telephone

- Extending the number of rings before a caller receives a message
- Changing telephone messages daily
- Setting telephones to go directly to a message when someone was away from the desk
- Returning all calls within four hours
- Decreasing the number of calls by giving customers needed information
- Printing often-requested information on forms
- Stocking departments with the most common forms
- Sending out posters with key benefits telephone numbers
- Encouraging the use of E-mail

Over the next several months, calls answered by a person on the first try steadily increased. To date, a response rate of 80 percent to 95 percent has been consistently maintained. Customer complaints are nonexistent.

The success of the staff benefits team prompted formation of additional teams. A variety of issues have been analyzed.

Another staff benefits team found that roughly 3 percent of the people leaving university employment were not provided timely notice of their benefits continuation rights (COBRA). While 3 percent does not seem to be a high percentage, untimely notice of even one employee was unacceptable. After examining the issue, the staff benefits team learned that university departmental personnel who submitted termination notification paperwork to DHR did not understand the various processes that were driven by such notification. Additionally, a lack of understanding existed regarding timeliness issues. The staff benefits team focused on communication devices that would make departmental employees as well as terminating employees aware of issues associated with untimely notification. The number of untimely notices subsequently dropped to zero and has remained there for more than one year.

The layoff process for university classified, union-represented staff is a clearly defined, seniority-based agreement. In early 1991, OSU eliminated more than 200 classified positions, of which 135 were occupied. The impact was devastating. A DHR-sponsored TQM team tackled the issues surrounding the process, including the loss of productivity, deflated morale, and minimization of disruption in the workplace. The solutions focused on creative communication models. A layoff road map was designed as a flowchart to guide employees and supervisors through the process. A survivors' video was produced in which employees who had survived the process spoke of their experiences and provided advice. Additionally, support groups for affected employees and their families were established.

Other issues addressed by human resources employees included the position reclassification process, employee awards, processing of personnel action forms, performance management, and workers' compensation claims management.

DHR's TQM teams have had varying degrees of success. All have been worthwhile endeavors, and each team has contributed to improving the overall operation of DHR. Using a team approach has become DHR's way of doing business. Quality tools are regularly used. In fact, DHR's integration of quality practices into daily management contributed to the department receiving the College and University Personnel Association National Award for excellence in human resource management in 1993. Further, DHR's personal experience with TQM has increased to its ability to effectively advise and assist other departments attempting to implement quality principles.

USING TQM TO IMPROVE TEACHING

There are a number of success stories about using TQM to enhance the teaching process. One concerns a professor who continually received disappointing course evaluations; indeed, his students were even becoming antagonistic toward him (Howard and Rudolph 1993). After trying a number of techniques that did not work, he decided to apply TQM principles.

He analyzed the situation and decided his product was instruction delivery and his customers were the students. He then formed a quality team of students to work on the problem of improving his teaching. The team surveyed his classes and discovered that one major problem involved assignments using the computer. The professor had received hints that there was a problem, but he had believed it involved the complexity of the programs.

The quality team discovered that the real problem was the interface with the printers in the computer lab: The printers were not compatible with the software he was having the students use. Students were spending hours trying to accomplish the nearly impossible task of formatting their homework assignments to look like the textbook examples. Now that the professor had a handle on the problem, he was able to modify the homework assignments to focus student efforts on the real goal of completing the assignments rather than wasting time with trying to improve the appearance of the printouts. Moreover, the professor believed that the TQM approach helped him to understand student needs better, and changed the classroom atmosphere from one of confrontation to one of teamwork. Students comment that they feel involved in the teaching process in his course.

A second case involves using TQM to design an academic curriculum (Kleinsorge and Seville 1995). A department decided to review its curriculum to ensure that students were getting the best possible educational experience. Department faculty formed a quality team to study their academic offerings.

The team surveyed representatives of major employers as external customers to identify knowledge, skills, and experiences that employers desire in graduates. The team members also surveyed other academic departments in their college to determine academic competencies students needed to complete the core requirements of the college. From the survey data, the team analyzed redundancies in academic delivery, inappropriate course topics, and depth of course coverage. The end result was a course delivery system that met the objectives of the college and the employers hiring their graduates.

Several benefits resulted from this process. First, the faculty developed an up-to-date curriculum. Second, department members gained a better understanding of courses that emphasized content crossing several traditional disciplines. Third, the department enjoyed better public relations with both internal customers in the college and external customers (employers in the community). Finally, quality team members enhanced their teamwork skills and decreased the traditional territoriality that kept their disciplines apart.

HUMAN RESOURCE ISSUES AND TQM

A number of human resource issues have surfaced as OSU implements TQM. Because OSU classified employees are union represented, one of the first implementation issues encountered was defining the appropriate degree of union involvement. From the beginning, university leaders struggled to strike a balance between management rights and union direction of TQM implementation. On one side of the scale, some believed it is management's prerogative to implement process improvement teams as desired. The opposite perspective demanded that union leaders actively participate in TQM implementation from the outset. OSU pursued a middle ground. Management planned implementation, with input and active participation from local union leaders. Clearly, an organization desires to implement TQM successfully, so seeking the appropriate level of union involvement is necessary for TQM to flourish.

Another issue that surfaced was how to define empowerment. Some employees thought implementation of TQM meant no more managers. They felt they no longer had to take direction from their supervisor. They saw TQM as a way to define their job duties as they pleased. Conversely, some supervisors saw TQM as a threat to their power base. They feared the loss of control. Other managers saw it as an opportunity to abdicate all decision-making responsibility. Some employees found themselves in situations in which they were woefully unprepared.

Like many organizations, the university had not invested enough time training employees how to work in teams. Nor did employees have enough time to develop and use consensus skills. OSU found that human resource professionals have a key role in helping both employees and managers define and implement empowerment. DHR implemented a comprehensive supervisory skills training program. Managers spend a week studying core competencies for effective supervisors. Defining and understanding employee empowerment is a significant part of the training. Further, TQM training for team leaders and participants devotes time to discussing and defining empowerment. Performance management also presents HR with opportunities to help individuals understand empowerment.

Another significant HR issue encountered is dealing with dysfunctional units. TQM cannot be implemented in a dysfunctional unit. When individuals are plagued with infighting and backbiting, or when employees are actively working to undermine one another, trying to implement TQM only serves to make the situation worse. Dysfunctional units are encouraged to pursue organizational development prior to implementing TQM. Frequently, an external consultant can be engaged to help the individuals reestablish appropriate and effective lines of communication. TQM can be pursued when the working environment improves.

LESSONS LEARNED

The most important lesson learned is that opportunities abound for quality specialists and HR professionals to collaborate. There is a natural affinity between the two stemming from their mutual dedication to helping employees thrive and be successful in the workplace. Quality specialists can draw on the years of experience and expertise that HR professionals possess. Conversely, HR professionals can learn from the often-unique and varied perspectives of quality advocates. Quality and HR have tremendous potential for synergy.

Another lesson learned is that while talk is easy, action is difficult. It is easy to extol the virtues of TQM. The concepts are simple and appeal to common sense. But it is more challenging to motivate individuals to change behaviors rooted in years of conduct. In many cases, reaching a crisis point was the only way to motivate change. Further, constant vigilance is required, or employees slip back into the old way of doing business.

Implementing TQM takes time. In the beginning, employees must learn new skills. Time away from regular duties must be devoted to quality improvement activities. At OSU, time constraints continue to be a concern for many. After several years of pursuing quality practices, maintaining the momentum is still a constant challenge. External distractions, including legislative actions and requirements, divert time and energy from HR professionals and others.

Finally, the issue of recognizing and rewarding individuals and teams for quality pursuits is a continual struggle. A suitable recognition and reward process has not yet been defined.

CONCLUSION

OSU's implementation of TQM has been enriched by a close, collaborative relationship with DHR. The expertise and support of HR professionals throughout implementation has been invaluable; and HR's own utilization of quality practices has augmented its evolution into a high-performance work unit. While the pursuit of TQM has many challenges, the potential benefits are limitless. Working together, HR professionals and quality specialists can achieve great success.

REFERENCES

Coate, L. Edwin. 1990. *An analysis of Oregon State University's total quality management pilot program.* Corvallis, Oreg.: Oregon State University.

————. 1991. Implementing total quality management in a university setting. In *Total quality management in higher education new directions for institutional research,* no. 71, edited by L. A. Sherr and D. J. Teeter. San Francisco: Jossey-Bass.

————. 1992. *Total quality management at Oregon State University.* Corvallis, Oreg.: Oregon State University.

Howard, Nancy L. 1993. The role of the quality manager. In *Pursuit of quality in higher education: Case studies in total quality management new directions for institutional research,* no. 78, edited by D. J. Teeter and G. G. Lozier. San Francisco: Jossey-Bass.

Howard, Nancy L., and Jacquelyn T. Rudolph. 1993. Implementing TQM at Oregon State University: Moving into academe. In *Quality and its applications,* edited by J. F. L. Chan. Newcastle upon Tyne, England: Penshaw Press.

Kleinsorge, Ilene, and Mary Alice Seville. 1995. *Using total quality concepts for curriculum development.* Corvallis, Oreg.: Oregon State University.

Chapter 10

Team-Oriented Performance Management: An Alternative to Traditional Performance Appraisal*

Michael A. White and Delbert M. Nebeker

Performance appraisal (PA) is as common in modern organizations as gossip is around the water cooler. Almost all employees experience some form of PA, and then they talk about it during those water cooler sessions. Typically, employees gripe about PA; they don't seem to like it very much. Employees often complain that PAs are superficial; their supervisors are biased and unfair; the feedback isn't helpful; or their supervisor doesn't even hold PAs at all. Supervisors don't like PAs much better either. Supervisors complain that PAs take too much time; they don't improve performance much; the forms don't relate to the employees' jobs; they're too hard to do right; and they just upset everyone.

It seems that everybody agrees that PAs are a problem. If that's true, why do organizations keep using them? Are they that important? If they are so important, can they be made more effective? These are the questions addressed in this chapter. Specifically, what is known about PAs, and what they can do for an organization, will be reviewed. Then, how to improve PAs will be discussed.

The system described in this chapter is based on multiple ratings from many sources. It is called team-oriented performance management (TOPM). The TOPM system was originally designed for U.S. federal government organizations and specifically the Department of the Navy civilian workforce. While not currently being tested, in recent years this approach has received a great deal of attention from many parts of the federal government. This approach had also been recommended by the Office of

*The authors appreciate the contributions of Barrie Cooper, David Dickason, Paula Konoske, and Larry Marler. The views expressed here are those of the authors, are not official, and are not necessarily those of the U.S. Navy.

Personnel Management as one of the three possible alternates to the traditional PA system practiced in the federal government.

PERFORMANCE APPRAISAL AND PERFORMANCE MANAGEMENT

Organizations are created to accomplish goals. This does not occur spontaneously or without directed effort. The performance of those within the organization, that is, their directed effort at organizational tasks, is required if organizational goals are to be met.

PA is typically considered a central component of an organization's need to manage its people's performance and an integral part of the organization's performance management system. This is just what its name implies: a system to help the organization manage its people's performance and thereby to accomplish its goals.

The performance management system usually involves a process of (1) goal specification; (2) action; (3) performance measurement; (4) feedback; and (5) corrective action. PA can fulfill several roles in this process. Historically, PAs were designed to tell employees how they were performing over a specified period of time. According to Decenzo and Robbins (1994), today's human resource officers cite three reasons for conducting PAs: (1) feedback; (2) employee development; and (3) documentation for a personnel action, such as disciplinary action. Clearly, these are efforts that can assist in an organization accomplishing its goals. Table 10.1 lists 10 other reasons for conducting PAs.

There are many good reasons listed for performing PAs, and some serious consequences for the resulting appraisal as well. In spite of the rational basis for PA and its noble intentions, however, the recent literature seriously questions whether the goals outlined for the PA have been, or even can be, met.

PROBLEMS IN CONDUCTING INDIVIDUAL PERFORMANCE APPRAISALS

There are many different ways PAs can be done, such as using supervisor ratings, mechanical piece counts, customer ratings, peer ratings, and so on. The most common, and the one that has drawn the most criticism in the literature, is supervisory ratings. It was about supervisor ratings that McGregor (1957) first voiced an "uncertain feeling" regarding the accuracy of individual PA. Since that time, researchers have been exploring the limitations and appropriate use of the individual performance appraisal (Landy and Farr 1980).

TABLE 10.1 Psychological, personnel, and management literature citations of reasons for conducting individual performance appraisals.

1. Meet legal requirements. (Use in grievance proceedings; comply with union contracts or demands.)

2. Assist in employee development. (Establish individual and organizational training objectives.)

3. Provide performance feedback to improve performance.

4. Provide basis for personnel decisions. (Promotions; justify merit increases and raises; termination and layoffs; placement and transfer; disciplinary actions; selection and hiring decisions.)

5. Improve goal setting. (Evaluate goal achievement; assist in goal identification and set priorities.)

6. Increase motivation. (Basis for employee recognition and rewards; increase employee involvement.)

7. Improve organization development. (Foundation for planning and development; modify work behavior; relate work behaviors to results; help personnel planning; reinforce authority structure; increase employee role understanding and clarify responsibilities; input for organizational decisions; increase focus on organizational effectiveness; assess employee potential.)

8. Improve supervisor and employee interaction. (Increase supervisor and employee interaction; improve supervisor and employee relationship; enable supervisors to get to know employees better.)

9. Provide research criteria. (Validate selection procedures.)

10. Other. (Provide information to senior managers; establish performance standards; evaluate personnel systems; performance comparison.)

Since McGregor's first misgivings, investigators have shown that the individual PA can be quite inaccurate when compared to objective performance measures (Drenth 1984; Holzbach 1978; Landy and Farr, 1980; Schmitt 1976). Some of the common types of errors are presented as follows.

Researchers report varying degrees of error depending on the perceived purpose of the evaluation. Performance ratings with potentially serious consequences for the subordinate (such as disciplinary action) have been shown to be more favorable than ratings for the same level of performance with little or no real consequences (McIntyre, Smith, and Hassett 1984). Organizational researchers also report systematic error in subjective appraisal related to the sex of those being evaluated (reviewed in Nieva and Gutek 1980); the evaluator's position in the organization (Berry, Nelson, and McNally 1966); and the general errors of leniency (everyone receiving the same high rating) and halo (a person receiving uniformly high ratings on all rating factors even when they are very different attributes) (Drenth 1984).

Measurement Scales

New types of rating scales have been developed that attempt to correct the problems observed in individual PAs. For instance, a forced-choice rating system requires the rater to choose between two descriptions of the employee that are either equally positive or equally negative, but qualitatively different in their description of the employee's performance. It has been argued that this type of rating system eliminates halo and leniency error, since the rater does not know which of the two choices is the "good" rating. This form of PA results in a single global rating for the employee. Therefore, feedback is based on only a global evaluation (Landy and Farr 1980), and little specific performance feedback is available. This is a drawback because performance feedback, and the development of the employee based on that feedback, are considered the two primary purposes for employee evaluation (Latham 1986).

What is evaluated may be another problem with rating scales. At the time of McGregor's (1957) original misgivings about the individual PA, most appraisal systems evaluated employees' traits, rather than behaviors, and made no attempt to validate how appropriate the traits were for the position and person being evaluated. Researchers began questioning whether these traits were relevant to the positions being rated; thus, questioning content validity.

Scales with improved content validity have been suggested to replace the trait rating scales (Campbell et al. 1970; Wernimont and Campbell 1968). Generally, these scales are based on a job analysis that determines the most important characteristics of a job. Then, performance evaluations are then based on these job characteristics (Latham 1986). While there are several such scales currently in use, there is little reason to recommend one over another (Brumbeck 1988). None seem to be any better than trait scales at eliminating the errors associated with appraising individual performance (Feldman 1981; Ivancevich 1980; King, Hunter, and Schmidt 1980).

In summary, it may be that the problems observed in individual PA cannot be corrected by designing a new type of scale. Brumbeck (1988) concludes that organizations should stop experimenting with different rating formats, since none seem to make any real difference in terms of accuracy of PA ratings. The authors most heartily agree!

Cognitive Bias

Some studies indicate that even when there are no differences in actual performance, previous performance seems to lead to causal attributions and performance evaluations consistent with expectations—rather than with actual performance. Tucker and Rowe (1979) have explicitly examined the influence of expectations in causal attributions of past performance. Negative expectations led evaluators to attribute the cause of successful performance to external factors, rather than to the subjects. This attribution resulted in lower evaluations of expected future performance (Carroll 1978; Smith 1983).

Other research indicates systematic bias associated with individual performance judgments. Several researchers have shown that, in general, people tend to make internal attributions for their own success and external attributions for their failure (Arkin, Gleason, and Johnson 1976; Miller 1976; Scheumerhorn 1986; Schroeder 1984; Snyder, Stephan, and Rosenfield 1976). Other researchers have found that observers of poor performance tend to attribute it to internal causes, but that employees themselves attribute the causes of that same poor performance to external influences (Jones and Davis 1965; Jones and Nisbett 1972). This effect is generally known as the self-serving bias. Given these biases, supervisors are more likely to blame subordinates for poor performance and give less credit for good performance than do the subordinates themselves. What a formula for unhappiness and conflict!

Researchers have argued that to improve this form of evaluation, the psychological processes that underlie the subjective evaluation of performance must be better understood (Latham 1986; White 1991). Landy and Farr (1983), however, point out that, of all the research performed on PAs over the past several decades, the act of making a performance appraisal judgment itself is the one topic that has received the least amount of attention. It has been suggested that it is not known what "knowledge, skills, and abilities" are needed for a valid appraisal, and they don't know, with any degree of certainty, what should be measured. A review by Halachmi (1993) lends support to these conclusions.

What little is known about the cognitive processes involved in performance judgments does little to help rectify the problems. For instance, White (1991) has examined the influence of several known performance appraisal biases. He found that, together, these biases produce effects that could not be predicted from any one bias alone. The study concluded that the complexity of the appraisal judgment is so great that it could not be reliably used as a form of PA. Clearly, the current understanding of the cognitive processes that underlie the PA judgment help little in improving the appraisal of individual performance.

Further, when the performance to be evaluated extends over a lengthy time period, such as a year, there is a tendency for the rater to give almost everyone the same positive rating. Considering the number of events relevant to a subordinate's performance occurring over this extended period of time, it may simply be unreasonable to expect a supervisor to analyze all of these events in order to make an accurate appraisal. This inability could naturally promote a lenient evaluation for all. Leniency error has been described as the most undermining influence on any PA system, and it has been credited with the destruction of several widely used PA systems (Drenth 1984; Miner 1972).

Finally, numerous authors report that those who actually perform appraisals treat them as a nuisance or simply take them very lightly. One study concluded that "few management tasks are conducted so poorly or viewed more negatively than the Performance Appraisal" (Schneier, Geis, and Wert 1987). Brumbeck (1988) reports that one company president exclaimed that "16 elephants could not make a supervisor rate honestly when consequences like bonuses hinge on ratings;" and that "supervisors have nothing to lose in giving inflated ratings." Brumbeck concludes that there was an "unwillingness" for supervisors to rate accurately.

Systems Problems with the Annual Performance Appraisal

W. Edwards Deming (1986) points out that, in addition to the problems noted, there are three problems associated with the individual measurement of performance.

1. Individuals cannot be evaluated without consideration of the work process or system of which they are a part.

2. Performance appraisals may establish individual goals and objectives that are not necessarily congruent with those of the work group, let alone those of the overall organization.

3. There are negative personal consequences for individuals resulting from individual PAs.

The individual is one part of a process. As shown in Figure 10.1, a process is made up of the people, machines, materials, and methods that together produce a given product or service. Situational constraints are such that any employee's work is tied to numerous systems and processes, while performance evaluations focus only on individuals. Further, Brumbeck (1988) argues that work is increasingly being organized into teams, which makes it extremely difficult to define individual jobs.

Focusing PAs on individuals, however, assumes that they can be evaluated as isolated units, apart from the process and teams in which they work.

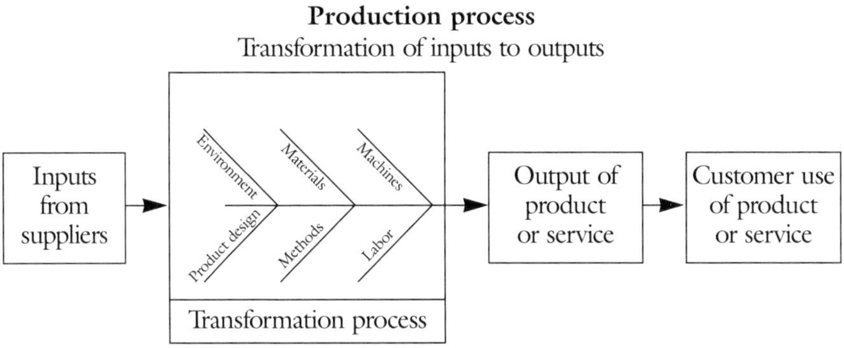

Production process
Transformation of inputs to outputs

FIGURE 10.1. Important inputs supplying and then interacting within a process to produce a product for customers.

In fact, employee accomplishments may account for only 15 percent of the variation of the process, while the majority of the problems in an organization stem from problems with its processes and not its employees (Siegel 1982; Tribus 1983; Deming 1986; Hoffer 1988; Juran, Gryna, and Bingham 1951).

Finally, focusing on individuals tends to result in blaming them for systems problems—those over which individuals have little or no control or authority to change. Instead, it has been argued, the focus should be on development of individuals and their contribution to the team (Bowen and Lawler 1992; Joiner and Hacquebord 1988).

Individual goals not linked to long-term organizational goals. Long-term strategic planning is a necessary component of any good performance management system, which in turn coordinates the organization's major control systems (such as suppliers, personnel, production, and distribution) so as to guarantee that the organization's goals are met. In any good performance management system, organizational goals are the starting point for developing increasingly specific goals as they are translated into departmental, divisional, and work team goals. This is a top-down, rather than bottom-up fashion.

In the past, individual PAs have been used as though they were a performance management system, even though they are woefully inadequate to fulfill that task. In the PA situation, individually determined performance standards are often, if not usually, bottom-up, and therefore do not necessarily link to overall organizational goals (Metz 1984). Thus, the typical individual PA cannot coordinate the organization's work process to a successful completion of the organization's goals.

Further, bottom-up individual performance standards tend to promote competition, instead of cooperation. Kohn (1987) cites many studies supporting the idea that cooperation enhances the motivation, creativity, and accomplishment of the organization's goals, while competition undermines cooperation and the positive outcomes that result from it. This is because a competitive situation requires that for someone to win, someone else must lose (Kohn 1987). Standards that reflect individual success or failure in individual PA (especially a forced-ranking system) support competition among organizational members, rather than cooperation.

Suboptimization and the undercutting of teamwork are two other negative outcomes that may be encouraged by individual PAs. Even with overall organizational goals, objectives for any single individual, shop, or division are often not integrated well with those of the total organization. Local objectives often take priority over organizational objectives. Appraisal and reward systems based on a system designed to maximize localized success can result in damage elsewhere in the organization (Ohio Quality and Productivity Forum 1989).

Individual PAs often make a bad situation worse by encouraging managers to meet short-term objectives and not long-term process improvement efforts. Instead, specific performance goals should stem from joint agreements between different levels of managers and between the manager and employee so as to guarantee a coordinated effort in maximizing overall organizational goals (Derven 1990; Locke and Latham 1990).

Negative personal consequences of individual performance appraisals. The merit system or annual individual appraisal is asserted to be the most powerful suppresser to quality and productivity in the western world (Deming 1987). Deming alludes to the merit system as a "destroyer of people," while the Ford Motor Company maintains that the merit system and annual appraisal is a "management weapon to control people" (Deming 1986; 1987; 1989).

It has been argued that individual PAs discourage risk taking and encourage mediocrity by rewarding those who set safe goals. As noted, individual PAs may also increase competition and reduce teamwork in the organization. Deming (1987) maintains that the individual PA promotes employees pushing themselves forward for their own good and not for the good of the system. Problems associated with individual PA can also produce such detrimental effects as learned helplessness, poor employee morale, and absenteeism (White 1991).

Conclusion

In summary, there has been a general tendency for PAs to produce biased results, which cannot be corrected with new types of measurement scales. The appraisal process may be too complex for any single appraiser to conduct with any degree of accuracy. But even if accuracy could be achieved, individual PAs may produce results that are not supportive of the major goals of the organization, and the PAs may even undermine the goals. Even if the problems could be easily corrected, there is some question whether supervisors would be sufficiently motivated to supply accurate PAs for their subordinates.

The natural conclusion to draw from the information presented is simply to stop doing individual PAs. This is a conclusion strongly recommended by Deming (1986) and others (Joiner 1994). This is not, however, a realistic option for many organizations. A much different approach to appraisal can be taken for the individual, team, and overall organizational performance. A new model for performance management that focuses on team accomplishments, yet allows individual evaluation and feedback, is presented.

A MODEL FOR A TEAM-ORIENTED PERFORMANCE MANAGEMENT SYSTEM

This approach was designed to provide a model of team-based performance management that would be consistent with quality principles and still meet many of the objectives of PA. Further, TOPM is a team-focused approach to PA. Some researchers believe that within a short time the majority of PAs will be team based rather than individual based (Green 1991; Thornburg 1991).

Finally, after reviewing many alternative approaches, a recent federal government panel, the Interagency Advisory Group on Performance Management and Recognition (1993), recommended that government organizations move from individually oriented performance appraisal to team-oriented approaches with some corresponding organizational redesign. The method recommended, which resulted in both team and individual appraisals, was the TOPM system.

While some human resource researchers recognize the new emphasis on teams, many still rely on the traditional recommendations of developing accurate individual performance goals and supervisor-subjective appraisal, rather than taking the team and organizational goals and other measurement approaches into account (Halachmi 1993). It might be useful to list the steps needed to develop a team approach to performance appraisal. It is based on achieving six major design objectives. They are

1. The performance management focus must shift from individuals to teams.

2. Appraisals must be accurate and not subject to bias.

3. An improved system for performance feedback, which provides individuals with useful information in a timely manner, must be developed.

4. Individual performance goals must be consonant with and contribute to overall organizational goals.

5. An atmosphere of blame must be changed into one of trust so that the appraisals can be used to develop employee skills and abilities.

6. Awards and recognition must emphasize teams.

A Team Focus

The first component involves shifting away from an individual focus in performance management to one on the team. Here, using self-directed work teams is recommended. These are teams organized around a process, without the day-to-day oversight of a supervisor (Wellins, Byham, and Wilson 1991). Self-directed work teams can increase team productivity, improve employee satisfaction, reduce absenteeism, and lower overhead costs (Travieso and Coray 1994). While self-directed work teams aren't necessary for a team approach to performance management, and TOPM could certainly be implemented without them, it is seen as a logical extension to the team management concept.

In spite of the team focus, it is often necessary to assess individual contributions to process improvement and individual skill development. Such assessment is designed to support team process improvement. These appraisals are best performed by peers and others in a multisource assessment appraisal that has been shown to be quite accurate (Lutsky, Risucci, and Tortolani 1993; Murphy and Cleveland 1991). The use of multiple raters substantially reduces errors and systematic bias in ratings. Employee development needs can be identified by comparing existing skill levels against process requirements. The identification of needed skills originates from a cross section of observers, including team peers, and can be gathered in either a formal or informal manner. This information can then be used to coach individuals on how to improve their performance.

Process Measurement

The second design objective is the accurate measurement of performance. This can be achieved by measuring process and team performance. This will result in accurate objectives and performance measures. This component relies on the information technology associated with process improvement (Davenport and Short 1990; Hammer 1990). To do this,

1. The boundaries of an organization's key work processes must be defined.

2. Those working in these key processes as well as their customers and suppliers should be identified.

3. Measures of the process must be developed to provide the team with the most important information concerning process improvement.

Four types of measures of a process are typically important to obtain. These are

1. Outputs, such as quantity and quality

2. Outcomes, such as results and customer reactions

3. Quality of the process, such as responsiveness to internal customers

4. Quality of supplier inputs, such as reliability and responsiveness

Process measures reflect the efficiency (unit costs) and quality (waste, rework, errors, and so on) of an organization's internal processes due to system factors (materials, machines, personnel, and methods) and are vital for diagnostic purposes. Precise process measures are critical because they have a direct effect on output quality. Unfortunately, only recently have organizations started establishing systems to collect accurate data on process characteristics. When such data are not available, it is necessary to develop those process measures. Process improvement opportunities can be identified by examining the four types of measures previously identified.

New process measurements might well require some organizational redesign. Simply revising the measurement system or automating it may not be enough (Hammer 1990). It is highly likely that a basic shift from an organization that is structured around function to one that is structured around process will be required.

Timely Feedback

The third component in the development of the TOPM system involves a method to deliver timely and relevant feedback. This approach involves both objective and subjective measures. The objective measures must be designed around an organization's processes. Process feedback should be provided to team members on a regular basis to guide work team performance and to assist in process improvement. This measurement system should use at least three measures of quality: (1) customer satisfaction with the overall quality of the product or service produced by the team; (2) quality of the product measured directly, based on customer requirements; and (3) efficiency of the processes used by the team to produce the product.

Feedback regarding process improvement efforts should occur frequently, while team and supervisor feedback might occur on a longer basis, perhaps quarterly. These feedback cycles will be dependent on the process and the organization.

Organization Performance Goals and Driving out Fear

The fourth and fifth points proceed jointly. Once individual goals are replaced with team and organizational goals, the focus shifts away from one of blame on the individual to a focus on improving the process for the organization. Further, an emphasis on teamwork and the use of individual appraisals to identify needed training conveys an additional message of cooperation rather than competition and blame. This is advantageous for both the individual and the organization.

Team-Based Awards

The final component of the TOPM system should entail the implementation of team-based awards. This system will involve group-based monetary awards, with the size of the awards dependent on the value of the team's increases in process improvement. The exact nature of the team-based awards should be developed by the organization in accordance with its own culture. Most gain-sharing plans have a philosophy consistent with the emphasis on cooperation and process improvement.

Because instituting team-based awards and changing the focus of the appraisal system from individual to group may constitute a change in the conditions of work, the TOPM system may be subject to collective bargaining. It is highly recommended that any union(s) be brought into the design of any such system as early as possible.

Performance Appraisal in a TOPM Organization

Following the TOPM approach, individual PAs for each team member consist of at least three elements. These are

1. The amount of improvement over a baseline in process quality achieved by the team as a whole

2. The individual employee's contribution to the team process improvement efforts

3. The extent to which the employee is developing skills relevant to continued process improvement and team contributions.

A formula for the appraisal rating is given in the following equation where the weights applied to each element are indicated by *W*s.

$$\begin{matrix} \text{Overall} \\ \text{performance} \\ \text{appraisal} \end{matrix} = W_1 \times \begin{matrix} \text{process} \\ \text{improvement} \\ \text{over baseline} \end{matrix} + W_2 \times \begin{matrix} \text{Individual} \\ \text{contributions to} \\ \text{process improvement} \end{matrix} + W_3 \times \begin{matrix} \text{Individual} \\ \text{skills} \\ \text{development} \end{matrix}$$

The first element is the amount of process improvement the team achieves as measured by the outcome, output, process measures, and customer satisfaction. These measures are weighted and combined into a single score. This score is assigned to each member of the team.

The second aspect is the individual's score for his or her contribution to the accomplishment of the work team's goals and/or the contribution to process improvement. Possible measures of an individual's contribution might include input made in team meetings and performing process analysis and improvement tasks, such as data collection. Contributions made to the team should be reflected in improved team performance. Multisource assessments (Kurtz et al. 1993) or peer ratings on these dimensions should be obtained to estimate this individual element. Using these multiple sources reduces the amount of error in ratings.

The third aspect of the individual's PA is the supervisor's rating of the employee's efforts to develop new skills relevant to process improvement and team participation. The purpose of this rating is to recognize and reward the employee's technical development. This rating is then combined with the others to produce an overall employee rating.

In summary, an individual's performance appraisal consists of a process quality improvement score; a team contribution score; and an individual development score. Obviously, these scores may not be equally weighted. Determining their weights should be decided by relevant organizational members. The relative size of these weights is not a trivial matter. If the weight placed on process improvement exceeds that placed on individual elements, then the emphasis is clearly on team performance and process improvement. In fact, it is this aspect of the system that has the potential to make one of the most powerful statements about the importance of team performance and process improvement. Therefore, the weights chosen should be carefully considered.

THE IMPLEMENTATION OF TEAM-ORIENTED PERFORMANCE MANAGEMENT

Preliminary Requirements

Certain developmental responsibilities in TOPM are unique to the executive level. These are as follows:

1. Review customer feedback.

2. Determine customer requirements.

3. Develop the strategic plan.

4. Provide organizational directives for developing the performance management system.

Collecting and reviewing customer feedback will provide the basis for determining customer requirements. These will then be used to guide the development of the strategic plan. At a minimum, the plan will specify long-term organizational objectives, plans designed to achieve those goals, and resource allocation strategies.

The executive level must also provide organizational directives for developing the TOPM system in conformance with the organization's strategic plan. Test directives should be developed with labor union(s) and other interested persons or organizations.

Directives must be developed to support the TOPM system, with care taken to link this performance management system to other personnel systems. TOPM is not meant simply to replace the current PA system, but rather to promote an integration of all existing performance control systems (for example, suppliers, personnel, production, and distribution) (Booz-Allen & Hamilton 1990).

Designing the New Performance Management System.

As shown in Table 10.2, there is a set of responsibilities in the design of the new TOPM system that is common to all levels of management (executive, mid-management and first-level supervision). Responsibilities at each level are not carried out independently but in association with other levels. In situations where TOPM has been adopted along with the concept of self-directed work teams or another similar approach, employees would participate in these design activities instead of first-level supervisors.

TABLE 10.2. Performance management design responsibilities for all levels in the organization.

1. Review executive steering committee responsibilities and directives (customer requirements, strategic plans, and organizational directives pertaining to system).
2. Define critical processes.
    a. Identify critical processes.
    b. Define process boundaries.
    c. Identify critical subprocesses.
    d. Identify personnel in processes/subprocesses.
    e. Conduct and/or review results of process capability studies.
3. Define organizational goals at process/team level.
4. Develop product/service outcome measures.
5. Specify requirements or steps for teams to meet goals.
6. Specify requirements or steps for individuals to meet team goals.
7. Develop performance feedback and rewards system.
    a. Develop performance feedback and reward mechanisms for process teams.
    b. Develop performance feedback and reward mechanisms for individuals.

Responsibilities for Implementing a Team-Oriented Performance Management System

Responsibilities for implementing the TOPM system for the executive level, midlevel managers, and supervisory level personnel are as follows:

1. Educate organizational personnel in
    a. Performance management.
    b. Process measurement and improvement.
    c. Performance expectations.
    d. Reward mechanisms, such as productivity gain sharing.
2. Collect product/service and process measures.
3. Monitor performance relative to objectives.
4. Provide corrective feedback.
5. Modify processes as necessary.
6. Provide performance feedback to teams.

7. Recognize and reward teams based on process improvement.

8. Assign individual performance ratings.

Because of this shared responsibility, the first step in implementation is the education of all organizational personnel. It should be recognized that education is a continuing process. Not only do new personnel need to be integrated into the system through education but veteran personnel also need to be updated on new and existing process improvement techniques.

The next three management responsibilities are fairly straightforward: (a) collect product/service measures; (b) monitor performance relative to objectives; and (c) provide feedback for corrective action.

Modify processes as necessary (TOPM management responsibility no. 5). At this point relevant performance feedback should be provided to work process teams. Process feedback must be a continuous, ongoing responsibility, not just an annual occurrence. By providing regular feedback, management will be in a position to reward and recognize the teams based on process improvement.

Provide performance feedback to teams (TOPM management responsibility no. 6). As part of TOPM implementation, multisource assessments and/or peer ratings of individual contributions to team performance should be completed (Edwards 1990). These measurements are primarily intended to assist in employee development. Ratings are based on elements and standards related to the job being performed and the extent that they contribute to team process improvement. Because all objectives are not equally important for purposes of rating, they should be weighted according to their importance to process development and improvement. All measures are combined to form an overall score.

In setting individual performance objectives and standards, supervisors and managers should consider the extent to which team members satisfy both internal and external customers. Internal customers are those that the process team supports within the organization; external customers are those that use the organization's final product or service. Table 10.3 shows a number of additional elements that might be included in individual standards and how they might be assessed.

In appraising the individual, the emphasis should be on multiple objectives that will be evaluated by several raters. This approach is recommended because of its expected level of reliability (Lawler 1967) and its removal of the supervisor as the sole judge. As a result, the supervisor can have reliable ratings and can easily act as a coach to the employee. As such, the supervisor can focus on problem solving to help employees achieve their performance potential.

TABLE 10.3. Examples of what aspects of individual performance might be assessed and how to assess them in a TOPM system.

What to assess?

1. Performance resulting in improved customer relations (internal and external)
2. Effort resulting in the removal of special causes in process variation
3. Work performance that improves team processes
4. Effort that results in better teamwork and cooperation in and outside of the work group
5. The quality of an individual's task performance
6. An individual's contributions to team productivity
7. An individual's technical competence in specific work skills

How to assess?

1. Customer ratings
2. Supervisor ratings
3. Peer ratings
4. Subordinate ratings
5. Self-ratings

It is often difficult for employees to persist in solving quality problems over extended periods of time (White and Konoske 1989). Constructing objectives and standards that support quality-oriented behavior sends a message to employees that this activity is important to the organization. It places an emphasis on efforts to identify special causes of undesired variation and helps improve team processes. It is important to convey to employees the minimum acceptable level of quality and productivity, while at the same time promoting process improvements above these levels.

Recognize and reward teams based on process improvement (TOPM management responsibility no. 7). Here, it is recommended that team performance above a certain baseline, standard, or target be rewarded. The rewards can be both monetary and nonmonetary; both are highly effective (White and Culbertson 1992).

Monetary rewards can be directly proportional to the gain over the goal or may be decided on a less rigid basis. Individual components of a team reward can be divided equally among team members or on the basis of their perceived contribution to team performance. Whatever method of reward distribution is selected, it is important that team members understand it well before implementation. Disappointments and misunderstanding concerning the reward system can seriously undermine future process improvement efforts.

Assign individual performance ratings (TOPM management responsibility no. 8). This is the last and possibly the easiest of management responsibilities in the TOPM system. Individual ratings are computed based on the formula presented on page 205, and come from a variety of sources. As noted, the supervisor can serve as a coach and advisor for anyone who may be having difficulty performing their job. The supervisor would not be burdened with defending his or her personal rating of the individual's performance.

While the assessment roles and responsibilities would fall to supervisors and management in a traditional organization, this need not be the case. With an empowered workforce and an emphasis on self-directed teams, employees at all levels of the organization can participate in implementing the TOPM system.

CONCLUSIONS

The challenges and problems associated with traditional PA as a performance management system were reviewed. Traditional PA was found inadequate and often destructive. A team-based perspective that focused on process improvement and personal development was recommended. Then, an approach to performance management that is designed to foster a systems perspective in process improvement was presented.

TOPM is a coherent approach to the improvement of organizational processes that is congruent with individual goals instead of being in conflict with them. It also encourages cooperation and teamwork instead of competition within work groups. Individual development is encouraged to target improving future performance. Finally, TOPM seeks to reduce blame for past performance problems.

While the methods embraced in this approach are promising, only multiple applications of the approach and careful evaluation of it will show if TOPM has met its objective. The TOPM approach is so new that it is just beginning to be implemented. It has yet to be formally evaluated. Only time will tell how well it will achieve its promise.

REFERENCES

Arkin, Robert M., James M. Gleason, and Shawn Johnson. 1976. Effect of perceived choice, expected outcome, and observed outcome of an action on the causal attributions of actors. *Journal of Experimental Social Psychology* 12, no. 2:151–158.

Berry, Newell H., Paul D. Nelson, and Michael S. McNally. 1966. A note on supervisor ratings. *Personnel Psychology* 19, no. 4:423–426.

Booz-Allen & Hamilton, Inc. 1989. A study of performance management systems compatible with total quality management (TQM). Unpublished manuscript prepared for the Department of the Navy.

Bowen, David E., and Edward E. Lawler. 1992. Total quality-oriented human resources management. *Organizational Dynamics* (spring): 29–41.

Brumbeck, Gary B. 1988. Some ideas and predictions about performance management. *Public Personnel Management* 17, no. 4:387–402.

Campbell, John P., Marvin D. Dunnette, Edward E. Lawler III, and Karl E. Weick. 1970. *Managerial behavior, performance, and effectiveness.* New York: McGraw-Hill.

Carroll, John S. 1978. Causal attributions in expert parole decisions. *Journal of Personality and Social Psychology* 36, no. 12:1501–1511.

Davenport, Thomas H., and James E. Short. 1990. The new industrial engineering: Information technology and business process redesign. *Sloan Management Review* 31, no. 4:11–27.

Decenzo, David A., and Stephen P. Robbins. 1994. *Human performance management.* New York: John Wiley & Sons.

Deming, W. Edwards. 1986. *Out of the crisis.* Cambridge, Mass.: MIT Center for Advanced Engineering Study.

———. 1987. *The merit system. The annual appraisal: Destroyer of people.* Washington, D.C.: W. Edwards Deming.

———. 1989. Foundation for management of quality in the western world. Paper presented at the 1989 meeting of The Institute of Management Sciences (TIMS), 24 July, Osaka, Japan.

Derven, Marjorie G. 1990. The paradox of performance appraisals. *Personnel Journal* 69, no. 2:107–111.

Drenth, Pieter J. D. 1984. Performance appraisal. In *Handbook of work and organizational psychology,* edited by P. J. D. Drenth, H. Thierry, P. J. Willems, and C. J. de Wolff. New York: John Wiley & Sons.

Edwards, Mark R. 1990. A joint effort leads to accurate appraisals. *Personnel Journal* 69, no. 6:122–128.

Feldman, Jack M. 1981. Beyond attribution theory: Cognitive processes in performance appraisal. *Journal of Applied Psychology* 66, no. 2:127–148.

Green, J. 1991. Teamwork may revamp appraisals. *TQM Quarterly* (Washington, D.C.: Defense Logistics Agency) (October): 4.

Halachmi, Arie. 1993. From performance appraisal to performance targeting. *Public Personnel Management* 22, no. 2:323–344.

Hammer, Michael. 1990. Redesigning work: Don't automate, obliterate. *Harvard Business Review* 68, no. 4:104–112.

Hoffer, W. 1988. Errors on the job can be reduced. *Nation's Business* 76, no. 4:62–64.

Holzbach, Robert L. 1978. Rater bias in performance ratings: Superior, self, and peer Assessment. *Journal of Applied Psychology* 63, no. 5:579–588.

Interagency Advisory Group Committee on Performance Management and Recognition. 1993. *Evaluating team performance: A report of the working group on evaluating team performance*. Washington DC: Office of Personnel Management.

Ivancevich, John M. 1980. Behavioral expectation scales versus nonanchored and trait rating system: A sales application. *Journal of Applied Psychology* 65, no. 2:131–133.

Joiner, Brian L. 1994. *Fourth generation management: The new business consciousness*. New York: McGraw-Hill.

Joiner, Brian L,. and Heero Hacquebord. 1988. Six strategies for beginning the quality transformation. Part II. *Quality Progress* (August): 44–48.

Jones, Edward E., and Keith E. Davis. 1965. From acts to dispositions: The attribution process in person perception. *Advances in Experimental Social Psychology* 65, no. 2:219–266.

Jones, Edward E., and Richard E. Nisbett. 1972. The actor and the observer: Divergent perceptions of the causes of behavior. In *Attribution: Perceiving the causes of behavior,* edited by E. E. Jones, D. E. Kanouse, R. E. Nisbett, S. Valins, and B. Werner. Morristown, N.J.: General Learning Press.

Juran, Joseph M., Frank M. Gryna Jr., and Richard S. Bingham Jr. 1951. *Quality control handbook.* New York: McGraw-Hill.

King, Larry M., John E. Hunter, and Frank L. Schmidt. 1980. Halo in a multidimensional forced choice performance evaluation scale. *Journal of Applied Psychology* 65, no. 50:507–516.

Kohn, Alfie. 1987. No contest: Contrary to what you think, your company will be a lot more productive if you refuse to tolerate competition among your employees. *Inc* (November): 145–146.

Kurtz, David P., James M. Gaudin, John S, Wodarski, and Phyllis T. Howing. 1993. Maltreatment and the school-aged child: School performance consequences. *Child Abuse and Neglect* 17, no. 5:581–589.

Landy, Frank J., and James L. Farr. 1980. Performance rating. *Psychological Bulletin* 87, no. 1:72–104.

———. 1983. *The measurement of work performance, methods, theory, and applications.* New York: Academic Press.

Latham, Gary. P. 1986. Job performance and appraisal. In *International review of industrial and organizational psychology,* edited by C. L. Cooper, and I. T. Robertson. New York: John Wiley & Sons.

Lawler, Edward E. III. 1967. The multitrait-multirater approach to measuring managerial job performance. *Journal of Applied Psychology* 51, no. 5:369–381.

Locke, Edwin A., and Gary P. Latham. 1990. Work motivation: The high performance cycle. In *Work motivation,* edited by U. Kleinbeck, H. Quast, H. Thierry, and H. Hacker. Hillsdale, N.J.: Lawrence Erlbaum Associates.

Lutsky, Larry A., Donald A. Risucci, and Anthony J. Tortolani. 1993. Reliability and accuracy of surgical resident peer ratings. *Evaluation Review* 17, no. 4:444–456.

McGregor, Douglas. 1957. An uneasy look at performance appraisal. *Harvard Business Review* 35, no. 3:89–94.

McIntyre, Robert M., David E. Smith, and Catherine E. Hassett. 1984. Accuracy of performance ratings as affected by rater training and perceived purpose of rating. *Journal of Applied Psychology* 69, no. 1:147–156.

Metz, Edmund J. 1984. Managing change: Implementing productivity and quality improvements. *National Productivity Review* (summer): 303–314.

Miller, Dale T. 1976. Ego involvement and attributions for success and failure. *Journal of Personality and Social Psychology* 34, no. 5:901–906.

Miner, John R. 1972. Management appraisal: A review of practices nad procedures. In *Motivation and compensation: A selection of readings,* edited by Henry L. Tosi, Robert J. House, and Marvin D. Dunnette. East Lansing, Mich.: MSU Business Studies.

Murphy, Kevin R., and Jeanette N. Cleveland. 1991. *Understanding performance appraisal.* Needham Heights, Mass.: Allyn and Bacon.

Nieva, Veronica F., and Barbara A. Gutek. 1980. Sex effects on evaluation. *Academy of Management Review* 5, no. 2:267–276.

Ohio Quality and Productivity Forum. 1989. *Commentaries on Deming's fourteen points of management: Deming's point seven: Adopt and institute leadership.* Piqua, Ohio: Ohio Quality and Productivity Forum.

Schermerhorn, John R. 1986. Team development for high performance management, training, and development. *Training and Development Journal* 40, no. 11:38–41.

Schmitt, Neal. 1976. Social and situational determinants of interview decisions: Implications for the employment interview. *Personnel Psychology* 29, no. 1:79–101.

Schneier, Craig E., Arthur Geis, and Joseph H. Wert. 1987. Performance appraisal: No appointment needed. *Personnel Journal* 66, no. 11:80–87.

Schroeder, James E. 1984. Attribution and attrition in the U.S. army basic training program. *Journal of Psychology* 117 (July): 149–157.

Siegel, James C. 1982. *Managing with statistical methods.* SAE Technical Paper Series No. 820520. 22–26 February. Warrendale, Pa.: Society of Automotive Engineers.

Smith, Stephanie H. 1983. Performance expectations and causal attributions for older and younger workers on speed and experience-related jobs. *Representative Research in Social Psychology* 13:54–65.

Snyder, Melvin L., Walter G. Stephan, and David L. Rosenfield. 1976. Egotism and attribution. *Journal of Personality and Social Psychology* 33, no. 4:435–441.

Thornburg, L. 1991. Performance measures that work. *HR Magazine* (May): 35–38.

Travieso, Charlot, and K. E. Coray. 1994. Will self-directed teams work in government? Paper presented at the Symposium on Employee and Labor Relations, January, Williamsburg, Virginia.

Tribus, Myron. 1983. *Managing to survive in a competitive world.* MIT video course. Cambridge, Mass.: MIT Center for Advanced Engineering Study, 2 March.

Tucker, David H. and Patricia M. Rowe. 1979. Relationships between expectancy, causal attributions, and final hiring decisions in the employment interview. *Journal of Applied Psychology* 64, no. 1:27–34.

Wellins, Richard S., William C. Byham, and Jeanne M. Wilson. 1991. *Empowered teams: Creating self-directed work teams that improve quality, productivity, and participation.* San Francisco: Josey-Bass.

Wernimont, Paul J. and John P. Campbell. 1968. Signs, samples and criteria. *Journal of Applied Psychology* 52, no. 5:372–376.

White, Michael A. 1991. *The influence of attributions on the subjective performance appraisal.* Ph.D. diss., Claremont Graduate School, Claremont, Calif.

White, Michael A., and Amy L. Culbertson. 1992. *Recognizing, awarding, and appraising people in a total quality leadership organization: The naval aviation supply office model.* (TQLO Report 92-04). Washington, D.C.: Navy Total Quality Leadership Office.

White, Michael A., and Paula. J. Konoske. 1989. *An evaluation of quality circles in Department of Defense organizations.* (NPRDC Technical Report 89-9). San Diego, Calif.: Navy Personnel Research and Development Center.

Part III

International and Diversity Issues

Chapter 11

Human Resource Management and TQM in the United Kingdom

Graham Godfrey, Adrian Wilkinson,
Michael P. Marchington, and Barrie G. Dale

The importance of human resource (HR) issues to the successful introduction of total quality management (TQM) has been highlighted in previous chapters. This chapter reviews how human resource management (HRM) and TQM interact in the specific circumstances faced in the United Kingdom. Naturally many of the problems and issues raised are faced by companies throughout the industrialized world, but differences in national culture, industrial relations history, and the economic and political climates all have an effect on the approach taken to HRM and how TQM is introduced and advanced. TQM in Britain can be problematic because of the short-termism inherent in management decision making and the history of adversarial industrial relations associated with deep social divisions in the United Kingdom.

The empirical evidence referred to in this chapter is largely based on research into U.K. companies undertaken by staff at the Manchester School of Management, University of Manchester Institute of Science and Technology (UMIST). This includes research carried out for the Institute of Management Quality and the Manager program, the Institute of Personnel Management (IPM)—now called the Institute of Personnel and Development—Quality: People Management Matters program; and a current research project, Quality and the Human Resource Dimension, funded by the Engineering and Physical Sciences Research Council (EPSRC).*

---

*The authors acknowledge the funding provided by the EPSRC for the current research project "Quality and the Human Resource Dimension."

THE U.K. CONTEXT

The writings of the internationally recognized quality management experts (Crosby 1979; Deming 1982; Feigenbaum 1991; Juran 1988) tend to be prescriptive in nature, with TQM deemed to be universally applicable; however, consideration needs to be given to the cultural base and the management styles that exist in each organization. Atkinson (1990) claims that many quality initiatives fail because management undertakes the application in an environment and culture that is hostile to its development. Similarly Garvin (1988, 27) argues that "there is no single successful model of quality management . . . . A successful implementation programme at one company might well fall flat at another."

Given the likely cultural differences found among companies operating in different parts of the world, and the need for a contingent approach to quality management, it is probable that differences will be found in the approaches taken to TQM. The timing of TQM initiatives is also an important consideration as it appears that quality management is more established in many American companies than in their counterparts in the United Kingdom, due to a later take-up of these ideas in Britain (IPM 1993). British industry, however, is now positively responding. There is now a considerable momentum behind quality management, and interest in quality is spreading beyond the traditional industrial locus of quality control into the health service and other public services (Wilkinson et al. 1994; Dale 1994).

It is not only in TQM that differences in approach are likely to be found between the United States and the United Kingdom. Though the development of HRM in the United States compares quite closely to that in the United Kingdom, discrepancies are likely in the form that HRM takes in the two countries. Many British academics and practitioners have remained skeptical about the promises of HRM because,

> Despite certain undoubted similarities in particular practices, the British context is very different, and it is only sensible to expect that any "take-up" of American-style/Japanese-style human resource management, will involve, at best, some considerable adaptation. (Storey 1989, 3)

Legge (1989) notes that American definitions of personnel management clearly assume a unitary frame of reference whereas the British definitions appear to adopt a pluralist perspective. This difference is carried over to the concept of HRM, where the American view maintains its unitary perspective, but many British writers see that HRM stance as problematic.

Similarly, the ambiguity in TQM—on the one hand stressing employee involvement and teamwork but on the other an increased control resembling

Taylorism (Wilkinson et al. 1992)—is seen as potentially threatening to its successful introduction. Much of the evidence in the United Kingdom is that firms have concentrated too heavily on the hard aspect of TQM, such as the tools, techniques, and systems, to the neglect of the softer issues, such as culture change, teamwork, and gaining the commitment of the workforce to the goal of continuous improvement. There is also similar evidence that organizations have rushed into TQM before the basics of quality assurance were in place.

A study carried out for the IPM (1993) included a telephone survey of American companies. Based on this evidence, the study concluded that

> The quality initiatives discussed with American practitioners all appear to have embraced the human aspects of quality management. All . . . were clear about the interface between quality improvement and people issues in their particular organisation. Many said this had only recently become apparent and that their quality programme had been reassessed or relaunched as a result. Most of the practitioners' organisations were in the third or fourth phase of a quality initiative . . . in most cases QM had become more people-orientated. (p. 81)

This finding was in contrast to the evidence from the United Kingdom, which suggested that many firms had yet to fully integrate the human dimension to quality management. The HR professionals in the United States also felt that they were involved in both a wider range of quality management activity and enjoyed more involvement at the strategic level than their counterparts in the United Kingdom (IPM 1993). This difference may be due to the generally later introduction of quality management initiatives in the United Kingdom. In a survey of British managers for the Institute of Management carried out in 1993, Wilkinson, Redman, and Snape (1993) reported that, of those organizations currently involved in a quality management campaign, 30 percent stated the initiative had been introduced in the past 12 months, and 56 percent one to five years ago. Only 14 percent reported that the quality management initiative at their company had been running for at least five years.

Furthermore, in the United Kingdom, the successful introduction of TQM has required a substantial change to the adversarial industrial relations of the past, with attitude and behavior change required not only from employees and the unions representing them, but also—and perhaps more importantly—from management. TQM required "a major adjustment to the corporate culture and style of managing for most U.K.-based organisations" (Wilkinson 1994, 281).

THE U.K. EXPERIENCE
The Spread of TQM

There is a long history of quality campaigns in Britain going back to the British Productivity Council's Right First Time campaign of the late 1950s. During the 1980s quality gained a new impetus with the government's National Quality Campaign and over the last decade quality management appears to have become de rigueur in the United Kingdom. The Institute of Management study, with a sample of 880, showed 71 percent of firms claiming to have a formal quality management campaign and a further 11 percent planning to introduce one (Wilkinson, Redman, and Snape 1993).

As in the United States, British firms were faced with intense international competition, particularly from Japan, and were forced to change their attitude on quality—from viewing it as a negative cost to seeing it as a source of competitive advantage (Garvin 1988). British and other customers increasingly turned to Japanese products, which quickly gained a reputation for reliability, in contrast to the poor quality reputation of their British competitors. More than 20 years ago, British firms occupied the first four places, as well as eight others, in the *Fortune* league of the world's top 50 companies outside the United States. By the end of 1986 British companies held only six places, the top two and four others (Dale 1994). Quality was now perceived to be a matter of survival. When the British Department of Trade and Industry launched the National Quality Campaign in April 1983 it was contacted by some 50,000 companies for quality management information over the next four years (Lascelles and Dale 1989).

In some cases the pressure to change was indirect—the change being imposed by the demands of large and powerful customers such as Ford Motor Company (Preece and Wood 1995) and in other cases from foreign-owned parent companies. This imposition may have meant that, in some companies, wholehearted support for the concept was lacking from senior management. The establishment of manufacturing bases by major Japanese companies has also been a key factor influencing not only their own staff but that of their suppliers.

In Britain, TQM spread from manufacturing to the private service sector and then into the public sector (for example, the health service and local government), where the concept of TQM appeared to mesh with the political arguments of the "New Right" for the championing of market forces and customer rights. The motives, however, behind the spread of TQM into the public sector "appear to have at least as much to do with driving down costs as with promoting quality" (Pollitt 1993). This has been partly responsible for a more critical reception to quality ideas in the United Kingdom than in the United States.

Finally, ISO 9000 series registration has proved very popular in the United Kingdom with upwards of 25,000 registrations to date. Unfortunately, many of these companies have failed to progress toward a holistic TQM approach. ISO 9000 series registration can be considered as a useful first step toward TQM. There is a huge gap, however, between the requirements of ISO 9000 and what is portrayed in the TQM model underpinning the U.S. Malcolm Baldrige National Quality Award (MBNQA) and the European Quality Award (EQA). Those organizations that have ISO 9000 registration but are not advanced in their quality management activities would benefit from studying one or more of these models in order to develop a holistic TQM approach to managing their businesses.

Success or Failure? The U.K. Evidence

An Institute of Personnel Management survey (IPM 1993) found a variety of different approaches to and aims for quality management among the 346 organizations involved. Five percent saw achieving ISO 9000 series quality management system registration as the central or only objective behind their quality initiatives; 38 percent of the organizations stated that their aim was to move toward or become a total quality organization and 13 percent of the organizations implementing quality management initiatives had as their main aim the development of a quality workforce, committed to the vision of quality.

The evidence of the studies on TQM in Britain falls far short of painting a picture of total success. Table 11.1 shows that the research evidence is mixed, reflecting the fact that British companies have faced considerable difficulties with TQM implementation (Geary 1993). Cruise O'Brien and Voss (1992, 3) conclude that "most U.K. firms are a long way from TQM and finding it difficult to get there."

THE CAUSES OF DIFFICULTIES

The growing evidence that TQM in Britain has not achieved its objectives has led to the identification of a number of major problems. In the IPM survey, 83 percent of respondents reported problems in the implementation process. The most common of these was resistance to changing the organizational culture, mentioned by 45 percent, and resistance from middle managers. In order to overcome these problems, it was felt greater awareness training and better communications were needed—a problem-solving process that usually involved the HR function.

By attempting to emulate the success of Japanese manufacturing industry, many British employers adopted only certain aspects of the Japanese approach to quality management. For example, in introducing quality circles

TABLE 11.1. Recent research.

Study	Approach	Sample	Findings
A. T. Kearney (1992)	survey	100 UK	80% failure (either had no information on performance or did not report any improvement)
London Business School (1992)	self assessment against Baldrige criteria	42 UK	Most firms in the UK sample would rate between 100 to 400 points out of 1000 rated against Baldrige. This is not sufficient to apply for let alone win the award.
Economist Intelligence Unit (1992)	case studies	50 plus 6 'stars' (Europe)	Report massive cynicism. 'We got the religion and then we lost it.' TQ initiatives found to be inconsistent with TQ principles.
Durham University Business School (1992) (1993)	survey	235 (north of England) 650 (Scotland)	'TQM is still an innovation and there are many initiatives.' Half the expected benefits have still to be delivered. But is the bottle half empty or half full?
Institute of Management (1993)	survey plus interviews	880 UK	Only 8% claim QM is very successful.
Bradford (1994)	focus on externally reported information	29	A high proportion exhibit above average industry performance.

Source: Hill and Wilkinson 1995. By permission MCB University Press.

British employers failed to comprehend the broader context of TQM (Hill 1995). This partial approach failed to change attitudes and culture necessary for the successful transformation of British industry under TQM (Plowman 1990).

Central to many of these issues is the human dimension to TQM. Many of the problems faced in implementing TQM can be at least partially attributed to a neglect of HR policies and their integration with TQM (Wilkinson 1994). This lack of understanding appears to be a common problem in the United Kingdom. In the IPM case studies, four out of every five organizations had experienced problems in the introduction of TQM that were associated with HR issues, particularly in terms of generating acceptance and commitment (IPM 1993). Wilkinson and Witcher (1991) identified four potential problems in introducing and sustaining TQM initiatives in the United Kingdom: (1) short-termism; (2) organizational segmentalism; (3) reluctant managers; and (4) industrial relations and the associated social divisions.

Short-Termism

According to Dale (1994, 316),

> Total Quality Management is a long-term process. It can take up to ten years to put the fundamental principles, procedures and systems into place, create an organisational culture that is conducive to continuous improvement and change the behaviour and attitudes of an organisation's people.

In the Institute of Management survey, senior managers were accused by their middle management colleagues of being skeptical, unenthusiastic, and unwilling to commit resources and of treating quality management with a "short-termist" perspective. More than 60 percent of organizations saw "emphasis on short-term goals" as a difficulty (Wilkinson, Redman, and Snape 1993). This concentration of effort on satisfying short-term goals can be linked to the ownership of British industry and the dominance of the finance function (Wilkinson and Witcher 1991). This approach to business management is illustrated by the lack of investment in training in Britain, when compared to major overseas competitors, and by the low percentage of Gross Domestic Product that is spent on research and development. According to the *Guardian* (26 May 1995), in 1991 the percentages for the United Kingdom, United States, and Japan were 1.28 percent, 2.07 percent, and 2.16 percent respectively. These situations have serious implications for TQM (Geary 1993).

Pressure from financial institutions led British companies to seek new initiatives that could provide fast financial gains. Therefore, British managements were faced with contradictory pressures: on the one hand to implement quick-fix solutions through cost cutting, but on the other hand to satisfy pressure from customers to introduce TQM elements. In some cases, the result was the introduction of TQM without the substantial investment in resources required, proceeding in a "half-hearted, unsystematic and partial way" in the hope of a quick-fix (Hill 1995, 48). These pressures were passed on to managers through performance-related pay schemes to which the long-term cultural change required for TQM was largely irrelevant. This quick-fix mentality is also at the root of the claims that TQM is not working, as found by the surveys previously noted. This has resulted in managers switching their attention to other concepts, such as business process reengineering, which are claimed as the latest means to deliver efficiency. Many managers do not appear to realize that a single approach on its own will not produce major savings. These will only be delivered by the cumulative affect of many approaches integrated together under a common umbrella.

Under this short-term mentality, management delayering has occurred, with the prime motivation being to reduce labor costs rather than to increase employee participation in decision making. One firm involved in the authors' current research had made both layers of shop floor supervision redundant and replaced them with team leaders. This is in line with the devolving of responsibility put forward in a TQM approach, but the delayering did not appear to be aimed at increasing shop floor empowerment, nor did it appear to be part of a planned culture change. It was implemented—with no consultation or employee participation in the process—mainly as a cost-saving exercise. The result of the changed structure was to create an uncertain role for the the new team leaders and the demotivation of the reluctant team members. This provides an example of where "the Japanese model has provided British management with a useful ideological legitimisation for their actions, actions which are rarely consonant with the espoused values of TQM" (Geary 1993, 31).

Organizational Segmentalism

According to Wilkinson and Witcher (1993, 52),

> By introducing the market into the organisation, TQM promises to break down bureaucratic dysfunctionalism which encourages conflict between interest groups, functions and departments, and only serves to isolate managers and other employees from the customer.

TQM is meant to help solve the problem of departments retaining specialist knowledge for themselves and not fully cooperating with other functions within the organization. TQM, however, comes up against its most difficult problems when it addresses interunit and company quality issues. Cross-functional teamwork is required but this leads to a reduction in expert power, and as such goes against the existing power culture in many organizations (Giles and Starkey 1988). Progress does seem to have been made in this area since this finding. In the authors' current research, most managers interviewed expressed the opinion that interdepartmental cooperation had increased significantly with buck-passing mostly a thing of the past.

Reluctant Managers

According to Oakland (1989, 15),

> The middle management have a particularly important role to play, they must not only grasp the principles of TQM, they must go on to explain them to the people for whom they are responsible, and ensure that their own commitment is communicated.

The findings of a major survey of middle managers in the United Kingdom (Scase and Goffee 1989) reported that most of them have been reluctant managers, with compliance rather than full commitment being the norm. Senior managers must take this reluctance into account as middle managers are the channel through which they can communicate with, and influence, rank-and-file employees (Wilkinson and Witcher 1991).

There is evidence in at least some companies to support the argument that middle management reluctance can have a detrimental effect on the TQM message. One union convenor felt that, although the union and the directors were moving in the same direction and were committed to promoting TQM, "the message gets changed as it goes down through the ranks of managers. What started as cooperation at the top, ends up as an order to shop floor employees." At another company, a great deal of training had been put into developing the team leaders, but some of these felt that the TQM message had not been fully taken on board by their immediate superiors, thus holding back progress on quality management. At another company, the board of directors was developing action plans based on an assessment of strengths and areas for improvement against the European Quality Award's TQM model of Business Excellence. The board was concerned about the lack of commitment by middle management to TQM and discussed various ways of overcoming this.

In Hill's 1991 study of the way in which companies in Britain have attempted to develop employee participation, first through the use of quality circles and then TQM, he reported that the lack of managerial commitment was overcome by a system of rewards and penalties. This conflicts with traditional textbook TQM theory, which argues that all that is required is sufficient education and communication.

Indeed, when faced with the issue of incentives and rewards, many companies appear to face difficulty in putting TQM theory into practice.

Many of the more traditional advocates of TQM strongly oppose the use of financial incentives to reward high-quality work. Individual incentives and performance-related pay schemes are argued to be damaging to the teamwork and cooperation that is required for TQM, in that they may emphasize short-term targets at the expense of long-term goals. Recognition of efforts in the form of verbal acknowledgement or token prizes of minimal value, rather than larger financial rewards, are seen as the key to improving quality performance. In practice, however, it is clear that many companies utilize financial incentives in their search for increased employee performance and that, in a number of cases, these have been successful. For example, see Piddington, Bunny, and Dale (1995).

One reason for the continued use of such incentives, against the advice of many of the quality gurus, is that they are seen as a way of underpinning the TQM culture (Snape, Wilkinson, and Redman 1995). The incentives indicate to employees exactly what sort of behavior is seen as desirable by the company, to indicate the seriousness of the issues surrounding quality management, and as a way of overcoming any resistance to the changes in the required behavior. The compromise view is that traditional output-based payment-by-results schemes are likely to inhibit moves to improve quality; but if incentives are restructured to support quality improvement and teamwork, they may be beneficial. Incentives may include senior management bonuses being dependent on customer and employee satisfaction figures, and scores achieved against the MBNQA and EQA models. Snape, Wilkinson, and Redman (1995) found no evidence that the presence of financial incentives undermined the perceived effectiveness of TQM, and if anything there was a positive impact, particularly if group- or company-level bonuses were used instead of individual performance-related pay.

Industrial Relations and Social Divisions

According to Wilkinson and Witcher (1991, 50),

> In the U.K. there seems to have been a particularly strong divisive social culture. For historical reasons, leadership and managerial skills are still much associated with certain background qualities, which have been usually based on social class orientations.

The class differences found in British society are reflected in U.K. organizations, leading to a more confrontational working relationship than is assumed under the unitarist perspective by many of the quality gurus. The situation is made worse where top managers cling to the trappings of privilege, such as segregation of staff facilities and privileged car parking, and where there is a social remoteness in employee relations (Wilkinson and Witcher 1991). The importance attached to these status differences by shop floor workers is not necessarily appreciated by senior management, but they can have a significant impact on reinforcing a them-and-us attitude. The author's current research indicates that management delayering can also be an obstacle to breaking down this perceived division between the shop floor and senior managers if the latter do not make themselves visible on the shop floor.

The history of adversarial industrial relations, with class-based social divisions leading to a strong them-and-us perspective from both managers and employees cannot be easily ignored or removed. This barrier to the creation of a feeling of common interest is proving harder to break down than the unitarist writings of the quality gurus would suggest. In their survey of 235 companies, Whyte and Witcher (1992) found that about 20 percent of companies saw greater involvement, more teamwork, and improved employee attitude as some of the main consequences of TQM, whereas a much higher percentage—about one-third—thought that culture and attitudes were its main difficulties (Wilkinson and Witcher 1993, 53). In short, the pre-existing culture may be too strong for TQM to succeed.

Despite changes in the management approach under TQM, it is not clear to what extent employee trust in management has grown, and it is probable that it remains low (Kelly and Kelly 1991). This lack of employee trust in management can have a significant impact on how otherwise well-intentioned HR policies are interpreted by the workforce. One company involved in the current research, under new management following a Japanese takeover, issued a two-year no-redundancy promise to show its commitment to employees and to encourage improved productivity to eliminate delivery arrears. Because the workers had endured years of broken promises by the previous management, this new deal was met with almost universal suspicion and cynicism. "It's not worth the paper it's written on" was a common response. Any positive changes, such as moves toward a single-status organization, were felt to be minor when compared to the negative actions of the previous management.

Nor is it clear how much managements trust employees. This managerial lack of trust displays itself in the HR policies of another company, where clocking-on for shop floor workers still exists, because it is feared that workers may abuse an alternative system. Similarly, although more information has been provided to employees to encourage their commitment to the company, this does not extend to giving them information on company profits since it is felt that they may use this to justify increased wages. This lack of trust is also reflected in the approach taken to quality, with each product bearing the identification of the employee responsible so that disciplinary action can be taken if the employee is negligent in his or her work.

As stated earlier in this chapter, TQM requires substantial changes to the traditional adversarial nature of industrial relations in Britain. Postwar full employment and the voluntary approach to industrial relations in Britain left the trade unions in a position of relative strength. The change in government approach in 1979, and the associated high levels of unemployment experienced since then, have had a dramatic effect on trade union power in the workplace. This decline in power, however, should not be overstated. Compared to the 15 percent of American employees who are members of a union, U.K. union membership density, though itself having substantially declined, is still more than double the U.S. figure (Bird and Corcoran 1994). In five out of the six companies involved in the current research, union membership among shop floor workers is very high (over 80 percent), a situation not untypical for many British manufacturing companies introducing TQM. Union attitudes, however, do not appear to be hindering TQM's introduction and development.

Though TQM seems to require substantial changes to working practices and job controls, both of which are traditional areas of trade union influence, the implications for industrial relations are rarely discussed in the quality management literature. In practice, however, as TQM works down the hierarchy, industrial relations issues become increasingly involved, particularly in the manufacturing sector (Wilkinson 1994).

Some managements have used this shift in the balance of power to seek to marginalize the unions. For some firms HRM and TQM were seen as useful tools in that marginalization process, enabling employees to be incorporated into managerial thinking through the increased use of direct communication and employee involvement. At least one company in the case studies that formed part of the IPM research saw the aim of TQM as a diminution of union roles, and others recognized that this had happened, although it was not an expressed aim.

In unionized companies, a partnership approach (Godfrey and Marchington, forthcoming) seems to be most applicable if union involvement and support for the TQM initiative is to be achieved. In a partnership approach, management attempts to build a high-trust relationship with the union representatives, involving joint working parties and the increased involvement of the union representatives in the business. A joint problem-solving approach is adopted (Kessler and Purcell 1994), in which the parties take part in nonadversarial dialogue, with the shop stewards working with management in the search for the best solutions to jointly identified problems. A successful partnership approach requires a genuine change in the attitudes and behavior of management, if the role of the shop steward is to change to one that more suits the needs of the business. In the companies involved in the authors' current research, there is a feeling that, given an open relationship, unions can play a positive role in introducing and advancing TQM. Mohrman et al.'s (1995) survey evidence shows that unions have not been an obstacle to TQM in the United States. Other results in the United States support the view that, in unionized firms, TQM is more likely to be successful if the trade unions are brought on board at the commencement of the initiative (Kochan, Gittell, and Lautsch, forthcoming).

Of the 11 unionized companies in the IPM case studies, in only three cases had there been explicit union opposition and resistance to quality management initiatives. It was argued that this did not necessarily reflect a lack of concern over issues such as job security, increased workloads and responsibilities, and the threat to the role of unions. Rather, the unions found it difficult to challenge the logic of quality management, particularly when major customers were insisting on initiatives to be taken in this direction. One union representative in the current research asked, "How can we challenge management when they are giving us what we've been asking for for years?"

This type of comment reflects the problem facing the wider union movement in Britain. Having called for new forms of work organization and increased employee involvement for decades, unions are now faced with a managerial strategy that purports to grant employees increased discretion and participation at work, but they are suspicious of what these initiatives may conceal and fearful of their effect on the unions (Geary 1993). After generally opposing TQM initiatives in the past, the union movement has now changed its strategy to one of seeking to work with employers to build a high-trust, partnership relationship in which the unions can continue to have a role (Guest 1995).

The Role of the HR Function

In the 1993 IPM survey, 75 percent of organizations that had experienced quality management reported that the HR function played a role in the introduction and development of quality management. In 53 percent of these, this role was limited primarily to operational activity, providing or administering training in quality procedures, but in 25 percent of cases the HR practitioners described themselves as primary facilitators. There was strong evidence that the HR function was supporting the quality management initiative through personnel policies and practices, such as performance management and training and development programs.

Increased involvement of the HR function in quality management has had an impact on the long-term objectives of the initiative. Where HR specialists were involved in quality management at a strategic level, organizations were likely to see this as a search for continuous improvement and to be concerned with the behavioral aspects of quality. Without this HR strategic involvement, the goals were likely to be defined in terms of achievable, quantifiable goals with an emphasis on quality systems.

The evidence from the 1993 IPM survey was that British-owned companies were less likely to have this HR strategic-level input into quality management initiatives than American-owned subsidiaries (37 percent and 61 percent respectively); and, consequently, the HR practitioners in the American-owned companies enjoyed a higher degree of influence over the manner in which quality management was introduced and later developed. This discrepancy was also evident, though to a slightly lesser degree, when comparing British-owned and European-owned subsidiaries operating in Britain.

Seventy-four percent of the respondents also reported that quality management had led to changes in the HR function with a decentralization of people management, accompanied by a more business-orientated, customer-led approach to HRM. Based on the evidence of the IPM case studies, Marchington, Wilkinson, and Dale (1993) analyzed the breadth and depth of HR involvement in quality. The breadth of involvement is defined by the range of areas in which the function is able to make a contribution. The depth of HR's involvement in quality management was assessed by indicators such as the managing director's perception of HR's contribution to quality management; the number of employees trained by HR on quality; the number of quality teams facilitated by HR; the contribution of HR to the quality steering group; and the link between HR and quality functions. Marchington, Wilkinson, and Dale (1993) found that the breadth and depth of HR involvement varied considerably, though increasingly a link was being made between quality of service or manufacture and the quality of staff. There was an increasing recognition of the centrality of HR issues to quality management initiatives.

Marchington, Wilkinson, and Dale (1993) also analyzed HR input in terms of level (strategic versus operational) and profile (high versus low). By combining these two dimensions, four categories of HR input can be created: (1) strategic/high profile; (2) strategic/low profile; (3) operational/high profile; and (4) operational/low profile. Each category is characterized as follows:

• *The change agent (strategic/high profile)*—This role is characterized by a high-level (board or equivalent) contribution that is highly visible to others in the organization. The HR function is seen as the driver for the quality initiative.

• *The hidden persuader (strategic/low profile)*—The HR function operates at a strategic level, working closely with the chief executive of the company and highly regarded at that level. The visibility of the HR function's input to quality was much less visible to others in the organization.

• *The internal contractor (operational/high profile)*—The HR function has no presence at board level and does not play a strategic role. It has no particular primacy in the quality process and instead concentrates on providing services that will obtain and maintain a productive workforce.

• *The facilitator (operational/low profile)*—This is based at the operational level, often providing hands-on support to line managers, such as the provision of training courses, newsletters, or other information.

These roles are not mutually exclusive, and, in particular, an HR function is likely to carry out the facilitator role alongside at least one of the other roles described. Wilkinson and Marchington (1994) stress that although each role allows the HR function to make a positive contribution to quality management, there are likely pitfalls as well. The change agent, while potentially the most influential of any of the roles because of its high profile and strategic contribution, also runs the risk of significant costs if problems occur with quality management, creating enemies within the organization. The low profile of the hidden persuader and facilitator roles produces the opposite problem in that little recognition is given for the part the HR function plays in developing and maintaining any successful quality management initiative. The likely pitfalls for the internal contractor arise if the service targets are not met or if the organization decides to contract out the services the HR function has previously provided.

Marchington, Wilkinson, and Dale (1993) also say that the HR functions in companies operating in the United Kingdom have made a greater contribution to quality management than might be expected and that, if anything, this role is increasing in significance. The role played varied considerably, however, depending largely on the history and culture of the organization, the market in which the organization operated, and the imagination shown by the HR professionals themselves. Marchington, Wilkinson, and Dale (1993) also report that the role played can vary over time and within the organization; for example, with different roles being played at corporate and establishment levels.

They conclude that a major reason for the failure of early quality management initiatives was that HR issues were not given sufficient attention and that this view is gaining ground in the organizations themselves, thus providing the opportunity for HR professionals to become more involved in quality improvement.

SUMMARY

Despite a relatively slow start to quality management in the United Kingdom, British industry is now positively responding to TQM, and initiatives have become common practice. It appears, however, that in the early initiatives the emphasis was on the hard tools and techniques of TQM with insufficient attention paid to the softer issues, such as teamwork, employee commitment, and culture change. The evidence from the authors' current research indicates that this is now starting to be addressed and that the people issues are being seen as vital to eliminating non–value-added activity, taking cost out of the product, and becoming increasingly competitive.

This neglect of the HR dimension in part explains the lack of success experienced by some U.K. companies with their quality management initiatives. Another factor that helps explain the difficulties in implementing TQM is the history of social division and adversarial industrial relations in Britain. TQM, with its associated culture change, is a long-term process. In companies that have experienced low-trust, conflictual employee relations in the past, this process will take even longer.

Employees and employers need to learn to trust and cooperate with each other, so that the teamwork and devolved responsibility that is so critical to TQM can develop. Management must make sure that its HR policies actively support and reflect this desire.

REFERENCES

Atkinson, Philip E. 1990. *Creating culture change: The key to successful quality management*. Bedford, England: IFS Publications.

Bird, Derek, and Louise Corcoran. 1994. Trade union membership. *Employment Gazette* (June): 189–197.

Crosby, Philip B. 1979. *Quality is free*. New York: McGraw-Hill.

Cruise O'Brien, Rita, and C. Voss. 1992. In search of quality. London Business School working paper.

Dale, Barrie G., ed. 1994. *Managing quality*. 2d ed. Herts, England: Prentice Hall.

Deming, W. Edwards. 1982. *Quality, productivity, and competitive position*. Cambridge, Mass.: MIT Press.

Feigenbaum, Armand V. 1991. *Total quality control*. 3rd ed. New York: McGraw-Hill.

Garvin, David. 1988. *Managing quality*. New York: Free Press.

Geary, John F. 1993. Total quality management: A new form of labour management in Great Britain? In *Participation and involvement in Great Britain,* edited by M. Ambrosini, and L. Saba. Milan: Franco Anglei.

Giles, Eileen, and Ken Starkey. 1988. The Japanisation of Xerox: New technology. *Work and Employment* 3, no. 1:125–133.

Godfrey, Graham, and Mick Marchington. Forthcoming. Shop stewards in the 1990s: A research note. *Industrial Relations Journal.*

Guest, David E. 1995. Human resource management, trade unions, and industrial relations. In *HRM: A critical text,* edited by John Storey. London: Routledge.

Hill, Stephen. 1991. Why quality circles failed but total quality management might succeed. *British Journal of Industrial Relations* 29, no. 6:541–568.

———. 1995. From quality circles to total quality management. In *Making quality critical,* edited by Adrian Wilkinson, and Hugh Willmott. London: Routledge.

Hill, Stephen, and Adrian Wilkinson. 1995. In search of TQM. *Employee Relations* 17, no. 3:9–26.

Institute of Personnel Management. 1993. *Quality: People management matters.* London: Institute of Personnel Management.

Juran, J. M. 1988. *Quality control handbook.* 4th ed. New York: McGraw-Hill.

Kearney, A.T. 1992. *Total quality: Time to take off the rose-tinted spectacles.* Bedfordshire, England: IFS Publications in association with *TQM Magazine.*

Kelly, John, and Caroline Kelly. 1991. Them and us: Social psychology and the new industrial relations. *British Journal of Industrial Relations* 29, no. 1:25–48.

Kessler, Ian, and John Purcell. 1994. Joint problem solving and the role of third parties: An evaluation of ACAS advisory work. *Human Resource Management Journal* 14, no. 1:1–21.

Kochan, Thomas A., Jody H. Gittell, and Brenda A. Lautsch. Forthcoming. Total quality management and human resource systems: An international comparison. *International Journal of Human Resource Management.*

Lascelles, David, and Barrie Dale. 1989. The UK department of trade and industry national quality campaign: 1983 to January 1989. *International Journal of Operations and Production Management* 9, no. 6:1–46.

Legge, Karen. 1989. Human resource management: A critical analysis. In *New perspectives on human resource management,* edited by John Storey. London: Routledge.

Marchington, Mick, Adrian Wilkinson, and Barrie Dale. 1993. The case study report. In *Quality: People management matters.* London: Institute of Personnel Management.

Mohrman, Susan A., Ramkrishan V. Tenkasi, Edward E. Lawler III, and Gerald E. Ledford, Jr. 1995. Total quality management: Practice and outcomes in the largest U.S. firms. *Employee Relations* 17, no. 3:26–41.

Oakland, John S. 1989. *Total quality management.* Oxford, England: Butterworth Heinemann.

Piddington, Harley, Heather Bunny, and Barrie Dale. 1995. Rewards and recognition in quality improvement: What are the key issues? *Quality World* (March): 12-18.

Plowman, B. 1990. Management behaviour. *TQM Magazine* 2, no. 4:217–219.

Pollitt, Chris. 1993. *Managerialism and the public services.* Oxford, England: Blackwell.

Preece, David, and Michael Wood. 1995. Quality management: Who is using the sums and for what purpose? *Human Resource Management Journal* 5, no. 3:41–55.

R&D tax breaks must be part of long-term strategy. 1995. *Guardian,* 26 May.

Scase, Richard, and Robert Goffee. 1989. *Reluctant managers.* London: Unwin Hyman.

Snape, Ed, Adrian Wilkinson, and Tom Redman. Forthcoming. Paying for quality: A demeaning gesture or just desserts? *Human Resource Management Journal.*

Storey, John. 1989. *New perspectives on human resource management.* London: Routledge.

Whyte, John, and Barry Witcher. 1992. *The adoption of total quality management in Northern England.* Durham, England: Durham University Business School.

Wilkinson, Adrian. 1994. Managing human resources for quality. In *Managing quality,* edited by Barrie Dale. Hemel Hempstead, England: Prentice Hall.

Wilkinson, Adrian, and Michael Marchington. 1994. TQM—Instant pudding for the personnel function. *Human Resources Management Journal* 5, no.1:33–49.

Wilkinson, Adrian, Mick Marchington, John Goodman, and Peter Ackers. 1992. Total quality management and employee involvement. *Human Resource Management Journal* 2, no. 4:1–20.

Wilkinson, Adrian, Tom Redman, and Ed Snape. 1993. *Quality and the manager: An IM report.* Corby, England: Institute of Management.

———. 1995. New patterns of TQM in the U.K. *Quality Management Journal* (winter): 37–51.

Wilkinson, Adrian, and Barry Witcher. 1991. Fitness for use? Barriers to full TQM in the U.K. *Management Decision* 29, no. 8:46–51.

———. 1993. Holistic total quality management must take account of political processes. *Total Quality Management* 4, no. 1:47–56.

Chapter 12

Human Resources Management and TQM in Australia

Alan Brown and Amrik S. Sohal

INTRODUCTION

This chapter examines the human resource management (HRM) practices of some quality award-winning companies in Australia within the context of the HRM model as proposed by several authors.

The notion of HRM as being more than simply a change in name for personnel management has been debated for a number of years. Some see it simply as a change in title, while Beer et al. (1985) consider it to be an integrated approach to managing people that is aligned with a broad business strategy. Others, such as Legge (1991), are more cynical, expressing doubts that the enactment of HRM will actually achieve its aspirations. In practice, many organizations have simply changed the title for the same function, where HRM remains an administrative type of function rather than adopting a strategic focus.

According to Guest (1987, 503), "HRM comprises a set of policies designed to maximise organizational integration, employee commitment, flexibility and quality of work." This sounds very much like the requirements of an organization that has TQM, especially if the following quote from the Australian Quality Award (1992) guidelines is considered. The focus of the people category is on

> Examining the effectiveness of efforts to realise the full potential of people, and to maintain an environment conducive to participation, trust, teamwork, empowerment, personal leadership, personal growth, and pride in performance. (p. 17)

Guest (1987, 507) compares personnel and HRM on dimensions such as the planning perspective, psychological contract, and employee relations and roles. HRM is seen as having a long-term focus, based on employee commitment and something that is devolved to line management. Guest adds that collective industrial relations plays only a minor role in the HRM model.

Four characteristics of what can be considered a strong HRM approach are listed by Storey (1992). They are

1. Human resources (HR) make the difference and distinguish successful from less successful organizations.

2. Decisions regarding people in organizations is of strategic importance.

3. People must be the intimate concern of line managers.

4. Key levers are required to activate HRM. They are required to gain employee commitment.

Storey (1992, 35) has identified 27 points of difference between personnel and HRM around the categories of beliefs and assumptions, strategic aspects, line management, and key levers. Some are similar to those proposed by Guest and others. They include HRM as being based on unitarist ideas, customer focused, based on nurturing employees, using teamwork, and often incorporating performance-related pay.

HRM AND QUALITY

Using this as a reference point, it could be hypothesized that quality-driven organizations, and in particular quality award winners, would have adopted many of these features of what could be termed an HRM approach. Effective management of human resources is a central platform of quality management with all major national quality awards including a category devoted to people that accounts for up to 20 percent of the total points allocated to the awards. Other categories also implicitly include people.

Subcategories within the people management group in the Australian Quality Award (AQAF 1995) are

- Human resource management planning
- Employee involvement
- Performance management
- Education and training
- Well-being and morale
- Communication

Organizations are required to demonstrate their activities in these areas and how they link with a quality focus.

There is an abundance of literature that addresses the issue of links between HR and quality or the importance of HR in the quest for quality. For examples, see Bowen and Lawler (1992); Ulrich (1993); Wright and Kusmanadji (1993); and Carr (1987). Several roles for HR are usually identified and include HR as a change agent; the need to change HR practices; or the need for HR sections to practice quality principles themselves. Few examine the HR practices in leading quality organizations.

Some exceptions include Blackburn and Rosen (1993) who examined HR in U.S. Baldrige Award-winning organizations and developed a profile of 14 ideal HR practices. They also looked at various HR activities and compared these in a traditional organizational paradigm with that of a quality-focused organization.

An extensive study by Wilkinson, Marchington, and Dale (1993) examined the contribution of HR to quality in a number of U.K. organizations. They developed a model that looked at the depth and breadth of involvement of HR people in the quality push. Breadth is a measure of the range of activities for which HR plays a role in the quality push, while depth is a measure of the influence of HR principles on the development of TQM; for example, HR's contribution to TQM steering groups. Wilkinson, Marchington, and Dale's research findings suggest that HR has played a significant role in the quality-oriented organizations that they examined.

Schonberger (1994) studied the role that HR has played in major quality-focused organizations. He discussed some changes that organizations have made in areas such as jobs, teams, position titles, managers, and leadership. Shadur et al. (1994) found certain HRM practices that tended to differentiate high and low efficiency organizations in the Australian automotive industry. Organizations considered as more efficient tended to use employee welfare schemes and performance-related pay.

Storey's (1992) U.K. research found that many companies were adopting HRM and quality management. Wilkinson, Allen, and Snape (1991) suggest that TQM is consistent with HRM on several grounds. First, its emphasis is on employee commitment; second, line managers take on a key responsibility for managing people; and third, a strategic approach to managing labor is adopted. They also add that HRM is critical to the successful implementation of TQM. Furthermore, industrial relations considerations can play a significant role in TQM.

How then do quality-focused organizations align their HR strategies so that they reinforce the quality drive? One way of exploring if the ideas of HRM are being implemented in practice would be to examine some organizations that can be considered as leading edge in quality, since the criteria for major quality awards is that a strategic approach to HRM is made.

A recent Australian study (Sohal 1995) shows that a high proportion of organizations are using TQM, and there has been a substantial increase in the use of quality certification and benchmarking. These are the dominant quality practices of the 1990s and are driving the implementation of TQM and quality improvement programs in Australian industry. Disappointingly, quality management practices are still concentrated in the manufacturing function, with little increase in the use of these techniques in other areas. Around one-third of the companies indicated that quality management practices were not being used at all in the HR, administration, and marketing functions.

The following section looks at strategies used by some Australian quality-oriented companies to deploy and integrate HRM into their overall business plan. Most have either won or applied for an Australian Quality Award in recent years. All are large organizations and all except those in the public sector operate in internationally competitive marketplaces. Many are global corporations with headquarters outside Australia, and as such, face competition from not only other companies in their industry but other plants in the same company in various global locations.

Information was obtained both from interviews with senior HR managers, quality managers, and other managerial employees and by examining documented material from each organization. Private sector organizations come from the following industries: photographic and imaging, motor vehicle manufacturing, pharmaceutical manufacturing, vehicle rental, document processing, mining and mineral processing, and air conditioner manufacturing. Public sector organizations are in electricity generation and distribution, water and public buildings maintenance, design, and construction.

The discussion is presented under the following headings.

- Recruitment, Selection, and Promotion
- Training and Employee Development
- Performance Management
- Rewards and Compensation
- Employee Well-Being and Morale
- HR Specialist's Role and HR Planning
- Union-Management Relations
- Job Design, Work Organization, and Employee Involvement

The chapter concludes with a summary and two case examples that illustrate the range of activities undertaken by the companies as part of their quality improvement initiative.

RECRUITMENT, SELECTION, AND PROMOTION

A quality-focused organization requires employees and managers who are committed to quality improvement, both as individuals in their everyday activities and as members of teams. Recruitment and selection practices for new employees are based on obtaining people who display the best characteristics for working in a quality organization. These include working in a team setting and problem-solving abilities. Organizations attempt to make new recruits aware of the type of company they might be joining through job advertisements and interviews. Criteria for internal selection and promotion also provide an important message for what attributes are important.

The vehicle manufacturer uses an extensive recruitment and selection process for screening new employees and identifying those who are considered the most suitable for the company's quality culture. A list of factors that are considered to be important were developed by the HR division. These are teamwork, problem identification, problem solution, work standards, adaptability, initiative, job fit, motivation, communication, production proficiency, and practical learning. Various techniques, including aptitude tests and group exercises, are used during the recruitment process to assess a potential candidate's strength on each of these factors. Targeted interviews are used to assess behavior. New applicants are subjected to about seven hours of interviewing and assessment before an offer is made. Only one in four job applicants is successful. The HR division, which devised and used these procedures, is now devolving this task to managers throughout the company.

Beneficial outcomes reported include hiring manufacturing employees who can read and write in English and who can articulate views that are seen as fundamental to participating in teams and process improvement activities. Traditionally, the Australian manufacturing industry employed people from a diverse range of cultural backgrounds, many of whom often do not speak English. This presents communication difficulties, particularly in an environment of continuous improvement. Initial analysis found participation in improvement activities to be substantially higher along with a higher participation in training, with better results for the new recruits. Offsetting this is the extra time required to recruit and select people.

The corporate HR section of the vehicle rental company acted as a consultant to individual branches, where recruitment and selection decisions were made. Advice included using turnover statistics and exit interviews. Effort has been spent on looking for selection criteria to identify the model sales agent, who has a strong customer focus.

In the document company, recruitment and selection centers just as much on a person's values, customer focus, and people interaction attributes as their competency and technical skills. For managerial positions the emphasis is on management through people skills and a focus on teamwork. The company has started to measure such attributes and their application in the workplace and is moving away from simply measuring the results achieved.

Modified recruitment and selection criteria are particularly important for managers and supervisors to reinforce a participative style of leadership, where communication and general people management skills are more or just as important as pure technical skills. In one case, a recently appointed head of accounting in a large quality-driven public sector organization is not a qualified accountant but someone who has team and process improvement skills. These have been regarded as more important than technical skills for this senior management post.

Another method of reinforcing organizational culture, in terms of demonstrating what is important, is to build teamwork and process improvement activities into job descriptions and criteria for promotion. For example, the mining company has altered its job descriptions for supervisory staff to emphasize team and people skills as equal to technical competence. Job descriptions have been developed by a number of organizations that include a proportion of time allocated to improvement activities and teamwork. Organizations that have been certified to ISO 9000 generally find that they need to include quality activities in job descriptions.

TRAINING AND EMPLOYEE DEVELOPMENT

Training plays a particularly important role in a TQM environment for several reasons, including communicating the vision of TQM, learning the tools and techniques for problem solving, and developing skills (Brown 1993). It is widely acknowledged that introducing TQM requires awareness training to help develop appropriate attitudes and values relating to quality and teamwork.

The survey by Sohal (1995) found that provision of training in quality management practices to all employees had increased significantly, and instances of no training in quality management decreased from 10 percent in 1991 to 3 percent in 1993. Training has clearly been recognized as an important success factor in successful quality management initiatives. Professional associations such as the Australian Institute of Management, the Australian Organisation for Quality, and the Australian Quality Council, as well as consultants, are a major source of quality management training for Australian organizations. Surprisingly, only about one-fifth of Australian companies consider universities and colleges as a source of quality management training. Furthermore, nearly 14 percent of the companies said that they were aware of the availability of training for quality management but considered it to be too expensive. So what are some of the leading quality companies doing in the area of training and employee development?

The group of companies studied spends a considerable amount of time and money for training in all activities, with some spending the equivalent of up to 7 percent of their company payroll budget on training. Most large organizations have found that training tends to become focused in a quality context. Modularized programs, which identify the various types of training that each employee will be given, are usually developed. These are directed at team building and leadership for managers and supervisors, and team working and meeting procedures for operators. The various modules, which might be based on a half or full day's training, are often scheduled over a period of time so that different employees can participate according to their particular needs and stage of development in TQM. It also means less duplication for those who may have previously participated in similar programs.

Induction programs take on an increased importance both in quality awareness raising and job-specific skills. Apart from including TQM/quality in their induction programs, other information concerning job roles, health and safety, and so on are usually given increased attention.

Introducing TQM can also highlight inadequacies in training programs or simply the lack of them, illustrating the significance of Deming's sixth point. One manufacturer discovered that introducing TQM required its employees to have a greater understanding of their job and the equipment they were using in order to consider improvement opportunities through TQM. The manufacturer developed an induction program that includes job roles, people, machinery, and safety.

Education in numeracy and literacy are also often overlooked in efforts to redesign jobs and run improvement teams. Companies with a multilingual workforce tend to put considerable effort into English or other relevant language courses. Otherwise, participating in a team is rather meaningless. Some large organizations have company-sponsored English language courses for their employees. The manufacturing companies and several public sector organizations have spent considerable money in examining this issue.

The electricity company has established a joint development agreement with its unions. The agreement provides scope for continuous learning and other initiatives. Both management and unions have responsibility for continuously monitoring and progressing items in the agreement. This provides a strong commitment to training by both parties to the agreement, which is designed to produce both pay and productivity benefits. This learning encompasses skill enhancement, competency training, and both on- and off-the-job learning opportunities.

Where organizations have introduced ISO 9000 quality systems, training also takes on increased importance. Particularly, improved and ongoing training and ensuring that records are kept in order are emphasized (Brown and van der Wiele 1994). Organizations report increased attention being given to training needs analysis and better training of new employees through improved induction processes. Part of the attention given to training is associated with the need to identify and deal with any deficiencies relating to employees.

PERFORMANCE MANAGEMENT

The primary case against performance appraisal by some quality management advocates, such as Deming (1986) and Juran (1989), is generally well known and is largely based on the argument that it focuses on individual achievement (or lack thereof) without acknowledging the influence of external factors. According to Deming (1982), performance appraisal produces short-term performance, builds fear, demolishes teamwork, and nourishes rivalry and politics. None of these enhance quality improvement. (Also see Scholtes (1987).)

In the quality organizations examined here, most attention on performance appraisal systems has been directed at managerial personnel. Some are experimenting with variations to the traditional systems, with proactive rather than reactive systems, peer review, and refocusing appraisal criteria on improving processes, teamwork, and systems. Peer review, which may be based on results of employee satisfaction surveys, requires care so as not to make it a threatening process. Those who have adopted this approach have managers openly discuss both their strengths and shortcomings, as highlighted in surveys, with relevant managers and subordinates. These discussions are often placed on the agenda for team meetings and help to reinforce continuous improvement in leadership style.

Several organizations have developed a proactive system that requires managers to outline their annual development plans, which must directly relate to the organization's strategic plan. This then includes people-related factors. For example, the photography company has managers identify key result areas in their plans. These must relate to the total company strategy.

Within the vehicle rental organization, management performance is based on the achievement of both financial and individual goals with the weighting being 70:30. Individual manager's goals are focused on people, particularly on increasing employees' involvement in employee participation groups (EPGs). The results of employee opinion surveys and participation in EPGs contribute to the individual performance assessment.

Within the document company, the last three to four years has seen a shift of focus from reliance on outputs to an input-output link. Performance appraisal used to rely quite heavily on actual outcomes against an agreed plan. Now performance and development review focuses on what employees set out to do, what they achieved, how it was done, and what they learned as a result. The focus has now moved to a learning orientation. Managerial performance is assessed by examining three areas: (1) business performance, (2) HRM effectiveness, and (3) leadership in deploying and practicing leadership through quality. These became generic areas for all management reviews and succession planning. Possible ratings given to managers are role model, adequate, and needs work, with the latter being a bar to promotion.

The HR processes of induction, performance planning, review, and succession planning are all aligned to formal criteria relating to quality principles. Standards for a role model manager help to define these principles and form the basis for management practice review. Once a year staffs assess their manager's behavior against a set of practices and the manager's own assessment. These are analyzed against role model management practices, communication, and use of quality principles and tools. Strengths and weaknesses are identified and tracked on a computer system. The reviews are not linked to a performance appraisal system per se, but are used for management self-awareness and teamwork improvement.

The pharmaceutical company has attempted to make values relating to quality more behavioral so that these became more meaningful. This has been achieved by incorporating the values into the performance management system for managerial employees. Building and instilling pride in teamwork, motivating others to achieve common objectives, and communication are important attributes for managers.

The mining company's team performance recognition system is designed to provide an incentive for improving team operation and not simply focusing on the results that teams produce. It illustrates how performance can be measured on a team basis. Some of the criteria for assessment include goals and objectives, leadership, communication, meeting format, and use of the continuous improvement steps.

Appraising performance for promotion purposes is another area where organizations with quality management can make modifications. Criteria such as facilitating teamwork and communication skills, rather than the ability to meet set targets, can be used as criteria for promotion.

REWARDS AND COMPENSATION

Two compensation issues that usually emerge in organizations with quality management are how to ensure that compensation systems are not counterproductive to teamwork and continuous improvement, and how any monetary benefits resulting from quality improvements might be shared.

To address the first issue, one trend is the movement away from hourly pay rates and toward annual salaries for operational-type employees. Some manufacturing and process-type companies have found continuous improvement activities usually result in fewer problems and breakdowns so that employees on hourly rates often experience pay reductions as less overtime is available. Ultimately, employees begin to question the benefits of quality improvement if they are personally financially disadvantaged. The downside to employees of annual salaries is that if there are problems that require longer work hours, then they work on their own time.

The movement to enterprise agreements in Australia has also promoted gain-sharing and profit-sharing schemes. One small company in the metal industry has an agreement that includes quality performance measures linked to a group bonus pay scheme, whereby the whole work team can receive bonus salary increases based on a formula. The formula monitors trends in indicators such as customer complaints per ton and conversion costs per ton. This provides a different financial link with the team's continuous improvement activities.

Gain sharing may lead to financial benefits being based on individual or team efforts. The vehicle rental company developed a financial participation scheme where contribution from the company into the scheme was based on an individual's gross earnings and the company's performance. One downside was that an employee would need to leave the organization in order to gain access to the benefits. The scheme was subsequently modified to allow employees to draw from the fund. This system allowed both individual and group performance to be rewarded.

At the document company many employees are employed in a sales environment where financial incentives are an important component of the reward structure. In order to retain these incentives, but at the same time to allow greater focus on medium rather than short-term contracts, a system is used that provides group incentives to plan strategically and offers individual incentives beyond the plan.

While it is generally accepted that pay is not the most important motivator at work, recognition is an important motivational force with quality. For individuals working in teams, this may be through having their ideas acknowledged. For teams, it may be recognition or presentation at a company meeting. The use of certificates and plaques, as well as shopping vouchers, is relatively common.

EMPLOYEE WELL-BEING AND MORALE

The notion of employees as internal customers is a core principle of quality management. Sohal's 1995 survey showed that 86 percent of

Australian companies recognize both internal and external customers. Analysis showed a clear link between recognizing both internal and external customers and the adoption of TQM.

Employee welfare and satisfaction have considerable impact on the quality culture, so measuring this is seen as equally important as measuring external customer satisfaction. Formal surveys are commonly used in this respect, and many larger organizations generally conduct these surveys annually. The results from these surveys may be widely distributed or discussed in relevant work areas. In some cases, section managers may be required to discuss the findings with their employees in order to develop strategies to deal with any problems, should any exist. In other cases, results of these surveys provide improvement opportunities for teams. In most cases these are linked to managers' performance reviews.

HR SPECIALIST'S ROLE AND HR PLANNING

The evidence here suggests that the HRM specialist has been given elevated status in quality-driven companies. In all organizations studied, the HR manager or director plays a significant role. For example, he or she may carry the role of both quality and HR manager; is a member of the strategic quality team; acts as a change agent and adviser to all parts of the organization; and is constantly searching for better ways of aligning HR systems to support the organization's quality effort. Many of the organizations were paying considerable attention on assisting line managers to take responsibility for their own HR activities using quality principles. This contrasts with research by Kochan and Osterman (1991), who found the HRM function in many U.S. organizations to be weak and to exert a much lower level of influence when compared with finance, marketing, and other functions.

The pharmaceutical company places people as one category among six key business goals in its five-year plan (1994–1998). Specifically, the goal is to "attract, develop and maintain a diverse team of motivated and talented individuals working in an environment that fosters accomplishment, ownership, creativity, mutual respect and the opportunity for each person to realise their full potential." As a measure of success, two factors are used: trust and personal growth. Employee surveys are used to evaluate employee perceptions of where the company is on these dimensions. As a measure of success, the company considers a ranking of 90 percent of employees rating satisfactory or better to be a target.

The electricity company, under a new CEO in 1991, specifically set out to win an Australian Quality Award. A new HR director was given the task of developing systems and processes that would support the quality culture.

Previously, the personnel management processes had essentially been administratively focused rather than strategically focused; however, job insecurity caused by downsizing has resulted in some dissatisfaction among employees.

The vehicle manufacturer faced the challenge of implementing quality management during a period of substantial plant rationalization. This involved closing one plant, commissioning a new plant, and moving production from a third plant to the new plant. HR played a central role in this change process.

UNION-MANAGEMENT RELATIONS

HRM in a heavily unionized environment is not unusual in Australia. The mining company and one of its mineral processing plants is a good example. Faced with five unions at the site and 1200 employees, management gave the opportunity for all unions to be involved in planning and implementing changes, which included TQM. Only one union, representing about half of the employees (mainly process workers), was actively involved at the outset. The second largest, representing tradespeople, oscillated between being and not being involved. As a result, over time, the proactive union was able to secure improved benefits for its members under a workplace agreement. The nonparticipation of three unions hindered some teams, since the members were not allowed to participate.

Other examples include the electricity company negotiating enterprise deals with unions that actively promote quality improvement. Some agreements include productivity and payment measures. Enterprise bargaining has been a significant trend in Australian organizations in recent years, and has been driven by changes in the industrial relations legislation and the desire to provide increased scope for flexibility and variation in pay, conditions, and so on.

This move to enterprise bargaining may have helped foster an environment that is conducive to promoting continuous improvement. Integrating TQM into wide organizational processes, such as industrial relations, helps to ensure that process improvement becomes a permanent fixture. Some enterprise agreements incorporate TQM as part of a total package, which includes workplace and job redesign, flexibility, and productivity improvements. It offers a mechanism for achieving productivity and efficiency gains to deliver pay increases.

One enterprise agreement incorporating TQM lists three performance indicators: (1) conversion costs per ton, (2) complaint cost per ton, and (3) frequency of complaints. The agreement also provides a bonus pay system for linking improvements in these performance indicators with pay.

Employee involvement through process improvement teams provides the vehicle for continuous improvement.

A number of enterprise agreements that incorporate TQM are also being negotiated in public sector organizations. These agreements typically include measures aimed at reducing demarcation problems and improving labor flexibility to permit productivity improvements. This requires specification of measures to assess productivity gains and how these will be distributed.

Union officials can act as drivers both as a party to enterprise agreements and in actively promoting involvement to their members. In some instances, unions can become so supportive of TQM that they drive the process with the same vigor as management. In the case of some public sector organizations, relevant unions have been involved in TQM from the outset.

JOB DESIGN, WORK ORGANIZATION, AND EMPLOYEE INVOLVEMENT

Employee involvement is a central tenet of HRM. Quality-driven companies have various systems and structures that are designed to empower and involve employees. Some use suggestion schemes modeled on the Japanese systems. Others use quality and process improvement teams that may be structured on work units or cross-functional processes. The scope of activities that employees can be involved in includes safety and health; work procedures; product and service quality; work allocation; and so on.

Few examples of what could be regarded as true employee empowerment with self-directed work teams can be found. Empowerment of teams to handle decisions without the need to refer to higher authority has been shown to be an important vehicle for quality improvement.

SUMMARY AND CASE EXAMPLES

Even though the sample of organizations examined here is smaller when compared with the U.K. study by Wilkinson, Marchington, and Dale (1993), it is comparable with the U.S. sample by Blackburn and Rosen (1993).

Evidence from the Australian organizations shows that HR's involvement in TQM has considerable breadth; that is, there are a range of activities in which HR has an active involvement. HR also plays a strategic role in the quality process. For example, HR directors or managers are on steering committees or other senior-level quality committees; their advice is frequently requested; and they often perform the role of quality manager. Table 12.1 provides a summary of HR practices in Australian quality organizations.

TABLE 12.1. Summary of HRM and TQM practices in Australian quality organizations.

HR activity	TQM practices
HR role	• At a strategic level • Part of the quality team • To align HR policies/systems to support quality principles • To act as consultant to line managers
Recruitment and selection	• Ability to promote quality values • Ability to work in a team • Problem-solving skills • Job descriptions include quality
Performance management	• Individual targets linked to the organization • Proactive, not reactive approach • Focused on management-level employees • Shop floor employees evaluate their managers • Emphasis on learning, not just achieving targets
Management promotion/ performance criteria	• Promoting teamwork and communication • Focusing on customer • Developing people skills
Rewards and compensation	• Group incentives based on quality measures • Individual incentives • Recognition schemes • Movement toward annual salaries and away from hourly pay scales
Training and development	• Employee skill development • Language education • TQM tools and techniques training • Induction training
Employee well-being	• Use employee morale/satisfaction surveys • Use Occupational Health and Safety as a focus for process improvement teams
Work design	• Multiskilled work teams • Increased responsibility • Employee involvement
Industrial relations	• Enterprise agreements • Union involvement • Agreements specify quality-based measures for pay

In terms of breadth of activities, not all organizations displayed strength in all aspects of HRM, although some clearly excelled in particular areas such as recruitment, selection, and training. All companies were continually developing improved HRM practices, in particular, performance and reward systems.

All companies used employee surveys to measure morale, attitudes, satisfaction, and cultural changes. These often formed the basis of team discussions or management reviews. This displays the significance of internal customers or employees in quality-focused organizations.

Some companies have enterprise agreements that include quality management principles. In these cases, unions are actively involved in negotiations and communication concerning the quality drive. Conflict is deemphasised by focusing on win-win outcomes, but management has not intentionally tried to create a unitarist, union-free environment. Many of the features of the HRM model as espoused by Storey (1992) are displayed in the sample of organizations examined here.

This chapter provides two case examples in the closing sections. Although these do not specifically focus on the role of HRM, the cases illustrate the range of activities undertaken by the two companies as part of their quality management initiative. In both companies the role played by the HR function had been critical in achieving success. Training, communication, and employee and customer surveys have been central to achieving the cultural change necessary in TQM implementation.

TQM at Van Leer Australia

Van Leer Australia Pty. Ltd. is a subsidiary of a multinational corporation involved in the manufacture of food packaging, plastic containers, and steel drums. The company has 15,000 employees worldwide, with its headquarters situated in Amstelveen, Holland.

Van Leer Australia employs approximately 120 people in Victoria and manufactures six products, including fruit trays, paper plates, egg cartons, plastic meat trays, and plastic service trays. These are supplied in high volumes to customers in the supermarket, farming, and meat industries. Van Leer management recognizes that to effectively compete, the company must focus on improving plant efficiency, reducing inventory levels, and increasing autonomy among employees.

The name given to the Van Leer quality program is Quartet, an acronym for Quality And Reliability Through Expertise and Teamwork. It was introduced to Van Leer Australia in 1985. Its evolution was driven by senior management continually stressing its philosophy. Projects that translate to directly measurable benefits to the company were selected, and employees at almost every level were given a chance to contribute. As improvements began to happen, employees were increasingly encouraged by the results they achieved.

Senior management believes that, through this slow and steady approach, Quartet is finally becoming a way of life within the organization. For example, every senior-level meeting includes Quartet on the agenda, and employee unions have also agreed to include Quartet objectives in position descriptions.

To increase awareness, a small handbook is given to employees as part of their training. The handbook contains the six crucial points of the Quartet philosophy, an introduction to the seven quality tools, and a systematic process for problem solving.

Van Leer Australia achieved certification to AS3901/ISO 9001, *Quality Systems for Design/Development, Production, Installation and Servicing,* in April 1991.

Data on customer expectations and perceptions are obtained in three ways: (1) individual sales contacts with customers; (2) focus groups; and (3) customer surveys. The surveys were a direct result of the quality system certification program, during which a need for quantitative customer feedback was identified. Customer surveys are now conducted every six months with 10–12 key customers. They focus on three areas—perception of Van Leer as a company, product quality, and service.

Communicating customer expectations and perceptions to low levels of the organization has been a key feature of the Quartet program. This involves operators visiting key customers to obtain a better understanding of their needs.

Cross-functional improvement teams have been in place for many years at Van Leer Australia. Each team has a leader who is nominated by the steering committee, composed of top managers who oversee the quality efforts, for the duration of the project. As a matter of policy, the team leader is given the authority to implement team recommendations within the scope of the project. Selection of improvement projects at Van Leer Australia is currently based on customer feedback and internal opportunities for improvement. Training in the application of the seven quality tools has been provided to every employee. At present, these tools are generally used by project teams for problem solving.

These teams have successfully completed a number of significant improvement projects, and the results of these have been reported through several media including notice boards, the staff magazine, and internal newsletters. The most successful projects are submitted to the Van Leer International newsletter for publication.

Van Leer Australia maintains a list of approved vendors—another outcome of the quality system certification program. The company is trying to establish sole relationships with some of its vendors by working with them on mutually agreed improvement projects.

One example was a project undertaken with a major supplier of raw materials, with whom the existing contract had to be reviewed to meet Van Leer's requirements. Representatives of the supplier spent a full day at the plant in Preston to understand Van Leer's needs. In return, Van Leer personnel visited the supplier's plant to understand the production technology and constraints. The exercise clearly indicated a lack of capability on the supplier's part to meet Van Leer's production requirements. Instead of resorting to other sources, however, Van Leer worked with the supplier to arrange an agreement that would benefit both parties. This shows a change of attitude from one of apathy to one of concern. Thus, the supplier committed to invest more than $1 million in plant upgrades.

Van Leer Australia has continued to survive and improve after 10 years of TQM and Quartet, despite a worldwide recession and an environment of stiff competition. The Quartet program has enabled management of each Van Leer site to measure progress and set future improvement objectives.

TQM at Varian Australia

Varian Australia, located in Melbourne, is a wholly owned subsidiary of an international, diversified, high-technology U.S.-based corporation. Employing about 400 people in Australia, Varian Australia is a completely autonomous operation that designs, sources, manufactures, and delivers optical spectroscopy instruments. Customers include those from the environmental industry, university and research laboratories, and industrial laboratories in the chemical industry. More than 90 percent of its products are exported, mainly to Europe and the United States.

It is difficult to define a starting point for TQM in Varian Australia. It is an organization which, for almost two decades, has focused on quality in its products and manufacturing processes. Various manufacturing programs, including just-in-time (JIT) and value-added management (VAM), have helped to provide a professional approach to manufacturing. Several quality-specific programs have been tried over the past few years. The current endeavor, called Continuous Improvement Process (CIP), was started in late 1991 and is seen to be the most effective program to date. The CIP initiative has enabled a quality organization to be established. This initiative has provided effective training, control, and monitoring of quality improvement activities. Some strengths of the CIP approach are

- Focus on satisfying both external and internal customers.
- Use a formal quality council, rather than the quality manager.

- Form natural work teams as the principal vehicle for continuous improvement (as distinct from cross-functional teams whose specific objectives are to solve problems).
- Emphasize getting runs on the board for small projects involving daily work.
- Use the train-the-trainer concept through to the shop floor.
- Support the goals of the worldwide operational excellence approach to business.

Varian Austrilia began by identifying the specific needs to be addressed by the program. Key areas included team building, process improvement, and problem-solving skills. A vision-setting workshop was then held for senior managers, at which the strategy to achieve the goal of becoming the supplier of first choice was discussed. The content of further training modules, strategies to meet operational excellence goals, and to launch the program were also planned.

Further courses were held to provide training for other managers and to facilitate implementation planning. One outcome of these activities was the appointment of a program manager to oversee CIP. Another outcome was the appointment of internal trainers to conduct further training within the organization. Two pilot teams were then identified, one consisting of senior managers only. Each team selected an improvement project to manage.

Full implementation and training followed for the rest of the organization. The first to be trained were indirect employees, followed by direct employees. While being trained, teams also started on their individual improvement projects. Progress is reviewed on a quarterly basis by the program manager and trainers, using information from internal surveys.

In November 1992, Varian Australia obtained certification to AS3901/ ISO 9001. Benefits resulting from this includes the following:

- Better control of processes, resulting in consistency from design through to delivery
- Increased measurement of performance, such as scrap rates
- Disciplined approach to business
- Increased need for TQM into other areas

A key competitive strategy of Varian Australia is to continually market new and improved products. As a company dealing with high-technology equipment, product specifications are inevitably well defined. Specifications are developed from data obtained from several sources including the following:

- Customer advisory boards established in several countries

- Surveys conducted worldwide with the Varian sales force
- Six monthly surveys conducted with selected customers
- Innovative ideas from within the company
- Competitive analysis

Four key indicators that relate to customer wants are used by Varian Austrialia. These are

1. On-time delivery of complete systems
2. Quick delivery response
3. Product quality
4. Number of warranty incidents per unit

To obtain this data, survey cards accompanying products sold are sent to customers.

Whereas the CIP program is primarily aimed at improving processes, Varian Australia has another well-established system to attack product problems. Corrective action teams (CATs) were started in August 1986 in most production lines. Generally, CATs consist of employees working in the same area as well as some cross-functional members. The teams meet once a week to discuss problems, as well as to implement other improvement initiatives in their work areas. Initially, the inputs to CAT meetings were internal problems, but the majority are now from worldwide field reports received through electronic mail. CATs have been instrumental in addressing product problems. Since their inception, CATs have resolved all but 200 of the more than 2000 problems identified (as of September 1992).

Varian Australia believes the CATs have played a significant role in making continuous improvement to products and operations. They have also allowed just-in-time performance to be achieved and have reduced warranty costs. With the CIP program extending to nonproduction areas, Varian Australia is aiming to make continuous improvement a way of life throughout the organization.

Varian initiated a value-managed relationships (VMR) program with its vendors in 1991. An objective of the VMR program is to rationalize the number of vendors that supply the 5000 active parts to the factory, and thereafter to move toward sole supplier relationships. To realize this goal, several initiatives have been undertaken, including conducting seminars with vendors to introduce VMR, training selected vendors to reduce their setup times, and implementing just-in-time (JIT) purchasing. Other measures include the tracking of on-time delivery performance for all suppliers on the VMR program.

Varian Australia is an organization that believes everything should be measured. Many graphs on display throughout the factory strengthen statistical thinking among employees. Approximately every two years, employees are retrained in the use of quality tools so that it has now become a standard way of solving problems. Supervisors have benefited through closer cross-functional links with other departments and CATs, and an increased team spirit among themselves.

A number of methods to recognize achievement are used. These include monthly *Operational Excellence* newsletters, storyboards displayed on notice boards for each team, and quarterly team presentations to the quality council.

Together with CIP, Varian Australia had to implement several major programs such as JIT and VMR. Effective organization as well as the ability and teamwork of senior managers are considered to be the critical factors in the successful management of these overlapping programs.

REFERENCES

Australian Quality Awards Foundation Limited. *Australian quality awards 1995 application guidelines.* Sydney: Australian Quality Awards Foundation.

Beer, Michael, B. Spector, P. Lawrence, D. Quinn Mills, and R. Walton. 1985. *Human resource management: A general manager's perspective.* Glencoe, Ill.: Free Press.

Blackburn, Richard, and Benson Rosen. 1993. Total quality and human resources management: Lessons learned from Baldrige Award-winning companies. *Academy of Management Executive* (August): 49–65.

Bowen, David E., and Edward E. Lawler. 1992. Total quality-oriented human resources management. *Organizational Dynamics* (spring): 29–41.

Brown, Alan. 1993. TQM: Implications for training. *Industrial and Commercial Training* 25, no. 1:20–26.

Brown, Alan, and Tom van der Wiele. 1994. Survey of western Australian experiences with ISO 9000. Working paper. Perth, Australia: Faculty of Business, Edith Cowan University.

Carr, Clay. 1987. Injecting quality into personnel management. *Personnel Journal* 66, no. 9:45–51.

Deming, W. Edwards. 1982. *Quality, productivity, and competitive position.* Cambridge, Mass.: MIT Press.

Guest, David. 1987. Human resource management and industrial relations. *Journal of Management Studies* 24, no. 5:503–521.

Juran, Joseph M. 1989. *Juran on leadership for quality.* New York: Free Press.

Kochan, Thomas A., and Paul Osterman. 1991. *Human resource development and utilization: Is there too little in the U.S.?* Paper presented for the Time Horizons Project of the Council on Competitiveness at the Massachusetts Institute of Technology, Cambridge, Massachusetts.

Legge, Karen. 1991. Human resource management: A critical analysis. In *New perspectives on human resource management,* edited by John Storey. London: Routledge.

Scholtes, Peter R. 1987. *An elaboration on Deming's teachings on performance appraisal.* Madison, Wis.: Joiner Associates.

Schonberger, Richard J. 1994. Human resource management: Lessons from a decade of total quality management and reengineering. *California Management Review* 36, no. 4:109–123.

Shadur, Mark A., John J. Rodwell, David E. Simmons, and Greg J. Bamber. 1994. International best practice, quality management and high performance: Influences from the Australian automotive sector. *International Journal of Human Resources Management* 3, no. 3:609–632.

Sohal, Amrik S. 1995. *Quality practices in Australian manufacturing firms.* Melbourne: Monash University and Cleveland, Ohio: Ernst & Young.

Storey, John. 1992. *Developments in the management of human resources.* Oxford, England: Blackwell.

Ulrich, Dave. 1993. A new HR mission: Guiding the quality mindset. *HR Magazine* 38, no. 12:51–54.

Wilkinson, Adrian, Peter Allen, and Ed Snape. 1991. TQM and the management of labour. *Employee Relations* 13, no. 1:24–31.

Wilkinson, Adrian, Mick Marchington, and Barrie Dale. 1993. Enhancing the contribution of the human resource management function to quality improvement. *Quality Management Journal* (October): 35–46.

Wright, Phillips C., and K. Kusmanadji. 1993. The strategic application of TQM principles to human resources management. *Training for Quality* 1, no. 3:5–14.

Chapter 13

Workforce Diversity and TQM

Stephen B. Knouse and David Chretien

The concepts of workforce diversity and total quality management (TQM) are two powerful forces in American business today. Although different in emphasis, both arose as reactions to the business status quo at the time. Business involvement with diversity began with the 1960s civil rights movement as a reaction against employment discrimination. While originally emphasizing race, equal employment opportunity (EEO) and affirmative action (AA) programs have added gender, ethnicity, and the disabled along the way (Twomey 1990).

Now diversity is expanding to include age (senior citizens as well as teenagers) and single parenthood. Indeed, US West defines diversity very broadly as

> A culture that promotes mutual respect, acceptance, teamwork and productivity among people who are diverse in work background, experience, education, age, gender, race, ethnic origin, physical abilities, religious belief, sexual affectional orientation and other perceived differences . . . . Diversity mirrors the communities in which we work and the customers we serve. (Caudron 1992, 40)

Several companies, such as Xerox, Kellogg, Avon, Chrysler, and Johnson & Johnson, have instituted equity management programs where corporate goals and AA goals are balanced in an environment of positive leadership support. For example, Xerox has integrated an aggressive AA hiring policy with a balanced workforce strategy for quality and productivity, which has resulted in one of the highest percentages of minorities in senior management positions among major U.S. companies (Yates 1993).

TQM strives for the "constant attainment of consumer satisfaction through . . . continuous improvement of organizational processes, resulting in high quality products and services" (Sashkin and Kiser 1991, 25). TQM in American business originated in the 1980s as a reaction against corporate overemphasis on producing quantity and an underemphasis on producing quality. While many see it as a set of statistical tools, such as statistical process control, others see TQM in people terms (Evans and Lindsay 1996). They view TQM as a set of values, such as commitment to quality and innovation. Moreover, they see successful TQM requiring interpersonal skills, such as teamwork, mutual respect, cooperation from employees, and leadership from managers (Bowen and Lawler 1992). Ultimately, TQM creates a corporate culture of shared employee values of quality and customer service (Blackburn and Rosen 1993).

When TQM is viewed from a people perspective, the linkages between TQM and workforce diversity become evident. Moreover, the authors can go further and propose that good TQM practice requires workforce diversity. In other words, a heterogeneous workforce may be a precursor to successful TQM.

ORGANIZATIONAL EXAMPLES OF DIVERSITY AND TQM

There have been surprisingly few direct attempts at tying diversity and TQM. A few successful TQM companies, however, have already emphasized the importance of diversity.

Motorola

Motorola was a 1988 winner of the Malcolm Baldrige National Quality Award (MBNQA). Motorola is well known for its Six Sigma program integrating measures of total customer satisfaction, strategic planning, participative management, and statistical controls. Motorola, however, also emphasizes employee diversity. It wants to attract the best and brightest workforce from the rich diversity of American citizenry (Donnelly 1992).

To accomplish this goal, Motorola targets recruiting toward diverse groups. In addition, it has programs for management development of women and minorities, for helping female employees balance work and family life, for outreach to diverse groups in the community, and for scholarships. To show its commitment to the management of diversity, Motorola named the CEO as the corporate champion for diversity. As a consequence, Motorola has won a number of awards including the U.S. Secretary of Labor Opportunity 2000 Award and was named one of the top 100 companies by *Working Mothers* magazine (Donnelly 1992).

Federal Express

Federal Express won the 1990 MBNQA. Although it had to show excellence in all seven sections of the award criteria, Federal Express was particularly attentive to section four: human resources development and management. Its focus is on improving the morale and well-being of employees as internal customers. To do this, Federal Express instituted a Safe Practices program for handling potentially dangerous goods and an extensive injury-reporting system.

In addition, Federal Express goes to great lengths to avoid employee layoffs. This is particularly important for the management of diversity because women and minorities, who many times are among the most recently hired, are particularly susceptible to layoffs. Further, Federal Express has a guaranteed fair treatment procedure that allows employees to appeal any issue to higher management. One consequence for management of diversity is that Federal Express has standardized minimum job requirements in order to guarantee fair assessment of qualifications of job applicants (Hart and Bogan 1992).

Oregon State University

Oregon State University has one of the most extensive TQM efforts in higher education. All facets of the university, not just academics, are involved in the TQM program. To show commitment to diversity, Oregon State has as one of its basic goals in its TQM strategic plan to expand opportunities to minorities, females, and the disabled. To meet this goal, Oregon State emphasizes recruitment of faculty, staff, and students from diverse groups. It strives for pay equity for women and minorities. And it is creating a campus environment conducive to the needs of diverse groups. In addition, Oregon State is trying to make the surrounding community increasingly attractive to diverse groups (Coate 1990).

Ford Australia

Australia is in a unique position. Its heritage is European, while it is geographically and economically tied to Asia. In order to trade with Asian countries, Australian companies must emphasize quality products. Ford Australia has a successful TQM program, called Q1, that defines quality in terms of maximizing customer satisfaction and minimizing production errors. It even employs a "Things Gone Wrong" check sheet. Ford Australia also uses innovative techniques, such as just-in-time (JIT) production management (Mathews 1991).

In the last 20 years, Australia has experienced large migrations of workers from Asian countries, such as Malaysia, and from Eastern Europe.

Consequently, the workforce of many Australian manufacturers is very eth-nically diverse. In fact, according to quality manager Doug Pederson, Ford Australia must issue its production notices in seven languages for employ-ees on the shop floor.

ADVANTAGES OF WORKFORCE DIVERSITY

A diverse workforce, composed of males and females, young and old employees, different ethnic groups, as well as other groups, can provide sev-eral unique advantages for a TQM program.

1. *Widely diverse perspectives (skills, knowledge, and experience).* Successful TQM depends on a multiskilled workforce (Bowen and Lawler 1992). Diverse employee groups possess a variety of acquired work skills, knowledge of products and processes, and experience with work tech-niques. Further, their diverse backgrounds present a wide range of aptitudes for skills training, which is so important to TQM.

2. *Diverse inputs into quality teams.* TQM relies on quality teams to monitor processes, identify problems, and arrive at solutions. The emphasis is usually on cross-functional teams in order to cover all important aspects of a quality problem (Evans and Lindsay 1996). Ensuring diverse work-force representation on teams, however, provides a number of different (and hence richer) perspectives on defining the problems, approaches to problems, and arriving at possible solutions (Sessa and Jackson 1995). Moreover, diversity produces broader critical thinking (Nemeth 1985), greater creativity (Cox, Lobel, and McCleod 1991), and greater innova-tion (Triandis, Dunnette, and Hough 1994) in group decision making. Indeed, the most effective diverse groups are able to appreciate their own members' different points of view; that is, the group knows how to focus on the views of appropriate group members in order to find the optimal perspective on a problem (Triandis, Kurowski, and Gelfand 1994).

3. *Input for TQM tools.* TQM uses a variety of problem solving tools, such as cause-and-effect diagrams, flowcharts, Pareto charts, and brain-storming (Evans and Lindsay 1996). A diverse workforce can enhance the use of these tools. For example, research has shown that heterogeneous groups (members with different needs, personalities, orientation, and back-ground) produce high-quality problem solving because they stimulate each other's abilities. Moreover, heterogeneous groups are particularly effective on complex tasks that require diverse problem-solving approaches (Szilagyi and Wallace 1990), which directly describes many quality problems. In the TQM setting, then, diversity as well as cross functionality should be con-sidered when composing quality teams.

4. *Diversity as a key to meeting customer needs.* Ultimately the customer drives the TQM effort; customer needs define quality for the TQM organization (Deming 1986). A diverse workforce has a large representation of the many types of customers American businesses serve. Such a workforce will better know and understand the needs of a diverse customer base. Moreover, these employees provide unique insights into the backgrounds of different customer groups that can be useful in understanding consumer decision making (Cox 1993). For example, the consumer behavior of Hispanics is influenced by the strength of identification with their ethnic group (Deshpande, Hoyer, and Donthu 1986).

Avon has found that its most profitable markets are customers in the inner city. Consequently, some of its top producers are African-American and Hispanic salespeople and managers who understand these markets. To facilitate its linkage with its markets, Avon sponsors a multicultural participation council where diversity issues concerning both internal and external customers can be aired (Cox and Blake 1991).

If the company is in the service sector, customers may feel more comfortable, and hence better served, if they see company employees similar to them. Further, if customers have particular needs, such as the need to translate information from one language to another for ethnic groups, workers of the same ethnic group may be the only employees who could fulfill this need. For example, US West focuses on Hispanic resource groups to help them understand and service the Hispanic market in the Southwest (Caudron 1992).

5. *Helping to diversify the surrounding community.* As a stakeholder in the surrounding community, TQM organizations directly affect employees as internal customers and clients and community groups as external customers. In diversifying its own workforce, TQM companies enrich the surrounding community. TQM companies can support activities of these diverse groups in the community through events such as concerts, plays, and community ethnic fairs. For example, Oregon State, as a cultural force in the community, emphasizes diversity in its community outreach activities (Coate 1990). And US West contributes financially to local and national ethnic groups (Caudron 1992).

ENSURING DIVERSE EMPLOYEE PARTICIPATION IN TQM

There are several techniques that serve both the goals of workforce diversity and TQM.

Top management support. TQM is a top-down approach to quality improvement, where top leadership drives the improvement process through modeling quality values for the organization, emphasizing quality in the strategic plan, and allocating resources to quality enhancement practices (Deming 1986). Similarly, effective diversity management requires top management support. In fact, recent research shows that strong top management backing, through modeling diversity values, allocating resources for diversity training, and emphasizing the benefits of a diverse workforce, is one of the primary factors in successful diversity programs (Rynes and Rosen 1995).

Hiring. American companies use a variety of means to increase workforce diversity: targeted recruiting; partnerships with educational institutions; partnerships with community groups; recruiting incentives; and internships (Morrison 1992). Many organizations also have AA plans for hiring. Bringing together AA goals and TQM in documents, such as policy statements, reinforces the commitment of the company both to workforce diversity and to excellence in quality. For example, Motorola emphasizes both in its human resources documents (Donnelly 1992). Federal Express supports diversity hiring through its guaranteed fair treatment procedure. Moreover, to emphasize teamwork, Federal Express maintains 18 recruitment centers where applicants are screened by possible peers (Blackburn and Rosen 1993). Once diverse groups are hired, Federal Express gives them time to establish themselves through its no-layoff policy.

Some companies, such as Xerox, have employed outside consultants to help them develop their equity management programs within the framework of their corporate productivity and quality goals. One prominent source of outside assistance is the American Institute for Managing Diversity affiliated with Morehouse College (Yates 1993).

An interesting experimental study by Williams and Bauer (1994) showed that potential recruits were positively attracted to a company if its recruiting materials stressed its diversity management programs. Most important, all groups—including white males—were positively influenced by these materials. Indeed, McDonald's stresses that diversity management adds value to the corporation (Solomon 1989) through its diversity programs.

Training. One of the unique features of TQM is its emphasis on extensive training for all employees (Bowen and Lawler 1992). This lends itself particularly well to skill building in diverse employee groups. Instead of focusing training on the homogeneous group of managers as do many American companies, TQM companies have goals for training time and expenditures for all employees. For example, Corning has a goal of two hours a week for TQM skills training for every employee (Shrednick, Shutt, and Weiss 1992). Xerox requires 28 hours of basic TQM training and has devoted $125 million to quality training, while Federal Express has 650 full-time trainers at sites around the world (Blackburn and Rosen 1993).

Effective training depends on effective assessment of individual training needs (Goldstein 1993). Moreover, TQM organizations must gauge individual employee skill development needs. Granite Rock Construction Company, a 1992 MBNQA winner in the small company category, accomplishes this through its Individual Professional Development Plan (see chapter 7). Employees meet with supervisors to define job requirements, review accomplishments, assess skill levels, and set skill development goals. Management then uses these data to plan external education and internal training programs (Caudron 1993). AT&T Consumer Communications Services, a 1994 MBNQA winner, combines training and restructuring activities. It provides new skills training and foreign language training to help employees relocate to new positions within the company (Phelps-Feldkamp 1994).

Communication. Open, direct communication is one of the key factors in successful TQM (Bowen and Lawler 1992). At the same time, increased communications difficulties and subsequent misunderstandings are one of the major hurdles in managing diversity (Rosen and Lovelace 1991; Cox 1993; Triandis, Kurowski, and Gelfand 1994). Management must have close informational links to employee teams, and these teams must be able to communicate within themselves and with each other. Ethnically diverse employee groups may have language problems that require additional training in English.

Communication problems, however, can also exist for employees for whom English is their first and only language. Old and young employees can misunderstand each other, and men and women can misunderstand the intention of communications. The upshot is that both management and quality team leaders should have their written communications read by diverse groups of employees to ensure that everyone shares the same meaning. Further, employees should be encouraged to express their concerns when difficulties arise (Christensen-Hughes 1992).

Motorola communicates with employees through a variety of media: electronic mail, talk sessions, town hall meetings, site publications, and video news magazines. To ensure that these messages are being received, Motorola uses focus groups and surveys of employees (Donnelly 1992). Federal Express uses in-house television networks where employees can call in questions to managers (Blackburn and Rosen 1993).

Employee-customer linkages. One of the major advantages of a diverse workforce is that it relates well to the diverse customer base of many companies. TQM organizations should emphasize direct links between its employees and target customer groups. For example, companies can recommend that employees join and participate in various specialized community groups. Thus, employees of certain ethnic, gender, and age groups can establish closer ties to those groups in the community. US West encourages African-American, Hispanic, Native American, and female employee groups to participate in its Pluralism Calendar of Events (Caudron 1992).

Rewards and recognition. Diverse teams should experience the rewards of successful interaction. This can be enhanced by organizing mutually enjoyable activities for team members, such as dinners, parties, or sporting events (Triandis, Kurowski, and Gelfand 1994).

TQM emphasizes employees working together in an atmosphere of mutual respect and cooperation. It is logical then that employees should share credit for accomplishments. Awards should focus on team efforts. For example, Motorola brings its total customer satisfaction teams together from its plants all over the world to compete in a quality Olympics. The finalists are published in a company booklet that describes their accomplishments and has color pictures of team members (Motorola 1992).

Best practices. TQM emphasizes that knowledge about the best practices of industry be disseminated through such techniques as benchmarking (Hart and Bogan 1992). In like fashion, the best practices of diversity management should be made known both within and between industries. Coopers & Lybrand, a large consulting firm, highlights the best practices of diversity management both of its own local offices and of other firms. It distributes information about these practices through a central clearinghouse. In addition, it provides training materials to groups desiring to try these practices (Deluca and McDowell 1992). Furthermore, organizations are cooperating to form interfirm diversity councils for the purpose of sharing ideas and training techniques (Reynolds 1992).

PROBLEMS WITH DIVERSITY

Diversity management is not without its problems. Some organizations are confused about what constitutes diversity management; they see it as simply EEO/AA with another name or as a focus only on women and minorities, according to a 1993 *HR Focus* article. Moreover, some research shows that greater workforce diversity is associated with a higher rate of absenteeism and turnover (Triandis, Kurowski, and Gelfand 1994). Indeed, the underlying factor appeared to be a lack of organizational commitment (Jackson, et al. 1991). The answer would seem to be to find some commonality of values among diverse individuals upon which organizational commitment can be built (Cox and Blake 1991). The emphasis in TQM on the values of customer commitment and continuous improvement might serve as a common focal point for such organizational commitment.

Even at the team level, diversity may create problems. Teams may start out on the wrong course if members do not initially feel comfortable with one another (De Valk 1993). Stress can result (Triandis, Kurowski, and Gelfand 1994). Discussion of differences and similarities early on can help, particularly if a facilitator can lead the team members around sensitive issues and prevent the discussion from degenerating into a gripe session about EEO/AA.

There may also be team problems over time. An interesting longitudinal study of racially and ethnically heterogeneous groups showed that such groups were less effective than homogeneous groups for the first 17 weeks of operation. For example, they had trouble agreeing on what was important and working together. After 17 weeks, however, the heterogeneous groups exceeded the homogeneous groups on some performance measures, such as range of ideas and perspectives (Watson, Kumar, and Michaelsen 1993). Apparently, diverse teams require a long start-up time until they are cohesive enough to run smoothly. This may require extended team-building training over several months. In addition, conflicts due to diversity may arise over time. Monsanto has addressed this problem through its pairs consulting program. Here, pairs of males and females or pairs of African-Americans and whites attempt to help resolve conflicts due to diversity among employees through the greater range of perspectives they provide (Laabs 1993).

These initial start-up problems within diverse teams may indicate that JIT training may be particularly effective for ensuring that the teams stay on track in solving quality problems. JIT programs deliver training as needed for the team, rather than overwhelming the group with substantial initial training. Coca-Cola, for example, starts teams with training on listening skills, brainstorming, and role taking. When the teams begin to coalesce into cohesive groups, training shifts to quality tools, such as data gathering and analysis and statistical process control (Caudron 1993).

DEALING WITH RESISTANCE TO DIVERSITY MANAGEMENT

Unfortunately for some employees, diversity management efforts have been linked to negative feelings about EEO/AA. Perhaps they see EEO/AA in terms of government regulation or legalistic machinations, or perhaps they have had personal experiences with discrimination (or reverse discrimination) that were not resolved by EEO/AA mechanisms to their satisfaction or perhaps even enhanced the problem. For whatever the reason, there may be negative attitudes toward EEO/AA that spill over into diversity management efforts.

One way that management might deal with such resistance is through an effort that (1) de-emphasizes the linkage of diversity management with the governmental and legalistic aspects of the entrenched EEO/AA; and (2) reemphasizes the importance of diversity to quality efforts and thus, in the larger sense, to doing good business.

1. *Write diversity management policy in terms of quality.* It would be a mistake in policy statements and in pronouncements to employees to portray diversity management as simply an extension of EEO/AA. Rather, top management should present diversity efforts as linked directly to quality efforts through the mechanism of achieving customer satisfaction. There should be strong statements that in order to understand what customers want, the organization must appreciate the diversity inherent in customer demands. In other words, customers must not be seen a monolithic group but rather as one composed of diverse segments with differing demands and requirements for products and services.

2. *Employ team-building exercises that focus on diversity appreciation.* Quality teams must develop cohesiveness if they are to work through complex quality problems. Therefore, the team-building stage, where cohesiveness is coalescing, is a good point at which to introduce an appreciation for team member diversity. One type of exercise that has been successfully used over a number of years involves superordinate (shared) goals where team members are forced to cooperate in order to achieve the goals (Aronson and Gonzalez 1988; Triandis, Kurowski, and Gelfand 1994; Triandis 1995). For example, team members must solve a problem where different subgroups (for example, males and females) each have parts to the problem but cannot solve the problem without the essential parts from the other subgroups in the team. As a consequence, the team learns that each subgroup may have vital information and that team members must work together using all this information if they are to succeed.

3. *Emphasize cooperative learning among team members.* Appreciation for individual member skills can also occur through emphasizing cooperative learning (Triandis 1995). Team members help each other in learning situations where they possess particular skills important for task mastery.

4. *Allow team members to interact with different types of external customers.* When team members have learned how diversity within their team may enhance success, they are ready to approach external customers. Management might require that team members contact customers who are

different in age, gender, race, or ethnicity in order to see firsthand that the customer's view of what is a satisfying product or service may be different from what the team member believes based upon his or her past experience. In order to reduce misunderstanding or missteps, at least initially, pairs of team members might contact customers where one team member is similar to the customer. For example, borrowing Monsanto's pair concept (Laabs 1993), a male and female pair may contact a female customer, or a young and old pair may contact a senior citizen customer. Thus, the customer may be willing to talk if he or she perceives that one of the pair may have a similar view of the world.

CONCLUSION

A workforce that is diverse in gender, race, ethnicity, and other unique characteristics is a valuable asset for a TQM organization. Diversity enriches the corporate culture through breadth of skills, values, and approaches to problems. TQM organizations should stress diversity in their strategic plans, practice diversity in their human resources activities, and recognize diversity in their internal and external communications.

REFERENCES

Aronson, Eliot, and A. Gonzalez. 1988. Segregation, jigsaw, and the Mexican-American experience. In *Eliminating racism*, edited by P. A. Katz and D. T. Taylor. New York: Plenum.

Blackburn, Richard, and Benson Rosen. 1993. Total quality and human resources management: Lessons learned from Baldrige Award-winning companies. *Academy of Management Executive* 8, no. 3:49–66.

Bowen, David E., and Edward E. Lawler III. 1992. Total quality-oriented human resources management. *Organizational Dynamics* (spring): 29–41.

Caudron, Shari. 1992. US West finds strength in diversity. *Personnel Journal* (March): 40–44.

———. 1993. How HR drives TQM. *Personnel Journal* (August): 48B–48O.

Christensen-Hughes, Jonathan. 1992. Cultural diversity: The lessons of Toronto's hotels. *Cornell Hotel and Restaurant Administration Quarterly* (April): 78–87.

Coate, Larry E. 1990. *Implementation of total quality management in a university setting*. Corvallis, Oreg.: Oregon State University.

Cox, Taylor H. 1993. *Cultural diversity in organizations: Theory, research, and practice.* San Francisco: Berrett-Koehler.

Cox, Taylor H., and S. Blake. 1991. Managing cultural diversity: Implications for organizational competitiveness. *Academy of Management Executive* 5, no. 3:45–46.

Cox, Taylor H., Sharon A. Lobel, and Poppy L. McLeod. 1991. Effects of ethnic group cultural differences on cooperative and competitive behavior on a group task. *Academy of Management Journal* (December): 827–847.

Deluca, J. M., and R. N. McDowell. 1992. Managing diversity. In *Diversity in the workplace,* edited by S. E. Jackson and Associates. New York: Guilford Press.

Deming, W. Edwards. 1986. *Out of the crisis.* Cambridge, Mass: MIT Center for Advanced Engineering Study.

Deshpande, Robit, Wayne N. Hoyer, and Naveen Donthu. 1986. The study of ethnic affiliation: A study of the sociology of Hispanic consumption. *Journal of Consumer Research* 13, no. 2:214–220.

De Valk, Steve. 1993. Holding up a mirror to diversity issues. *Training and Development* (July): 11–12.

Donnelly, James. 1992. *The quality of people at Motorola.* Schaumburg, Ill.: Motorola.

Evans, James R., and William M. Lindsay. 1996. *The management and control of quality.* 3d ed. Minneapolis: West Publishing.

Goldstein, Irwin L. 1993. *Training in organizations.* 3d ed. New York: Brooks/Cole.

Hart, Christopher W. L., and Christopher E. Bogan. 1992. *The Baldrige.* New York: McGraw-Hill.

Jackson, Susan E., J. F. Brett, Valerie I. Sessa, D. M. Cooper, J. A. Julin, and K. Peyronnin. 1991. Some differences make a difference: Individual dissimilarity and group heterogeneity as correlates of recruitment, promotions, and turnover. *Journal of Applied Psychology* 76, no. 5:675–679.

Laabs, Jennifer J. 1993. Employees manage conflict and diversity. *Personnel Journal* (December): 30–36.

Mathews, John. 1991. *Ford Australia plastics plant: Transition to teamwork through quality enhancement.* Kensington, New South Wales, Australia: University of New South Wales.

More businesses look at diversity as an obligation, not as a choice. 1993. *HR Focus* (October): 14.

Morrison, Anne M. 1992. *The new leaders: Guidelines on leadership diversity in America.* San Francisco: Jossey-Bass.

Motorola. 1992. *Total customer satisfaction team competition.* Schaumburg, Ill.: Motorola.

Nemeth, C. J. 1985. Dissent, group process, and creativity. *Advances in Group Processes* 2:57–75.

Phelps-Feldkamp, Diane. 1994. *AT&T Consumer Communications Services: 1994 Malcolm Baldrige National Quality Award winner.* Gaithersburg, Md.: National Institute of Standards and Technology.

Reynolds, Larry. 1992. Companies work together on workforce diversity. *HR Focus* (December): 17.

Rosen, Benson, and Kay Lovelace. 1991. Piecing together the diversity puzzle. *HR Magazine* (June): 78–84.

Rynes, Sara, and Benson Rosen. 1995. A field survey of factors affecting the adoption and perceived success of diversity training. *Personnel Psychology* (summer): 247–270.

Sashkin, Marshall, and Kenneth J. Kiser. 1991. *Total quality management.* Seabrook, Md.: Ducochon Press.

Sessa, Valerie I., and Susan E. Jackson. 1995. Diversity in decision-making teams. In *Diversity in organizations,* edited by Martin M. Chemers, Stuart Oskamp, and Mark A. Costanzo. Thousand Oaks, Calif.: Sage.

Shrednick, Harvey R., R. J. Shutt, and M. Weiss. 1991. Empowerment. *MIS Quarterly* 16, no. 4:491–505.

Solomon, Charlene M. 1989. The corporate response to work force diversity. *Personnel Journal* (August): 42–53.

Szilagyi, Andrew J., and Marc J. Wallace. 1990. *Organizational behavior and performance.* 5th ed. Glenview, Ill.: Scott, Foresman.

Triandis, Harry C. 1995. A theoretical framework for the study of diversity. In *Diversity in organizations,* edited by Martin M. Chemers, Stuart Oskamp, and Mark A. Costanzo. Thousand Oaks, Calif.: Sage.

Triandis, Harry C., Lois L. Kurowski, and Michele J. Gelfand. 1994. Workplace diversity. In *Handbook of industrial and organizational psychology,* edited by Harry C. Triandis, Marvin D. Dunnette, and Leaetta M. Hough. Volume 4, 2d ed. Palo Alto, Calif.: Consulting Psychologists Press.

Twomey, David E. 1990. *Equal employment opportunity law.* 2d ed. Cincinnati, Ohio: South-Western.

Watson, Warren E., Kamlesh Kumar, and Larry K. Michaelsen. 1993. Cultural diversity's impact on interaction process and performance: Comparing homogeneous and diverse task groups. *Academy of Management Journal* (October): 590–602.

Williams, M. L., and T. N. Bauer. 1994. The effect of a managing diversity policy on organizational attractiveness. *Group and Organizational Management* 3, no. 3:295–308.

Yates, William T. 1993. Equity management. *Change* (March/April): 40.

Part IV

Summary

Chapter 14

Bringing It All Together: Concepts, Practices, and Benchmarks

Stephen B. Knouse

Now that these different perspectives on human resource management (HRM) and total quality management (TQM) have been examined, what do they all mean? Obviously all of the authors' principles, concerns, and ideas cannot be distilled into one chapter. Rather, in this chapter what the authors offer is compared by looking at similarities and differences in their various concepts, techniques, and practices. Then, the fairly diverse material is integrated using benchmarking; that is, the new ideas are summarized that readers may want to copy, try out, modify, and build on.

HRM AND TQM: LOOKING FOR SIMILARITIES AND DIFFERENCES

A recent special issue of the *Academy of Management Review*, one of the top journals of management theory, was devoted exclusively to the interrelationships between management theory and TQM principles (Klimoski 1994). The lead article categorized TQM and HRM along three dimensions: concepts, practices, and techniques (Dean and Bowen 1994). This book unfolds along similar dimensions: Concepts, practices, and techniques are in Parts I and II. Part III expands both concepts and practices along an international-diversity dimension. Thus, this special issue will be used as a backdrop for looking at how the various authors present their ideas in this book.

Concepts

The authors describe how TQM addresses a number of traditional HRM areas.

Leadership and the organization. Among the shared concepts covered in the special issue of *Academy of Management Review,* leadership was the most strongly stressed in both traditional management theory and TQM (Dean and Bowen 1994). Visionary leadership at the top is emphasized in both camps (Anderson, Rungtusanatham, and Schroeder 1994). There is a contrast, however, in the perceived roles of management. Traditional management theory stresses directing and controlling activities, while TQM theorists emphasize that management's role is designing organizational systems (Spencer 1994) that create learning organizations—ones that continuously enhance their ability to shape their future (Senge 1992).

There is also a contrast between senior leadership of the direction of the organization and empowerment of the worker at low levels (Waldman 1994). Moreover, TQM has a "substitutes for leadership" perspective, where worker characteristics, such as empowerment and extensive training, can take the place of certain leader behaviors (Dean and Bowen 1994).

In chapter 1 of this book, Avolio and Yammarino examine the broad picture of leadership and TQM in the context of organizational cultural change. They point out that many firms have not considered the impact of TQM changes on ongoing organizational social processes. They advocate taking a multilevel approach similar to Waldman (1994); that is, the influence of TQM changes filter through differing "lenses" at the individual, dyad, group, and organization level. For example, leader vision may be interpreted differently at various levels, and thus require different methods of communication from the CEO, managers, and supervisors in order to create a shared vision at all levels. Moreover, communication techniques at each level may have to change over time as understanding of the vision coalesces.

Reward, recognition, and compensation. Both management theory and TQM cover reward extensively. They diverge, however, on the topic of recognition, which is pervasive in TQM but infrequently mentioned in the traditional management literature. In the area of compensation, management theory emphasizes individual-based incentive pay systems, while TQM advocates innovations in pay (Dean and Bowen 1994).

In chapter 2 Knouse describes several types of recognition awards (CEO awards, performance awards, peer awards, team awards, and customer-oriented awards). In addition, he borrows several principles from reinforcement theory to apply to the reward and recognition process: contingency (immediate reward directly associated with good performance); valued reward (customizing rewards through analyzing individual and team reinforcement histories); social reinforcement (recognition dinners, fairs); shaping (reinforcing small approximations of good performance, especially in new and difficult areas); and team competition (quality Olympics).

In chapter 4 Cleary states that compensation has three components that tie skills, performance, and expectations of the individual and the organization together.

1. Salary—a forward-looking agreement between the employee and company that takes into account skills the organization desires and the individual has to offer, individual experience, and market forces

2. Benefits—a package of supplements focused on equitable treatment of the workforce as a whole

3. Rewards—a backward-looking set of profit sharing and other financial options that rewards past performance

In order to create a compensation system that reflects the organization's commitment to employee pride in work and hence producing high-quality products and services, Cleary describes a number of principles that must be followed in developing the compensation system: fairness; ease of understanding; individual success aligned with organizational success; teamwork reinforced; salary separated from performance evaluation; skills tied to salary; profit-sharing incentives offered to all employees; and anxiety about salary equity among employees reduced.

In chapter 10 White and Nebeker incorporate team-based rewards in their team-oriented performance management (TOPM) system. Their version of gain sharing allocates monetary awards to teams based on the value of the teams' process improvements.

Performance evaluation. Perhaps the area with the greatest differences of opinion between traditional HRM ideas and TQM is performance evaluation. Traditional HRM focuses on individual evaluation for competitive rewards, such as merit pay, bonuses, and other types of compensation. TQM under Deming (1986) de-emphasized individual performance evaluation because it tended to promote individual competition over group cooperation toward TQM goals. Moreover, Deming emphasized the importance of system factors (techniques, training, machinery, and materials) in evaluating performance. Waldman (1994) tried to integrate both ideas by emphasizing person enhancers (skills training and motivation) as a primary system factor.

In chapter 3 Prince argues that adapting the traditional performance evaluation system to TQM will not work. Rather the organization should create a new performance evaluation system that fits the culture and strategy of the organization. The system should tie evaluation of outcomes, behaviors such as teamwork, and TQM criteria (continuous improvement, quality, and customer satisfaction) to performance planning (doing it better in the future), employee feedback, career planning, and personnel decisions, such as promotion.

In essence, the emphasis must be on managing the process of designing the evaluation system. The design team composed of people with varied expertise (HR professionals, managers, and employees) must understand appraisal issues in general and organizational concerns in particular. They must be able to connect the evaluation system with organizational strategy and values. And they must be able to make changes to the system as it evolves. Prince suggests that they experiment with a number of new ideas including using few rather than many rating categories, using multiple raters, using multiple reviewers in the feedback sessions, and using frequent individual and team reviews.

In chapter 7 Juneau describes the Individual Professional Development Plan (IPDP) used at Baldrige Award-winning Granite Rock, which is a nice compromise between traditional management by objectives evaluation and a Deming-type system evaluation. The IPDP not only assesses employee goal performance but it also is the basis for the firm's training and development systems. The IPDP incorporates employee self-evaluation and self-improvement of job skills and responsibilities (Waldman's person enhancers); mutual goal setting between employee and supervisor; feedback from the high-level management roundtable; and benchmarking with other firms.

In chapter 8 Carson, Carson, and Roe use the concept of "no-fault" policies to reiterate Deming's emphasis that organizations should get away from personal blame for problems and move toward emphasizing systemic causes of problems. Instead of wasting organizational time trying to pin blame on someone for a problem, quality teams can focus on identifying and solving system problems.

In chapter 10 White and Nebeker, using their TOPM system, combine individual and team performance in their assessment procedure. Their overall performance appraisal score contains three components: (1) team process improvement over baseline; (2) individual contributions to team process improvement; and (3) individual skill development. The third component nicely complements Waldman's (1994) idea of developing person enhancers.

Employee well-being and safety. The Baldrige Award guidelines for HRM (criterion 4.0) describe employee well-being as a subcategory. Well-being is generally couched in terms of employee satisfaction (Dean and Bowen 1994), although the HRM literature offers a number of approaches to understanding well-being.

One approach is safety. In chapter 5 Reber describes the similarities between the goals of TQM for employee welfare and safety management, and at the same time, deriving cost-effectiveness from doing it right the first time. He describes how several TQM tools (flowcharts, Pareto charts, and statsitical process control) can identify safe and unsafe behaviors and provide information about the effectiveness of safety suggestions.

Barriers and facilitators. A basic point stressed throughout several articles in the special issue of *Academy of Management Review* was the presence of system constraints on HRM and TQM (for example, organizational structure, organizational culture, and technology) (Waldman 1994).

In chapter 4 Cleary describes a number of constraints with traditional compensation systems. Commissions reinforce numbers sold rather than identifying and attempting to satisfy customer needs. Pay for meeting increasingly higher production quotas may actually force employees to reduce their workload in order to preserve reasonable pay levels. Fixed salaries produce the minimal performance on which to get by. Annual performance evaluation for pay raises reinforces achievement of individual rather than organizational goals. In all of these cases, workers are not behaving abnormally or in an unmotivated fashion. Rather they are acting rationally in their own self-interests under these pay systems.

Management must not criticize employees for acting rationally within these system constraints, but rather it must change the system. Salaries must reflect the skills that the organization wants and employees can offer. All employees must be able to equitably share in company profitability. And evaluation of performance must be continuous, immediate, and focused on improvement.

In chapter 6 Blackburn and Rosen report on a survey of human resources (HR) managers concerning barriers and facilitators to TQM. They found that the greatest barrier to successful TQM was pressure for short-term results. In addition, many managers complained of overly centralized authority dictating TQM efforts. A third barrier was unclear TQM objectives.

On the other hand, Blackburn and Rosen found that managerial support at all levels was the greatest facilitator of successful TQM. This support took the form of providing adequate resources to implement TQM practices and communicating clear TQM objectives. Moreover, they found that organizations with specific and intensive HR efforts (training and development, employee empowerment, and team-based job design) tended to be successful in TQM.

Most important, Blackburn and Rosen reported that organizations whose HRM department had implemented TQM within its own function had more successful levels of TQM overall. These HRM departments saw other departments as internal customers; evaluated satisfaction of other departments with HR activities; benchmarked HR practices; used TQM tools; had cross-functional quality teams; reduced response time for HR services; and set specific quality improvement objectives.

In chapter 8 Carson, Carson, and Roe identify several unique problems in the health care field that impinge on TQM. There is the problem of who is the customer—the patients, patients' support networks, staff, or third-party payers. Physicians historically controlled the process and want to maintain their independence. The current wave of downsizing facilities and staff creates overwork that detracts from time devoted to quality improvements. Moreover, the health care industry has traditionally focused on detection and correction after the fact rather than doing it right the first time.

On the one hand, pressure from the major accrediting body—JCAHO—drives quality initiatives. On the other hand, physicians, patients, and third-party carriers define quality differently, which greatly complicates quality improvement efforts. The HR specialist can play a crucial role in bringing all of these stakeholders together through various efforts, such as socialization into quality efforts, training, education, and career management.

In chapter 10 White and Nebeker identify a number of system problems with performance appraisal. Traditional performance appraisal systems attempt to evaluate individuals without regard to how their performance fits into work processes. The focus is on placing blame for problems rather than enhancing personal development. Moreover, traditional appraisal emphasizes meeting individual rather than organizational goals. And traditional evaluation suppresses risk taking while reinforcing mediocrity.

Organizational Techniques and Practices

Several authors examine what organizations in various sectors are doing.

Career management. In the area of career management, many speculate that the baby boomer wave has basically clogged the vertical promotion pipeline: Many levels of the organization find themselves plateaued. Therefore, organizations must look at alternative means of career progression, including horizontal and lateral career development (Dean and Bowen 1994).

In chapter 7 Juneau reports how Granite Rock has used the IPDP as a career management system for horizontal and lateral moves. The IPDP serves to focus on individual skills that can be enhanced through training and job experiences. Granite Rock then encourages these multiskilled employees to seek new job opportunities within the company.

In chapter 8 Carson, Carson, and Roe encourage health care organizations to look more to such horizontal and lateral career moves. In addition, they advocate clinical career ladders for health care providers.

Performance management. Performance management under TQM is seen as an interaction of system factors, such as procedures, policies, materials, and machines and person factors, such as skills and motivation. Although TQM leaders such as Deming (1986) stressed systems factors, present thought is that effective performance management under TQM must simultaneously look at both system and person factors (Waldman 1994).

In chapter 3 Prince describes how several quality organizations are experimenting with new evaluation techniques. Ford Motor Company moved from rating scales with several categories to only a few when it implemented its quality program. Consistent with a systems orientation, most employees fell into the acceptable performance category. Supervisors then did not have to focus on evaluating fine gradations of individual performance. IBM, Cadillac, and Federal Express emphasize self-evaluation in order to increase individual responsibility for performance and trust within the organization.

In chapter 8 Carson, Carson, and Roe advocate that health care organizations employ both individual and team evaluations and use both internal customers (other health care providers) and external customers (patients) to evaluate their members. In addition, the authors emphasize that an optimal time for patient evaluation of the quality of health care service may be 14–30 days after the service is delivered.

In chapter 10 White and Nebeker suggest that their TOPM system incorporates several important TQM principles: team rather than individual focus; process measurement; timely performance feedback to the team and the individual; individual goals consistent with organizational goals; and an atmosphere of trust supporting employee skill development. TOPM integrates customer requirements; goals from the strategic plan; measurement of critical organizational processes; evaluation of team performance; evaluation of individual performance contributing to team effectiveness; and reward of both team and individual performance.

Empowerment. In chapter 9 Howard and Rudolph report that Oregon State University had difficulties defining and implementing empowerment for employees and supervisors. Some employees believed that empowerment meant they were free from supervisory control and could define their jobs as they wished. Some supervisors thought empowerment eroded their control of the situation, while others used it as an excuse to remove themselves from decision-making pressures. Howard and Rudolph found that supervisory training in key skills and team leader training in empowerment were effective solutions.

Internationalization and Diversity

Part III expands concepts and practices along an additional dimension concerning differences: internationalization—differences across national cultures—and diversity—differences within U.S. culture). Surprisingly the special issue of the *Academy of Management Review* does not directly address internalization or diversity. (Surprisingly, because the TQM literature emphasizes differences in terms of building cross-functional teams and satisfying diverse customer needs.)

In chapter 11 Godfrey, Wilkinson, Marchington, and Dale survey British TQM programs and conclude that TQM in the United Kingdom faces a number of difficulties, some similar to those in the United States, some different. Similar to U.S. organizations, British companies experience financial pressure toward short-term results, bureaucratic inertia, and middle managers reluctant to adopt TQM. At the same time British companies face unique problems in the form of social class divisions and a large and intense union presence. In part, as a reaction to these problems, Godfrey et al. found that the HR function had evolved differing coping roles depending on the organizational climate: change agent (HR managers as high-level and high-profile drivers for quality programs); hidden persuader (HR managers with low visibility but working with top management); internal contractor (no central role for HR managers who, however, continue to provide HR services to assist quality efforts); and facilitator (hands-on support to line managers).

In chapter 12 Brown and Sohal examine Australian TQM organizations and find that a high percentage of manufacturing companies practice some form of TQM. Currently the emphasis is on quality certification and benchmarking. The authors describe the best practices of a number of firms that have stressed quality to compete on a global basis and consequently have won the Australian Quality Award. The Australian firms use many HR techniques similar to U.S. firms in the areas of recruiting, training, and reward and recognition. Their major difference appears to be having to deal with a stronger union environment. Managers have dealt with the situation by developing mutually beneficial agreements with the union in quality improvement efforts.

In chapter 13 Knouse and Chretien describe the advantages of diversity of membership on quality teams for both enhancing the perspectives and approaches to problem solving, and also for better understanding the complexities of a diverse customer base. The downside, however, is that diverse quality teams take longer to come up to speed than teams with the same types of member (for example, all male or all white). One implication is that diverse quality teams cannot be rushed but must be allowed time to coalesce. Another implication is that extensive team building is necessary to create the necessary team cohesion among the diverse members.

NEW IDEAS FOR BENCHMARKING

One of the important advantages of the TQM approach is that it emphasizes benchmarking (Camp 1995). TQM organizations are encouraged to seek out the new ideas of successful TQM efforts and then try them out—adopting those that work for them, modifying those that might work with some fine-tuning, and discarding those that are found not to fit the organization's unique situation. Through benchmarking, not only do organizations improve their processes in order to better serve their customers, but the entire field of TQM also grows. The knowledge base of the discipline is forced to remain constantly fluid and hence receptive to new ideas and changing perspectives. Innovation is encouraged, while established theories are less apt to become entrenched and eventually fossilized as has unfortunately become the case in some areas of management.

In this light, Table 14.1 summarizes several new ideas presented by the authors relating TQM to HRM.

Organizational Change

In order to understand how TQM affects organizational change, Avolio and Yammarino believe that TQM must be evaluated at different organizational levels. Each level may require different techniques for organizational change and hence different criteria for evaluating how this change occurs at that level.

The vision of where the organization is going with TQM is a prime example. If the vision is to be understood and shared at all levels of the organization, then there must be continual emphasis on the vision at different levels by the CEO, managers, and supervisors, who articulate the vision, model its values, and document its influence.

Recruiting

Recruiting is the first step in bringing new employees into the organization. Moreover, recruiting creates lasting expectations in newcomers about what will be required in the job (Wanous 1992). Carson, Carson, and Roe suggest a realistic job preview of what it is like to work in a TQM organization.

Prospective job applicants might view a videotape to receive a realistic picture of what it is like to work in a TQM organization. The video might show letters from satisfied customers and acknowledgments of appreciation from coworkers as positives, while time spent in team meetings, collecting data for solving quality problems, and dealing with hard-to-satisfy customers might be shown as negatives.

TABLE 14.1. Innovations for benchmarking.

HRM area	Innovation	Topic and chapter number
Organizational change	Shared vision through repeated articulation at various levels	Leadership and vision (1)
Recruiting	Realistic job preview of working within a TQM organization	Health care (8)
	Job descriptions including quality activities	Australia (12)
	Recruiting materials emphasizing that workforce diversity adds value	Diversity (13)
Employment interviewing	Team interviews of candidates with their prospective coworkers	Granite Rock (7)
Training	Separate TQM trainer coordinator from development director	Oregon State (9)
	Modularized training in leadership and team working	Australia (12)
	Appreciation for team member diversity in team building	Diversity (13)
	Appreciation for customer diversity through employee pair concept in on-the-job training	Diversity (13)
Performance evaluation and development	Integrated subordinate, peer, customer, and self-evaluations	Appraisal (3)
	Supervisor, team, peers, and customers included in review	Appraisal (3)
	Frequent individual and team reviews focused on future performance	Appraisal (3)
	TQM systems that require evaluation in the form of immediate and continuous feedback	Compensation (4)
	Major developmental objectives to improve personal skills	Granite Rock (7)
	Benchmarking visits to other firms to learn skill development ideas	Granite Rock (7)
	Optimal evaluations of customer (patient) service 14-30 days after treatment	Health care (8)
	Assessment of individual contribution to team process improvement and individual skill development	TOPM (10)

TABLE 14.1. (*continued*).

HRM area	Innovation	Topic and chapter number
	Multiple-source assessors of individual performance	TOPM (10)
	Peer review of managers based on employee satisfaction surveys	Australia (12)
Reward, recognition, and compensation	Alternative rewards for skill acquisition (one-time bonuses, further training as reward)	Reward and recognition (2)
	Understanding reward preferences through prior reinforcement history	Reward and recognition (2)
	Shaping (rewarding small improvements)	Reward and recognition (2)
	Profit sharing perceived as fair and easily understood by all employees	Compensation (4)
	Immediate and continuous evaluation and feedback for salary increases	Compensation (4)
	Safety awards that reinforce behavioral safety goals	Safety management (5)
	Gain sharing based on value of process improvements	TOPM (10)
	Group bonus based on quality measures	Australia (12)
Promotion	Future potential and current performance evaluated	Appraisal (3)
Safety	Plan of action meeting emphasizing safe behaviors	Safety management (5)
	Flowcharts identifying safety behaviors for safety checklist	Safety management (5)
	Pareto charts identifying causes of injury, illness	Safety management (5)
	Cause-and-effect diagrams identifying system causes of unsafe actions	Safety management (5)
	Benchmarking trips examining safety practices of other firms	Granite Rock (7)
Union relations	Buy-in of union members of quality initiatives by showing how they benefit (for example, work skill enhancement)	Granite Rock (7)

TABLE 14.1. (*continued*).

HRM area	Innovation	Topic and chapter number
	Balanced union involvement and management planning	Oregon State (9)
	High-trust partnering between union and management early in the TQM effort	United Kingdom (11)
	Joint development agreement on continuous learning for workers	Australia (12)
	Enterprise agreements incorporating TQM	Australia (12)
Discipline	Team administration of discipline	Health care (8)
	No-fault policies	Heath care (8)

Brown and Sohal report that in Australia, several firms have included time allocated to improvement activities and teamwork in job descriptions for candidates.

Knouse and Chretien find that emphasizing diversity in recruiting literature (for example, pictures of male and female employees and employees of various ethnic, racial, and age groups) attracts prospective employees of all backgrounds. Moreover, prospective employees see that a diverse workforce adds value through their unique perspectives and backgrounds to the organization's efforts.

Employment Interviewing

The interviewing process provides an opportunity for an active exchange of information between job applicants and the organization. Granite Rock uses a team interviewing process for hiring. The team consists of members of the prospective employee's department and a member of the HR staff. Prior to the actual interview, team members undergo a training session where they learn about the company's hiring philosophy, legal guidelines, and traits to look for in the candidates. The team is then split in two and each half interviews a candidate. Interview questions involve how the candidates would handle actual job situations. Candidates are evaluated on their communication skills in answering questions, how they can think quickly in potential work situations, and their chemistry with team members.

Training

Extensive and innovative training has been a hallmark of TQM organizations. As TQM evolved at Oregon State University, Howard and Rudolph found that team member surveys indicated an increased need for in-depth, specialized TQM training. The additional training load detracted from meeting the other training needs of the university. Thus, the HRM department created a manager of TQM training, allowing the training and development manager to return to providing the traditional training required by the university. Both positions, however, continued to coordinate TQM efforts and integrate TQM tools into other types of training.

Australian organizations have developed modularized programs that identify training for each employee. Emphasis is on leadership and team building for managers and team working and technical skills for workers.

Knouse and Chretien advocate that team training should emphasize an appreciation for employee and customer diversity. For example, team-building exercises can emphasize superordinate goals where a team cannot solve the problem without gathering the information that each member possesses. In on-the-job training, employee pairs (for example, male and female, European-American and African-American, old and young employee pairs) could contact customers of various backgrounds in order to better understand diverse customer needs.

Performance Evaluation and Development

Performance evaluation under TQM must integrate external customer needs, employee feedback and coaching (internal customer needs), quality process improvement, and individual skill development. Prince proposes a number of choices for designing the TQM-compatible performance evaluation system. He advocates combining subordinate, peer, customer, and self-evaluations with supervisory appraisals. These various sources provide crucial information from both internal and external customer perspectives as well as that of the organizational hierarchy. In addition, including all of these parties reinforces their importance in the process.

Prince also highlights the performance review process. He suggests that the supervisor, team, peers, and customers be included in review sessions. The importance of teams and internal and external customer input is thus emphasized, and these sources provide substantial feedback to the individual and the team.

The performance review process should have frequent sessions that focus on future performance planning and problem solving. The emphasis should be on how to do it better in the future.

Cleary describes how an organization has to replace its traditional end-of-year evaluation reviews with immediate and continuous feedback and coaching in order to set up other TQM systems, such as compensation.

Granite Rock's IPDP emphasizes major developmental objectives, where employees and their supervisors are encouraged to think of ways to improve employee skills in both their professional and personal lives. Employees are encouraged to benchmark skill development ideas by visiting other Granite Rock branches and other firms.

Carson, Carson, and Roe believe that there may be an optimal time for collecting customer data on evaluating employee service quality. For the health care industry they find that 14–30 days after delivery of the service is the time when patients have had time to reflect on recent treatments.

The TOPM system advocates evaluating individuals on various ways that they contribute to team process improvement: internal and external customer relations; contributions to reducing special causes of process variation; contributions to improving team processes; teamwork and cooperation; task performance; and contributions to team productivity. TOPM also suggests evaluating individuals on developing technical competence in work skills.

Moreover, TOPM recommends multiple-source assessment of individual performance in the form of customer, supervisor, peer, and self-ratings. These different sources contribute well-rounded process perspectives to the evaluation. One consequence is that this multiple-source perspective reduces the bias and errors that traditional one-source evaluations, such as supervisory ratings, may possess. In addition, they also take the burden off the supervisor to be a judge of performance and allow him or her to focus on coaching the individual.

Australian firms have focused their evaluation efforts on managerial performance. Criteria include improvement processes and teamwork. Some organizations have experimented with peer review of managers based on data gathered from employee satisfaction surveys.

Reward, Recognition, and Compensation

TQM organizations have evolved a variety of innovative reward and recognition programs (Knouse 1995). In the area of financial reward, a number of firms have experimented with skill-based pay. One of the problems with skill-based pay, however, is that the organization must pay now, and in the future, for skills that do not necessarily translate immediately into profitable goods or services for the firm. Knouse suggests some less expensive alternatives for reinforcing skill acquisition, such as one-time bonuses and further training as a reward for skill training.

Knouse also suggests some principles of reinforcement theory that may be applied to reward and recognition. For example, the reward and recognition team may better understand reward preferences within the organization by surveying the past reinforcement history of individuals and quality teams; that is, what are the important tangible and intangible rewards received in the past either in the company or elsewhere? In addition, shaping—the method of successive approximations—can improve the reward and recognition process. Rewarding small steps instead of large gains may be particularly effective when individuals and teams are trying to work in new, uncharted areas where risks are high and proven methods are scarce.

As a reward system, an effective compensation package must be perceived by employees as fair, easy to understand, focused on the profitability of the company, and not intertwined with the anxiety associated with performance evaluation. Cleary describes the profit-sharing program of a quality consulting firm that is based only on current salary and time with the company. Employees could easily calculate their own profit share, which was perceived as fair because it was clearly based on company profitability rather than on evaluation of individual performance.

Moreover, the perception of fairness is enhanced and anxiety reduced if the performance evaluation linked with salary increases is direct, immediate, and continuous. Annual evaluations create pressure on both employees and supervisors. Continuing to give salary increases across the board to poor performers does not help them and creates resentment among other employees. Cleary describes a private school where poor performers were observed and constantly coached by supervisors and peers. The focus was on improvement. In fact, feedback was given only for purposes of improvement and was not included in employees' official evaluation records.

Reber indicates that the reward and recognition system can both increase the performance of safe behaviors and decrease the incidence of accident rates with their accompanying costs. Awards to individuals and teams for safe time (no accidents for a period of time) reinforce intrinsic satisfaction of following behavioral safety goals.

White and Nebeker suggest a gain-sharing program where teams and individuals share a monetary award based on the value of their contributions to process improvements.

Brown and Sohal report that Australian firms are experimenting with financial rewards. One firm allocates group bonuses on such quality measures as number of customer complaints and cost of operation.

Promotion

With its emphasis on a systems orientation and team-based work, TQM has largely ignored how individually based personnel decisions, such as promotion, should occur. Prince recommends that decisions promoting individuals to higher-level jobs should be based on both current job performance and potential for future success in the new job (that is, an evaluation of skills, knowledge, and experience needed for the new job). An over-emphasis on current performance, even in the context of a TQM-oriented evaluation system, may result in a good performer being catapulted into a higher job for which he or she does not have the appropriate skills or experience. Moreover, the well-intentioned supervisor may even manipulate the process (purposefully give lower evaluations of current performance) in an attempt to prevent an employee from being promoted into a job that is over his or her head.

Safety Management

The Baldrige Award recognizes that a safe working environment underlies the quality of life in TQM organizations. Reber shows how various TQM statistical tools can enhance safe behaviors as they are being used to improve quality. At the beginning of each shift a work team can have a plan-of-action meeting incorporating features of the Deming cycle (plan-do-study-act). The duties to be performed are discussed, including safety behaviors, and suggestions for improvement made and then tried out. Process flowcharts which can be incorporated into behavioral safety checklists, can yield behaviors at each point in the process. Pareto charts can isolate important causes of occupational injuries and illness. Worker teams can brainstorm the causes of safety problems within the cause-and-effect framework of methods, materials, environment, equipment, and people.

Granite Rock maintains a safety record that is much better than industry average, in part by encouraging its employees to take benchmarking trips to other companies to examine safety practices.

Union Relations

Whereas traditional managers often viewed unions as a hindrance, TQM organizations have tried to involve unions in quality partnerships. Granite Rock used a quality team to introduce its IPDP to its unionized employees, who were at first reluctant to participate in the program. Showing the advantages of IPDP, particularly how employees could personally benefit by enhancing their work skills, dramatically increased participation.

From the beginning, Oregon State strove to balance union involvement with management planning, which has traditionally been considered a management right in collective bargaining. Oregon State struck a compromise whereby management planned the overall implementation of the quality effort while actively encouraging union leader involvement in the process.

While union influence is waning in many industrialized countries, it is more extensive in the United Kingdom than in the United States. Therefore, British TQM organizations have had to grapple with the union presence head-on in developing their TQM efforts. Moreover, the changes in job structure and work control advocated by TQM have historically fallen under the purview of the union. At the same time, historical union demands for increased employee involvement in work processes is precisely what TQM encourages. In short, both TQM and unions voice similar views on the importance of workers and their involvement.

Godfrey et al. point out that the TQM organization can capitalize on these similar views through a high-trust partnering approach between union and management. The important point is to bring the union into the TQM effort early in its inception and to build a continuing open relationship with the union. Godfrey et al. suggest high visibility for managers on the shop floor in order to break down the adversarial perception of "us" versus "them" that has evolved in unionized companies.

In Australia, management has not aspired to a union-free environment but rather has tried to work with unions in producing quality improvements. Firms have signed joint development agreements with their unions in which workers are assured continuous learning experiences. These efforts involve skill improvement and competency skill development in both on-the-job and off-the-job training. In addition, a number of firms have signed enterprise agreements with unions in which continuous improvement practices are recognized by both sides in the areas of job design, productivity, and efficiency.

Discipline

Organizations may naively assume that all members are highly motivated and highly productive under TQM practices. In reality, some employees will have problems no matter what management philosophy the company follows. Carson, Carson, and Roe believe that team-administered discipline may be effective in some situations. After all, the team probably knows better than management the source of a problem that involves one of its members, and team pressure can be a very convincing means of bringing a recalcitrant member in line with the program. Moreover, if the company follows no-fault policies, valuable time does not have to be spent trying to place the blame on an individual. Instead, that time can be productively used to identify and solve systemic causes of the problem.

ISO 9000

One area that is receiving increasing national and international attention is the ISO 9000 standards for quality. Basically, the ISO 9000 series is a set of criteria for certifying an organization's quality efforts for international trade. The emphasis is on documenting how the firm's processes create a quality system that controls incoming materials, inspection and testing, nonconforming products, and records. While the ISO 9000 series focuses on the documentation and measurement aspects of quality control, it does emphasize some HR processes, such as employee training (Peach 1994). Many firms that desire to enter international markets discover that they must have ISO 9000 certification to deal with international customers. The U.K. and Australian chapters touched on this.

Although many U.S. and foreign firms are seeking ISO 9000 certification as a first step to TQM, ISO 9000 does not necessarily mesh closely with TQM principles. Juran points out that the ISO 9000 series does not emphasize personal leadership by top management, quality goals in the business plan, continuous quality improvements, and empowerment of employees (Stephens 1994). It remains to be seen whether TQM and ISO 9000 will converge or diverge in the future.

CONCLUSION

The chapters in this book present a number of interesting ideas and principles to consider. One thing that continually struck me as I read through the chapters was the degree of difficulty encountered in attempting to implement TQM within the context of HRM in various organizational settings. Problems arose from trying to integrate a TQM culture with the organization's old culture; trying to identify the ultimate customer; economic pressure to downsize; internal and external pressure to show immediate results; misunderstanding of systems; reluctance of managers and professionals; mistrust of workers; trying to bring the union on board; and overall resistance to change. Perhaps the TQM literature has been too optimistic in its estimates of the time and difficulty required to change organizational behavior in order to reach a fully implemented TQM system.

At the same time, the chapter authors showed that managers and workers confronted these various difficulties with a number of innovative and effective HRM techniques. The basic point is that TQM must not be viewed as a static set of principles; that Deming's 14 points (or Juran's or Crosby's lists of principles) are not the final answer. Rather, TQM must be seen as a fluid, constantly changing entity that must continually evolve as new challenges and opportunities arise from both within and outside of the organization.

REFERENCES

Anderson, John C., Manus Rungtusanatham, and Roger G. Schroeder. 1994. A theory of quality management underlying the Deming management method. *Academy of Management Review* 19, no. 3:472–509.

Camp, Robert C. 1995. *Business process benchmarking: Finding and implementing best practices.* Milwaukee: ASQC Quality Press.

Dean, James W., and David E. Bowen. 1994. Management theory and total quality. *Academy of Management Review* 19, no. 3:392–418.

Deming, W. Edwards. 1986. *Out of the crisis.* Cambridge, Mass.: MIT Center for Advanced Engineering Study.

Klimoski, Richard J. 1994. A "total quality" special issue. *Academy of Management Review* 19, no. 3:390–584.

Knouse, Stephen B. 1995. *The reward and recognition process in total quality management.* Milwaukee: ASQC Quality Press.

Peach, Robert W. 1994. *The ISO 9000 handbook.* Milwaukee: ASQC Quality Press.

Senge, Peter. 1992. Building learning organizations. *Journal for Quality and Participation* (March): 30–38.

Spencer, Barbara. 1994. Models of organizations and total quality management. *Academy of Management Review* 19, no. 3:446–471.

Stephens, Kenneth S. 1994. ISO 9000 and total quality. *Quality Management Journal* (fall): 57–71.

Waldman, David A. 1994. The contributions of total quality management to a theory of work performance. *Academy of Management Review* 19, no. 3:510–536.

Wanous, John P. 1992. *Organizational entry: Recruitment, selection, orientation, and socialization of newcomers.* 2d ed. Reading, Mass.: Addison-Wesley.

Author Biographies

Bruce J. Avolio (Ph.D., University of Akron) is a fellow in the Leadership Studies Center at the State University of New York at Binghamton and a professor of human resources management/organizational behavior. He researches and consults in transformational leadership in North America, Europe, and Asia, and is coauthor of the *Multifactor Leadership Questionnaire* (Consulting Psychologists Press), the principal instrument for measuring transformational leadership. His clients include Exxon, IBM, Motorola, ITT, Digital, and Fiat. He has received $2 million in grants to study leadership from the Kellogg Foundation, the U.S. Department of Education, and the U.S. Army Research Institute. He is coeditor of *Improving Organizational Effectiveness Through Transformational Leadership* (Sage), which won the Society for Industrial-Organizational Psychology 1994 Distinguished Scientific Contribution Award. Currently he is building an international network of leadership centers.

Richard S. Blackburn (Ph.D., University of Wisconsin) is an associate professor of organizational behavior at the University of North Carolina at Chapel Hill, where he has received several teaching awards. His research interests include creativity, innovation, HRM practices, and TQM. He has consulted on leadership, motivation, and TQM with Cummins Engine, Gillette, Eli Lilly, and the U.S. Army Research Institute. He is the coauthor of *Managing Organizational Behavior* (Irwin).

Alan Brown (Ph.D., University of Western Australia) is an associate professor of management at Edith Cowan University in Perth, Australia. He is also the director of the Small and Medium Enterprise Research Consortium

297

there. He researches and consults in human resources management and TQM. He is currently examining the relationship between ISO 9000, TQM, and self-assessment.

Kerry D. Carson (Ph.D., Louisiana State University) is the Total Quality Management/Louisiana Education Quality Support Fund Regents Associate Professor of Management at the University of Southwestern Louisiana. He has worked in the private and public sectors of the health care industry in both clinical and administrative positions. His research interests are in TQM, health care management, and career development. He is coauthor of *Management of Healthcare Organizations* (South-Western).

Paula Phillips Carson (Ph.D., Louisiana State University) is the Professional Women in Business Associate Professor of Management at the University of Southwestern Louisiana. She has twice won the John F. Mee award for management research. She researches TQM, health care management, and the history of management. She is coauthor of *Management of Healthcare Organizations* (South-Western) and is presently writing a book on dysfunctional personalities in the workplace.

David Chretien (J.D., Louisiana State University) teaches business law at the University of Southwestern Louisiana. He researches and consults in equal employment opportunity/affirmative action and is active in local African-American community activities. He is the president of the Research Association of Minority Professors (RAMP).

Michael J. Cleary (Ph.D., University of Nebraska) is the founder and president of Productivity-Quality (PQ) Systems in Dayton, Ohio, and is emeritus professor of management science at Wright State University. He is a charter member and regional director of the education division of ASQC. He researches and consults in quality management, decision sciences, and statistics, and is the author of *Data Analysis Handbook* (Advocate Publishing).

Barrie G. Dale (Ph.D., University of Nottingham) is a reader in quality management and director of the University of Manchester Institute of Science and Technology (UMIST) Quality Management Centre, United Kingdom. His research interests involve HRM and TQM. He is the coauthor of seven books on TQM including *Quality Costing* (Van Nostrand), *Total Quality and Human Resources* (Blackwell) and *Managing*

Quality (Prentice Hall), and is coeditor of the *International Journal of Quality and Reliability Management.*

Graham Godfrey (M.Sc., University of Manchester Institute of Science and Technology) is currently a research associate at the School of Management at the University of Manchester Institute of Science and Technology (UMIST) in the United Kingdom. His research interests are in human resources management and TQM.

Nancy Howard (B.S., University of Oregon) directs the Office of Quality and Continuous Improvement at Oregon State University. She coauthored Oregon State's current quality training manual and codesigned Oregon State's facilitator/team leader training and quality improvement executive overview. She is an ex-officio member of the university's quality council. She has presented quality workshops for many universities.

Laura Junod (B.A., University of California at Santa Cruz) is certified by the Society of Human Resources Management as a human resources professional. She is currently managing the workers' compensation program for Granite Rock Construction Company and is developing a wellness program for the company.

Stephen B. Knouse (Ph.D., The Ohio State University) is the Alvin and Patricia Smith Professor of Management at the University of Southwestern Louisiana. His research interests are in TQM, human resources management, diversity management, and impression management. He has consulted on TQM and on diversity with the Office of Naval Research and had a sabbatical in 1992 to study TQM in Australia. He is the author of *The Reward and Recognition Process in Total Quality Management* (ASQC Quality Press) and coauthor of *Hispanics in the Workplace* (Sage).

Michael P. (Mick) Marchington (Ph.D., University of Manchester) is a professor of human resources management at the School of Management of the University of Manchester Institute of Science and Technology (UMIST) in the United Kingdom. His research interests are in TQM, employee relations, and employee involvement. He has coauthored five books on HRM and TQM, and is currently coauthoring a textbook on human resources management.

Delbert M. (Del) Nebeker (Ph.D., University of Washington) is a professor of psychology at the California School of Professional Psychology,

San Diego (Organizational Psychology Program). He has served as the director of the organizational systems department at the Navy Personnel Research and Development Center in San Diego. He researches reward systems, performance management, and TQM. He is also a consultant to government, academic and *Fortune* 500 companies on the subjects of performance management, compensation & reward systems, and quality.

J. Bruce Prince (Ph.D., University of Southern California) is an associate professor and chairperson of the management department at Kansas State University. He researches performance management, employee development, and TQM. He has consulted in North America, Europe, and Asia with such companies as Boeing, Hughes Aircraft, and General Electric. He has coauthored two books including *Organizational Behavior* (Prentice-Hall).

Robert A. Reber (Ph.D., Louisiana State University) is an associate professor of management at Western Kentucky University. His research and consulting interests include safety management, performance management, fair management practices, and compensation systems.

C. William Roe (D.B.A., Mississippi State University) is a professor of management and chairperson of the department of management and quantitative methods at the University of Southwestern Louisiana. He researches health care management, TQM, and social power, and has consulted on TQM extensively with local industry. He is coauthor of *Management of Healthcare Organizations* (South-Western) and is currently writing a text on TQM.

Benson Rosen (Ph.D., Wayne State University) is the Hanes Professor of Management and the senior associate dean for academic affairs at the Kenan-Flagler Business School of the University of North Carolina at Chapel Hill. He is also on the faculty of the Seminar in Technology Management, based in Switzerland, and is a fellow of the American Psychological Association. His research interests in human resources management, diversity, career management, and TQM won him the Distinguished Research Award from the Kenan-Flagler School. He has consulted with Burroughs Wellcome, SONOCO, IBM, and Sun Microsystems. He is the coauthor of two books.

Jacquelyn T. Rudolph (M.B.A., Oregon State University) is the director of human resources at Oregon State University. She was the primary author of the IBM/Oregon State Total Quality Management University Competition grant and directed the university's quality management program from 1991 to 1993, where she oversaw the integration of quality management university-wide. She is a member of the university's quality council.

Amrik S. Sohal (Ph.D., University of Bradford) is a professor of management and the director of the Quality Management Research Unit at Monash University, Melbourne, Australia. He researches TQM, manufacturing/operations management, and strategy and technology management in British Commonwealth countries. He is the founding editor of the *Asia Pacific Journal of Quality Management*. In addition he is the Asia Pacific editor of the *International Journal of Quality and Reliability Management* and the *International Journal of Operations and Production Management*. He is the author of four books on TQM and manufacturing.

Michael A. White (Ph.D., Claremont Graduate School) is an industrial psychologist with the Navy Personnel Research and Development Center in San Diego. His research interests are self-directed work teams, individual and group monetary incentive systems, performance management systems, and performance appraisal. He has consulted with U.S. federal government organizations on issues related to survey methodology, organizational redesign, and TQM.

Adrian Wilkinson (Ph.D., Durham University) is a lecturer in human resource management at the School of Management at the University of Manchester Institute of Technology (UMIST) in the United Kingdom. He researches the links between TQM and human resource management, and is currently investigating the implications of TQM for managerial jobs. He is coauthor of *Making Quality Critical* (Routledge).

Francis J. Yammarino (Ph.D., State University of New York at Buffalo) is a professor of management and fellow of the Center for Leadership Studies at the State University of New York at Binghamton. He is also a fellow of the American Psychological Society. He has consulted with the U.S. Navy, Air Force, and Department of Education. His research interests are in superior-subordinate relations, leadership, and research methodology. He is coauthor of four books and is the senior editor of *Leadership Quarterly*. He also serves on the editorial board of *Group and Organization Management*.

Suggested Reading

Anfuso, Dawn. 1994. Self-directed skills building drives quality. *Personnel Journal* (April): 84–93.

Bass, Bernard M., and Bruce J. Avolio, eds. 1993. *Improving organizational effectiveness through transformation leadership*. Thousand Oaks, Calif.: Sage.

Blackburn, Richard, and Benson Rosen. 1993. Total quality and human resources management: Lessons learned from Baldrige Award-winning companies. *Academy of Management Executive* (August): 49–66.

Bowen, David E., and Edward E. Lawler, III. 1992. Total quality-oriented human resources management. *Organizational Dynamics* (spring): 29–41.

Brown, Alan. 1993. TQM: Implications for training. *Industrial and Commercial Training* 25, no. 1:20–26.

Cardy, Robert L., and Gregory H. Dobbins. 1996. Human resources management in a Total Quality Organizational Environment. *Journal of Quality Management* 1, no. 1:5–20.

Carson, Kerry D., Paula Phillips Carson, and C. William Roe. 1995. *Management of healthcare organizations*. Cincinnati, Ohio: South-Western.

Chemers, Martin M., Stuart Oskamp, and Mark A. Costanzo. 1995. *Diversity in organizations*. Thousand Oaks, Calif.: Sage.

Cleary, Michael J., and Timothy J. Cleary. 1993. Designing an effective compensation system. *Quality Progress* (April): 69–72 and (May): 97–99.

Costigan, Robert D. 1995. Adaptation of traditional human resources processes for total quality environments. *Quality Management Journal* (spring): 7–23.

Cox, Taylor M. 1993. *Cultural diversity in organizations: Theory, research, and practice.* San Francisco: Barrett-Koehler.

Dale, Barrie G. 1994. *Managing quality.* 2d ed. Englewood Cliffs, N.J.: Prentice Hall.

Dale, Barrie G., and Cary Cooper. 1992. *Total quality and human resources.* Oxford, England: Blackwell.

Dean, James W., and James R. Evans. 1993. *Total quality: management, organization, and strategy.* Minneapolis: West.

Deming, W. Edwards. 1986. *Out of the crisis.* Cambridge, Mass.: MIT Center for Advanced Engineering Study.

Evans, James R., and William M. Lindsay. 1996. *The management and control of quality.* 3rd ed. Minneapolis: West.

Hart, Christopher W. L., and Christopher E. Bogan. 1992. *The Baldrige.* New York: McGraw-Hill.

Howard, Nancy Lee, and Jacquelyn T. Rudolph. 1993. Implementing TQM at Oregon State University. In *Quality and its applications,* edited by J. F. L. Chan. Newcastle upon Tyne, England: Penshaw Press.

Juran, Joseph M. 1988. *Quality control handbook.* 4th ed. New York: McGraw-Hill.

Klimoski, Richard J. 1994. A "total quality" special issue. *Academy of Management Review* 9, no. 3:390–584.

Knouse, Stephen B. 1995. *The reward and recognition process in total quality management.* Milwaukee: ASQC Quality Press.

Lawler, Edward E., III. 1990. *Strategic pay: Aligning organizational strategies and pay systems.* San Francisco: Jossey-Bass.

Lawler, Edward E., III, Susan Albers Mohrman, and Gerald E. Ledford. 1992. *Employee involvement and total quality management: Practices and results in Fortune 1000 companies.* San Francisco: Jossey-Bass.

Luthans, Fred, and Robert Kreitner. 1985. *Organizational behavior modification and beyond.* Glenview, Ill.: Scott, Foresman.

Morrison, Anne M. 1993. *The new leaders: Guidelines on leadership diversity in America.* San Francisco: Jossey-Bass.

Nebeker, Del, and Michael White. 1990. *Team-oriented performance management: A concept paper.* San Diego: Navy Personnel Research and Development Center.

Prince, J. Bruce. 1994. Performance appraisal and reward practices for total quality organizations. *Quality Management Journal* (January): 36–46.

Reber, Robert A., Jerry A. Wallin, and David L. Duhon. 1993. Preventing occupational injuries through performance management. *Public Personnel Management* (summer): 301–311.

Schoenberger, Richard J. 1994. Human resource management lessons from a decade of total quality management and reengineering. *California Management Review* (summer): 109–123.

Senge, Peter. 1990. *The fifth discipline.* New York: Doubleday.

Sohal, Amrik. 1995. *Quality practices in Australian manufacturing firms.* Melbourne, Australia: Monash University.

Wilkinson, Adrian, Mick Marchington, and Barrie Dale. 1993. Enhancing the contribution of the human resource function to quality improvement. *Quality Management Journal* (October): 35–46.

Yammarino, Francis J., and Bernard M. Bass. 1991. Person and situation view of leadership: A multiple levels of analysis approach. *Leadership Quarterly* 2, no. 2:121–139.

Author Index

Subject Index

Q

Quality. *See also* Total quality management
  compatibility with safety, 79, 87
  compensation and, 67
  of processes, 203
  of supplier inputs, 203
Quality assurance, compared to
    TQM/CQI, 161
Quality improvement. *See* Continuous
    quality improvement
Quality tools, 114, 115, 116, 264
Quality work the first time, 81–83,
    161–62
Quick fix. *See* Short-term perspective
Quota pay systems, 59–61

R

Race, and diversity, 261, 269, 289
Rating scales, 46–47, 50–51, 76–77,
    196, 201
Rational motivation, 11
Realistic job previews, 172, 285
Recognition systems. *See also* Reward
    systems
  in Australia, 247, 248
  benchmarking ideas for, 290–91
  development planning and, 133
  functions of, 31–32
  in higher education, 192
  importance of, 27
  OBM and, 34–38
  reinforcement theory and, 31–32,
    34–40
  for safety performance, 83
  team-based, 38–39, 209–10
  TQM success and, 112, 113
  TQM vs. HRM and, 278–79
  types of, 28, 30–31
  workforce diversity and, 268
Recruiting
  in Australia, 243–44, 285
  benchmarking ideas for, 285, 288
  in medical sector, 172
Regulations, safety, 80, 81, 84, 90
Reinforcement theory, 278, 291
  competition, 37–38
  contingent reinforcement, 35–36
  OBM and, 34–38
  in reward and recognition, 27, 29–32,
    34–40

shaping, 37
social reinforcers, 37
valued rewards, 36–37
Resistance
  to diversity management, 269–71
  in medical sector, 152–62, 165,
    168–76
  taxonomy of, 165, 168–71
  in United Kingdom, 165, 168–76
Resource availability, 109, 110, 118
Reward systems. *See also* Compensation
    systems; Recognition systems
  in Australia, 247–48
  as backward looking, 69
  benchmarking ideas for, 290–91
  destructiveness of, 59, 62, 69
  functions of, 29–30
  in higher education, 192
  importance of, 27
  OBM and, 34–38
  pay as, 28, 32–33
  quality and, 67
  reinforcement theory and, 27, 29–30,
    34–40
  for safety performance, 83
  team-based, 29, 38–39, 204, 209–10
  TQM success and, 110, 118
  TQM vs. HRM and, 278–79
  types of, 28–29
  in United Kingdom, 227–28
  valued, 36–37
  workforce diversity and, 268

S

Safety management, 79–81, 280–81, 292
  Baldrige Award and, 86–87
  costs and, 82–83
  development systems and, 140
  process orientation of, 80, 88
  TQM, and role of, 81–86
  TQM, similarities with, 80
  TQM techniques for, 87–94
Salaries. *See* Pay
Salary curves, 67–69, 77
Schools, compensation systems for,
    73–77
Selection systems, 112, 113
  in Australia, 243–44
  in medical sector, 172
Service recovery, 162